Liberating Your Passover Seder

An Anthology Beyond The Freedom Seder

Edited by

Rabbi Arthur Ocean Waskow

and

Rabbi Phyllis Ocean Berman

Ben Yehuda Press

Teaneck, New Jersey

Published by Ben Yehuda Press
122 Ayers Court #1B
Teaneck, NJ 07666

http://www.BenYehudaPress.com

To subscribe to our monthly book club and support independent Jewish publishing, visit https://www.patreon.com/BenYehudaPress

Ben Yehuda Press books may be purchased at a discount by synagogues, book clubs, and other institutions buying in bulk. For information, please email markets@BenYehudaPress.com

ISBN13 978-1-953829-06-1

21 22 23 / 10 9 8 7 6 5 4 3   20211103

Contents

In Loving Memory of Zeyde Zalman —
Reb Zalman Schachter-Shalomi —

And in loving commitment to our Grandchildren –
Yoni, Elior, Shifra, Kalman, Yaela

Prefatory Note

In Every Generation: Looking Forward

Rabbi Arthur Ocean Waskow and Rabbi Phyllis Ocean Berman

The Passover Haggadah ("Telling") calls upon all human beings, not only its Jewish celebrants, to free themselves in every generation from the pharaohs and would-be pharaohs who rise in every generation. Yet for two thousand years, until 1969, the text and form of the Haggadah itself was almost frozen. At most only once a century or in a few cases once a generation, it was as if the Seder (Order; Pattern of Service") itself had become a pharaoh, preventing acts of liberation from entering its sacred form. Individual sages or families might say or do something new, but "The Haggadah" and "The Seder" remained constant.

The Freedom Seder in 1969 said that the Seder could be about more than Jewish liberation. That broke the mold, and reinfused the evening with new ways of seeing what was old—and spread the word that we could do this. *Spreading* new words, new practices—that was what was really new. Jews and multifaith collectives exploded with new blossoms, new fruitfulness, new seeds of change.

More that 50 years later, stirred by a fiftieth anniversary Freedom Seder and by many aspects of liberation that had drawn on and reworked the Seder as a model, we have gathered some of those flowerings and fruits to look not backward but to what this teaches us about the future. The possible futures, plural. A multiplicity.

Among them: A sexy Seder for the Song of Songs. A joint Israeli-Palestinian Seder held, of all places, in Hebron. The stories behind the Orange on the Seder Plate and Miriam's Cup on the Seder table. A Zoom Seder for the 7th Night of Passover, with our own people poised at this moment to decide: surrender to horse-chariot militias or chance the Unknown, the Red Sea. A rousing Seder speech by a prophetic Black minister calling like Jeremiah for a protest at the king's own palace. Breaking the matzah so that it can be shared, changing from the Bread of Affliction to the Bread of Freedom.

The essays in this collection are organized into their own Seder— their own order or pattern:

1. The Original Freedom Seder and its Impact
2. Feminist Seders
3. Gay and Multi-Gender Seders
4. Earth and Refugee Seders
5. Israel-Palestine Seders
6. New Symbols: Friends and Families
7. The #FreedomSeder50
8. The Eleventh Plague: Virtual Seders
9. Mystical Seders
10. The Future: Spirit, Ritual, Politics

There is a tradition that the Seder begins by chanting the whole "Table of Contents," then chanting each section title as we meet it. Perhaps you will want to chant this Pattern and then proceed to explore each set, one by one. Act it out, dance it out, sing it out.

Free the Seder! Your own Seder!

The Original Freedom Seder and its Impact

Why I Wrote the Freedom Seder and Why It's Still Necessary 50 Years After Dr. King's Assassination

Rabbi Arthur Waskow

Fifty years ago, on April 4, 1968, the transformation of my life began with the volcanic news that Dr. Martin Luther King had been killed. Just a week later—a week of upheaval in my city and our country—the volcano of transformation entered within me, minutes before Passover began.

Passover? Why was that suddenly so shattering? I had always taken the Seder seriously, but I was astounded to feel this moment shaking me to my core. Why was this Passover different from any other Passover?

I was 34 years old, living in Washington, D.C. and working for peace and racial justice. I had grown up in a Jewish neighborhood in Baltimore with a strong sense that community—neighborhood itself—was warmly Jewish; that freedom and justice were profoundly, hotly "Jewish and beyond"—but that Jewish religion was boring boilerplate.

Except for celebrating the Passover Seder, which brought family, community, freedom, and justice around the same dinner table, I had long abandoned the rhythms of Jewish religion.

So as a grown-up I had found my community not in any Jewish neighborhood but in the network of organizers for racial justice, peace in Vietnam, and worldwide nuclear disarmament—a network centered in the Institute for Policy Studies, where I had been one of the founding fellows in 1963.

And then Dr. King's death and its aftermath in Washington undid me and rebirthed me.

I was not just a spectator to his passionate life and death. I had spent nine years in Washington working day and night against racial injustice and the Vietnam War—behind a typewriter on Capitol Hill; at the microphone on countless college campuses; sitting in unbearably hot back rooms of Convention Hall in Atlantic City in 1964, working alongside Dr. King when he came hobbling on a badly twisted ankle to rally support for the Mississippi Freedom Democratic Party; marching and sitting down against the Vietnam War in 1967, at the Pentagon; cruising D.C. streets in a sound truck (with my four-year-old son beside me), to turn out votes for Bobby Kennedy in 1968.

On the evening of April 3, Dr. King spoke to a crowd in Memphis: "I've been to the mountaintop... And I've seen the Promised Land. I may not get there with you. But I want you to know tonight, that we, as a people, will get to the promised land!" Echoes of Moses. By the next night, he was dead.

By noon the next day, Washington, my city, was ablaze. Touch and go it was, whether 18th Street—four houses from my door—would join the flames. Just barely, our neighborhood's interracial ties held fast. The President, who just a few days before had proposed peace talks with Vietnam, now begged the Black community to remain nonviolent—before, ironically, ordering the U.S. Army to occupy the Nation's capital city, taking over schools and traffic circles. A rifle-bearing soldier stood on the Capitol steps.

By April 6, there was a curfew. Thousands of Black protestors were being herded into jail for breaking it. No whites, of course; the police didn't care whether white people were on the streets. My white friends and I tried to turn their blindness to good use: For days we brought food, medicine, and doctors from the suburbs into the schools and churches of burnt-out downtown Washington.

And then came the afternoon of April 12. That night, Passover would begin. We would gather—my wife and I, our son, our daughter (just nine months old), with a few friends, for the usual ritual recitation of the Telling of our freedom. Some rollicking songs. Some solemn invocations. Some memories from seders of the past, in the families where our fathers had chanted—some of them in Hebrew or Yiddish, some in English.

But it was a bubble in time, a bubble isolated from the life, the power, the volcano of the streets. Perhaps, when the rituals were over and the kids had been initiated into the age-old ritual, had taken their first look into this age-old mirror in which Jews saw ourselves as a band of runaway slaves, we might put aside the ancient book and talk about the burning—truly, burning—issues of our lives.

So I walked home to help prepare to celebrate the seder. On every block, detachments of the Army. On 18th Street, a Jeep with a machine gun pointing up my block.

Somewhere within me, deeper than my brain or breathing, my blood began to chant: "This is Pharaoh's army, and I am walking home to do the seder."

"This is
Pharaoh's
army,
and I am walking home
to do
the Seder.
This is
Pharaoh's
army . . . "

King's speech came back to me. "I've been to the mountaintop... And I've seen the Promised Land..." The songs we had sung in Atlantic City four years before with Fannie Lou Hamer, who had come from a Mississippi sharecropper's shack to confront the Democratic Party: "Go tell it on the mountain, let my people go! ... Must be the people that Moses led, let my people go!" The sermons I had heard Black preachers speak, half shouting, half chanting: "And on the wings of eagles I will bring you, from slavery, from bondage, yes!—from slavery, to be My people—yes, my beloved people."

Yes, on the streets *is* Pharaoh's army, and I am walking home to do the seder.

Not again, not ever again, a bubble in time. Not again, not ever again, a ritual recitation before the real life, the real meal, the real conversation.

For on that night, the Haggadah itself, the Telling of our slavery and our freedom, became the real conversation about our real life. The ritual foods, the bitterness of the bitter herb, the pressed-down bread of everyone's oppression, the wine of joy in struggle, became the real meal.

For the first time, we paused in the midst of the Telling itself, to connect the streets with the seder. Every year since I had learned to read, I had recited the passage that says, "In every generation, every human being is obligated to say, 'We ourselves, not our forebears only, go forth from slavery to freedom.'"

Amazing!—not "every Jew," it says: "Every human being!"

In every generation. Including our own. Always before, we had chanted these passages and gone right on. Tonight we paused. Who and what is our oppressor? How and when shall we go forth to freedom?

To my astonishment, these questions burned like a volcano within me, erupting like the volcano in my city. Why did I care to make this connection? Why was this ancient tale having such an effect on me? How could I respond?

During the next six months, especially as a member of an anti-war, anti-racist delegation elected from D.C. to the Democratic National Convention in Chicago, some elements of the Passover story kept erupting inside me. The City of Chicago was infamously tyrannized by its mayor, Richard Daley, who ordered a police riot to bloody nonviolent demonstrators against the war. While his police tyrannized demonstrators outside, the same Daley, as chairman of the Convention, tyrannized us delegates inside. Powerful teachings about the modern pharaohs!

In the fall, I found myself preparing for the next Passover by writing a Haggadah, a Telling of my own—a script for what I imagined would be our own family Seder. I hoped it would deliberately make happen in the future what had already happened, with no deliberation, in the midst of turmoil. I dug out my old Haggadah, the one I had been given when I turned 13—the one with Saul Raskin's luscious drawings of the maidens who saved Moses from the river, the one that stirred my body each spring, those teenage years.

Into its archaic English renderings of Exodus and Psalms, I intertwined passages from King and Thoreau; Ginsberg and Gandhi; the Warsaw Ghetto Uprising against Nazism and the Nat Turner rebellion against slavery; the Christian radical A. J. Muste calling Moses the organizer of "Brickmakers Union Number 1" and a pacifist Russian rabbi named Tamaret—wove them all into a new Telling of the tale of freedom.

In that Telling, the then ongoing, even now unfinished, struggle of Black America for freedom was interwoven with the ancient story of the Israelites' struggle to end their slavery under Pharaoh.

Where the old Haggadah had what seemed to me a silly argument about how many plagues had really afflicted Egypt, I substituted a serious quandary: Were blood and death a necessary part of liberation, or could the nonviolence of King and Gandhi bring a deeper transformation?

I had written half a dozen books—on military strategy, disarmament, race relations, American politics—but this was different: This book was writing me. I had no idea whether it made any sense to do this; I knew only that I could not stop. When I had finished, I called around to find a Washington rabbi who might be sympathetic. I asked him— Rabbi Harold White—to read my draft: Was this a crazed obsession or a good idea?

Two days later, he called me:

"I love it, Waskow. It's an activist midrash on the Haggadah! You've taken the story into our own hands, as the rabbis said God wanted the fleeing slaves themselves to do. Do you know that midrash? The one where God refuses to split the Red Sea until one activist has gone into the water, up to his nose, about to drown?"

"What's a midrash?" said I.

"Oho!" said he, and even over the phone I could feel the excitement rise. "The rabbis would take the ancient text, and read it in new ways. On this one, where the Torah says the people 'went into the sea on the dry land,' the rabbis ask, 'Which was it? How could it be both sea and dry land?' And they answer that one of them went in while it was still sea; only then did it become dry land.

"You see?—the people had to act. The rabbis took the text into their own hands because they wanted the people to take history into their own hands. The text at first glance seems to leave the action to God; but the rabbis reread this oddity of text to mean the people acted.

"That's midrash. Can I share some midrash with you?"

So he lent me a volume of this *midrash*, and I fell in love. A whole new language that my heart had searched for all these years, a whole new language I had never known existed. A language of transformation-through-renewal, a language that drew on an ancient language to make it deeply new. A language of serious play that could, with a wink and a twirl, turn reality in a new direction and claim it was simply uncovering a meaning that was already there. A language of puns, serious and funny puns that took as cosmic teaching the clang of words and phrases with each other.

And this, the rabbi taught me, was what my new Haggadah was already: a midrash on the ancient text that turned it in a new direction. What neither he nor I expected was that as I was reinterpreting the text, the text was reinterpreting me. Turning me in a new direction, making a new "I" that was a midrash on the old me.

So I went ahead with the transgressive, transformative Haggadah that eventually was called "The Freedom Seder." In 1969 it was published in *Ramparts* magazine, where tens of thousands greeted it with joy: a religion they could share!

And on April 4, 1969, the first anniversary of Dr. King's murder and the third night of Passover, we held a Freedom Seder in the basement of a Black church in Washington, D.C., with about 800 people—Jews and Christians, Black and white.

It was not only my engagement with the Jewish text, with all the Jewish texts, that "rewrote" me. It was also my engagement with other Jews who were rewriting themselves, my engagement with communities that came together in the very process of wrestling with these texts.

For indeed, it turned out that others were entering this process, stirred by events in their own lives as I had been stirred by the streets of Washington. Stirred, some of them, by their need for community, and what many of them felt was the chilliness of conventional Jewish life. Stirred, some others, by their own spiritual yearnings and the flatness of what they had experienced as conventional Jewish life. Stirred, still others, by their hopes and fears for the State of Israel, which had stood on the edge of deeply dangerous waters in 1967, and crossed—they thought—in triumph.

But even that early, some were stirred to worry about warnings of a long Occupation. Some who had never been welcomed into the hidden places of Jewish thought and practice were stirred by the joy and triumph they saw as Blacks refuse to melt into America, and instead unfurl the hidden flags of their own culture. Still others—mostly women—were stirred by the possibility of reshaping the Judaism that had always ignored their needs and their perceptions. Still others who already had deep knowledge of hidden Jewish wisdom were stirred by the unexpected feeling that those riches could give new meaning to their lives.

And I found seeds and sprouts of a fiery Judaism where the Burning Bush was still aflame. I learned of a Rabbi named Heschel, who had marched alongside King at Selma.

Who had stood beside King when, exactly a year before his death, King spoke the words that some said were the warrant for his murder: Denouncing the U.S. war against Vietnam as an atrocity, warning that the deadly "triplets" of racism, materialism, and militarism were endangering America.

Who had stood beside King in Arlington Cemetery as they mourned the war dead—American and Vietnamese.

Who could write in the same essay that prayer was the joyful song the universe sang to itself, and that prayer was meaningless unless it was subversive.

Who had arranged with Dr. King to celebrate his first Passover Seder in 1968 with the Heschel family. The Passover when, though King was dead—*because* he was dead—he lived in thousands of seders across America, including mine. A living proof of death and rebirth, if not of resurrection.

And others who, like Heschel, had kept the Burning Bush aflame, even when their passion was criticized by colleagues—as indeed Heschel's colleagues at the Jewish Theological Seminary did, scorning his activist passion even while they admired his theology and scholarship.

Because I discovered I was not alone, because there were others for me to meet upon my journey, my journey became possible. As we discovered each other, we granted each other the truths of our own different stories, ultimately the truth that we could share a journey of many different journeys. We discovered how astonishingly rich were the Judaisms—plural—we had barely known, and how our forebears also had walked many different paths. And we discovered how astonishingly nourishing were the new Judaisms we ourselves could shape as we intertwined our own lives with each other and with the lives of our forebears.

But the process didn't end there; it simply began. Looking back, I can see that the Freedom Seder was the moment and the act through which I truly became a bar mitzvah: through it, I entered the gates of Jewish life; through it, I became an adult, shaping my own life. Given who I was, it was the only gate I could have taken: one I had to build myself.

And by the same token, looking back, I can see how it was the entry gate that a newcomer would build: clumsy, intuitive, marked by a blunder here and a blemish there, yet powerfully attractive to others who connected with its impulsive energy.

Plenty of people said I had no right, so new and raw, to raise the Jewish roof—but I was also able to find a community of searchers, for whom learning came out of the searching.

This process has now been the living center of my life for half a century. I have moved to a different city, taught and learned in different schools, prayed in different gatherings from other prayer books I have helped to write myself. I was drawn to a new understanding of the early rabbis as radicals, and studied to become a rabbi as radical as they had been—a rabbi who could join a rabbinate that was a midrash on rabbinic tradition. (Now I know what midrash is, and revel in the knowing.)

A feminist midrash on Judaism and the rabbinate. An ecological midrash on Judaism and the rabbinate. A transformative midrash on Judaism and the rabbinate, seeing Judaism as one wisdom among others looking toward the healing of our wounded country, our wounded world, our wounded Mother Earth.

Indeed, I have learned to understand midrash and all of Jewish time and Jewish thought as a spiral: neither a straight line that must go always forward, even into a precipice, nor a circle that must remain forever stuck in repeating past experience. Instead, a spiral, which curves always backward in order to curve forward.

Fifty years after that volcano erupted in my soul, I see it's time for another turn of the spiral. Facing Pharaoh in the White House and in the Corporate Carbon Pharaohs intent on burning our Earth to pile still higher pyramids of profit, I realize that never again can the Seder freeze. Now, again, we need a new Freedom Seder. "In every generation …" Indeed.

What makes time and life into a spiral, instead of either a straight line or an endless circle, is setting aside time for reflection, rest, renewal. The curve that moves the spiral onward is that renewal time—Shabbat, the Sabbath; each pause to bless Creation and say I-Thou(!) before we behave as if the world is only an *It*; the Great Shabbat when, we are taught, we must let the Earth have its own restful year.

Indeed, now I understand midrash itself as a spiral, in which we go back again and again in order to go forward. We draw on ancient wisdom to create new wisdom. What went before, we turn and turn like a kaleidoscope. With every turn, new beauty, new patterns, new complexity.

Facing new versions of the world. Birthing new versions of ourselves.

Father Dan Berrigan, Cornell University, and the Freedom Seder

Rabbi Arthur Waskow

It took a phone call in the spring of 1970 to start me into the adventure of the Freedom Seder at Cornell University.

The call came from a student at the university. He explained that in honor of Father Dan Berrigan, there would be a long weekend at Cornell expressing opposition to the U.S. war against Vietnam. Father Dan had been a deeply beloved chaplain at Cornell; had become a vigorous nonviolent resistor to the war; and he was now underground, resisting arrest by the FBI to face criminal charges for his resistance to the war.

The student who was calling explained that the weekend would take place during Passover. The organizers had heard of the Freedom Seder we held in 1969. They wanted to know whether I was interested in coming to Cornell for the Friday evening at the start of the weekend, and to lead a Freedom Seder on the campus. I said, "Of course I'll come!" And I made arrangements.

When I landed at the Ithaca airport, two students were there to pick me up. They asked, "Would you mind if we went to see the Cayuga River falls before we take you to the campus?"

Every once in a while, as an amusement in my life, I had sung the various school spirit songs of various universities. Among them was, "Far above Cayuga's waters / With its waves of blue, Stands our noble Alma Mater, / Glorious to view. / Lift the chorus, speed it onward, / Loud her praises tell; / Hail to thee our Alma Mater! Hail, all hail, Cornell!"

So: Was this a sacred initiation ritual for me as visitor, or for the weekend? Why not?

We stood close to the falls, roaring as the waters fell. Then the students explained: "The campus is crawling with the FBI, wanting to arrest Father Dan in case he shows up. The only place we could talk without being overheard by their mics was here—the roaring sound masks all conversations."

I blinked. (In silence:) *OK. This Freedom Seder might be even more exciting than last year's.*

Indeed. The students went on: "Suppose, just suppose, that Father Damien did indeed want to come out of hiding and take a public part in the Seder. When do you think would be the right time?"

Woo–hoo!

"Early in the Seder, we say 'Let all who are hungry come and eat. Let all who are in need come to celebrate Freedom.' I think that's when."

They said, "We thought that was one possibility. The other one we thought of was when we invite the prophet Elijah into the Seder."

My mind raced: *In Jewish tradition, Elijah comes just before the Messiah. In Christian tradition, John the Baptist was Elijah, proclaiming the advent of Jesus as Messiah. I admire Father Dan enormously. But—Do I want to certify him Jewishly as a messianic precursor?—I don't think so.*

"No," I said. "I prefer the earlier time."

"OK," they said. "It's up to you."

And off we went to the Cornell campus.

The Seder was held in the enormous Cornell Fieldhouse. There were a couple thousand people, sitting mostly in clusters on the floor. Each cluster had a paper plate with the crucial edible symbols of the Seder: matzoh, a bit of horseradish as the bitter herb, a sprig of parsley, and so on.

I thought to myself, *This might be the biggest Passover Seder since the Roman Empire's Destruction of the Temple! I wonder how many of these folks have any idea what a Freedom Seder is. Maybe they think it's the name of a new rock band.*

The designated leaders of the Seder, including me, were seated on a stage, a few steps higher than the thousands sitting on the floor. Off we went, into the recitation. When we reached the passage I had designated, a man who had been sitting on the floor, covered in a bulky overcoat that overshadowed even his face, arose, walked to the stage, climbed the steps, and took off the overcoat. It was Father Dan.

The fieldhouse went berserk with cheers and clapping. Campus radio was broadcasting the Seder live to dorms around the campus. Suddenly hundreds more students who had been listening on the radio came rushing into the fieldhouse. Many students came to the edge of the stage, sitting back to belly to make sure that no FBI agent could climb the steps to arrest Father Dan. They didn't try.

Father Dan joined in the recitation. About 15 minutes later, a procession of eight-foot-tall puppets, each with a puppet-player inside the tall costume, came marching through the fieldhouse. They were the Bread and Puppet Theater, an iconic group that use the arts of puppetry and pantomime to oppose the U.S. war against Vietnam. They came up on the stage, and mimed the Last Supper, which in Christian tradition was a Passover Seder led by Jesus with his closest comrades. They finished, and departed.

One of the organizers murmured to me, "I guess the Last Supper is the climax and conclusion of the Seder." Under my breath, I thought, *In Christian theology, probably so. In Jewish theology, certainly not. It's true that this is an interfaith Seder, but interfaith doesn't mean the Jewish origins get swallowed up in another tradition.* Aloud I said, "There is still some of the Freedom Seder that we need to recite." And we did.

When next I glanced around the stage, Father Dan was gone. I had no idea when or how he had vanished, once more underground. It took me weeks to learn that as the Bread and Puppet Theater left the stage, one of the puppeteers had ducked out of his puppet and Father Dan ducked in.

For one night, the Freedom Seder had actually liberated one human being. Weeks afterward, the FBI found where Dan was and arrested him.

We finished the Seder—and the first evening of the weekend that the students had named "America is hard to find," after a book of Father Dan's. The weekend went on, and I stayed around. There was lots of rock music, and thick clouds of marijuana smoke. I found myself getting unaccountably annoyed, even angry, and I asked myself why.

Finally it came to me: every Seder needs a Bitter Herb. Dan's presence and its reminder of the raging war had been our Bitter Herb. But now the bitterness had vanished into pure celebration. Instead of the traditional Passover wine alongside the Bitter Herb, we had ecstatic song and marijuana. I remembered Abby Hoffman saying that for the United States to outlaw marijuana was the same as the Soviet Union's outlawing matzah. For the Woodstock Nation, dope was a sacrament.

A sacrament of what? Of the mantra "Be Here Now." And what did matzah teach? Three thousand years of history and struggle, in every generation against new pharaohs and for new freedoms.

I thought, saddened, that simply "Be Here Now" was one truth, perhaps a truth for Shabbat. But I did not think that mantra alone, on its own, could stick it out for centuries against the bitterness of war and slavery and pharaohs. Even with all its internal contradictions, its backslidings, the Jewish People would outlast the Woodstock Nation.

The Influence of the Freedom Seder, 44 Years Later

Rabbi David Saperstein

(In October 2013, The Shalom Center celebrated the 80th birthdays of Rabbi Arthur Waskow and Gloria Steinem with a gathering of shared wisdom and joy called "This is What 80 Looks Like: The Elder as Activist, the Activist as Elder." Rabbi David Saperstein paid tribute to Rabbi Waskow with remarks that included observations about the impact of the Freedom Seder of 1969.)

My friend Arthur is both literally and figuratively an outsized presence in Jewish and American life with creative institutions, reimagined liturgies, and remade community in ways that can only be described as amazing. In fact, many of Arthur's accomplishments, if we had to be honest, seem so improbable that some of us have said that Arthur's ability to accomplish them is nothing short of magical.

What is striking about this, for those of you who happen to be Harry Potter fans, is, with his white beard, his avuncular nature and twinkly eyes, Arthur bears an uncanny resemblance to that magical wizard, Dumbledore. And I know for a fact that Arthur and Dumbledore have never been seen in the same place at the same time.

Arthur is also one of the most prolific writers in modern Jewish life. Every book and article or blog he writes is filled with truly dynamic thinking; he draws from his first career—a Ph.D. in American history and his influential work at the Institute of Policy Studies—as a writer on an array of liberal and radical causes.

There was a time when modern liturgical approaches meant new translations of the traditional liturgy or modern readings from modern sources to supplement it. And then there was 1969: Arthur published a Freedom Seder, integrating in inspiring liturgical modern language— okay, I do acknowledge sometimes over-the-top language—our traditional ritual with the most urgent moral issues our world faces. In that instant, the entire course of contemporary Jewish liturgical writing was altered.

Arthur helped as well to pioneer the Havurah movement, and he helped shape some of the best and brightest in his generation and in my much, much, much younger generation—seeding American Jewish life with some of the most creative and most influential thinkers of our era.

Through Arthur's merging (in the Freedom Seder and in his subsequent decades of creative prose, poetry and prayer), of new liturgies and rituals, the aesthetics of mystical strands of the tradition, the synergy of traditional prayer with meditation, and his passion for social justice—all rolled into the essential expression of who he is—he breathed new air and spiritual power into so many Jewish lives, including so many of you gathered here tonight. All this placed him in a pivotal role in helping to change the Renewal movement, once a marginal presence in Jewish life. Through many of your efforts, Arthur's relentless determination and creativity, matched and inspired by Reb Zalman (Schachter-Shalomi z"l) and by so many of his fellow Renewal rabbis and lay leaders who embraced that aesthetic, the Renewal movement has not only grown into a significant presence in its own right but it has had a profound impact on the Reform, Conservative, and Reconstructionist movements. And it's time, and then some, that that be acknowledged.

It's not surprising to me, that, often discomforting to the establishment, Arthur's amazing contributions to contemporary Jewish life have all-too-rarely been acknowledged. Though Arthur's style may not have been their style, may not be my style, might not even be yours, make no mistake about it: it's the style that Isaiah, Micah, and Amos would have recognized. And we are—every one of us here, every Jew everywhere—beneficiaries of his courage and eloquence and creativity and his relentless nudging.

Dumbledore may have been a great wizard, but even he would marvel at the way that Arthur's writing has enriched and continues to enrich our lives. It is a legacy that has transformed American Jewish life. I would note on this 80th birthday, that while at his age, Moses was just beginning his tenure of leadership, Arthur has been at it for four score and four years now and we celebrate his milestone with the prayer that someday soon he may help guide us to the Promised Land of justice and peace for all God's children he has pursued all these many years.

The Shalom Seders: Three Progressive Visions

Reena Bernards

The day after Ronald Reagan was elected president in November, 1980, I sent for my FBI file. What would I find in my Freedom of Information Act file? Did the government know about my activism? I wondered.

I was in shock, as were my fellow community organizer friends. Could it be that all the progress we've been working for in the decade of the 70s—women's rights, economic equality, a clean environment, was about to be thrown out the window? I was living in San Francisco at the time, running the East Bay office of a statewide organization for low- and moderate-income people. As we gathered for our Monday staff meeting, we looked like shell-shocked zombies.

Weeks later I received a letter from the FBI asking for my social security number. I threw the letter out. If I didn't have a file yet, I certainly didn't want to make it easier for the new administration to start one. In late December I found myself in Washington, D.C. at the "Conference for a New Jewish Agenda for the 1980s." The goal was to unite Jewish activists into a multi-issue organization to create a united front in the face of the Republican victory.

The conference exploded with the energy of over 700 young Jews. There were non-Zionist vegetarians, Modern Orthodox feminists, Reconstructionist pacifists, spiritual secular humanists, anti-nuclear rabbis and everyone in between. There were Middle East junkies—folks who only cared about ushering in Israeli-Palestinian peace and didn't much want to hear about anything else. Also attending were older folks like my parents, who were delighted to see so many young Jewish people so passionate, it didn't matter about what.

Participants stayed up until all hours hammering out by-laws, National Council membership and organizational positions. When it came to Israel, we debated how much of the forbidden terminology to use —Mutual recognition? Palestinian self-determination? Negotiations with the PLO? Two states? Where was the fine line we could draw that would assert what we believed while drawing as many Jews as possible into our circle? Finally on the last day, at 5 in the morning, the organization, New Jewish Agenda, was born. The Levity Caucus revealed a "New Jewish Gender," a person wearing only twisted balloons all over their body. Everyone collapsed in waves of laughter from relief, excitement, a sense of possibility, and utter exhaustion. I was dazzled and fired up.

That September I moved to New York and became director of the nascent national organization, known simply as Agenda. By 1984 we had forty chapters around the country holding vigils and demonstrations, hosting Palestinian and Israeli Jewish speakers in synagogues and Shabbat potlucks where a tofu stir fry was often the main dish. Without smartphones, email or fax machines, all our communication was done by telephone or snail mail. We spent lots of money bringing people together for in-person meetings, a process that was cumbersome, but strengthened our connections to each other.

Enter Esther Cohen, a woman with wild red hair and an infectious laugh. She was the head of a new publishing company, Adama Books, and she had a vision. When she was in college she had gotten to know Arthur Waskow, the famous author and organizer of The Freedom Seder. His Haggadah was written in 1969 for a seder that took place at the year anniversary of the killing of Martin Luther King Jr. Over 800 people poured into a Black church in Washington, D.C., a city still recovering from the aftermath of that tragedy. That Haggadah included quotes by Eldridge Cleaver, Nat Turner, Mahatma Gandhi, Hannah Arendt, Rabbi Tarfon, and Martin Buber.

Esther asked Arthur to update his Haggadah. He said that he had already done so, but he agreed to take another crack at it. Thus, The Rainbow Seder was created. Jeffrey Dekro, my co-director of Agenda at the time, gave Esther the idea of producing a compilation of three Haggadot, each representing a different strand of progressive Jewish thought, in partnership with Agenda. Jeffrey wanted to both promote Agenda, as well as infuse our organization with more *Yiddishkeit*.

The second Haggadah, Seder of the Children of Abraham, grew out of the Philadelphia Agenda's experience in Arab-Jewish dialogue. Added to this was A Haggadah of Liberation, a secular Jewish Haggadah, championed by the Seattle Agenda Chapter, Kadima. Adama Books published them into a paperback compilation, *The Shalom Seders*. The three Haggadot were revolutionary for their time, introducing a multitude of exciting new approaches to the Passover holiday.

In retrospect, each Haggadah also had an interesting, intentional omission. At the Agenda Conference in 1980, Arthur stood up during the discussion of the Israeli-Palestinian position paper, and said, "I'm not putting my head on that chopping block again," referring to the devastation brought upon activists in Agenda's predecessor, Breira, in the mid-

70s. Jewish professionals lost jobs. Others were vilified. So The Rainbow Seder does not include anything about Israeli-Palestinian reconciliation. Rather it speaks of an expansive view of the meaning of the Exodus. Escaping *Mitzrayim*, Egypt, is interpreted literally to mean getting out of a "narrow place." The vision of freedom is broad, and tied to religious symbolism. God's many names are included, and YHVH is encouraged to be pronounced as merely a breath. After the four questions, participants are invited to ask and discuss their own questions about freedom, hunger, homelessness and war. (Of course, since then Arthur has put his head on the Israeli-Palestinian chopping block many times over, including losing jobs, but he was still cautious in those early years following the crushing of Breira.)

The Seder of the Children of Abraham tells the story of the conflict as a dual narrative—a radical concept at that time. Yet it was written without direct input from Muslims, the direct descendants of Ishmael. Essentially, though Muslims could be invited, the seder was not meant to be a joint project. Rather it is a seder to take place after the main seders, aimed at educating Jews about the need to forge peace with the Palestinians. The four children it writes about are instructive. The angry child asks, "Why should I compromise?" The naïve child asks, "Why can't we just love each other?" The frightened child asks, "How can I be safe?" and the wise child asks, "How can we share the land in peace?" The answers to these questions include writings from Israeli Jews such as Abba Eban and Yehudah Amichai, as well as Palestinians including Abu Iyad and Issam Sartawi.

This seder was written by three Reconstructionist Rabbinical students and Agenda members who studied with Arthur in a class called Seasons of Our Joy. They were assigned to create a new holiday ritual. A Christian Armenian Middle East specialist was brought onto the drafting committee. The climate was tense in those days, and the Agenda folks had received death threats from the local Kahane activists. They struggled to find a synagogue that was brave enough to sponsor the seder. Finally after many turned them down, Rabbi Ivan Caine of the Society Hill Synagogue in Philadelphia agreed, though he himself was opposed to the politics of the dual narrative. Mordechai Liebling said, "We were so anxious leading up to the seder that Brian thought he was having a heart attack, Dvora thought she had a brain tumor and I thought I had testicular cancer." Nonetheless the seder was a huge success. The 100 people in attendance included Palestinian members of the Philadelphia dialogue group.

The third Haggadah, A Haggadah of Liberation, never mentions the word God in English. The story of the Exodus is told as a successful slave rebellion, but with humor, very different from the original Rabbinic version, which insists that "God brought you out of Egypt with a strong hand and outstretched arm." This secular version of the story says, "a new committee was formed—the 'How-to-Get-Out-of-Here-Committee.' They met every Tuesday and Thursday night for two months; at the end of two months, people weren't sure that much had been accomplished. Some preferred to remain in slavery rather than face the perils of committee life."

I still think of that committee every time we tell the Exodus story on Passover. The Haggadah powerfully re-centered the Hebrews as agents of their own liberation. The traditional Rabbinic Haggadah does not even include Moses in the story.

I did try to get Bria Chakofsky, soft-spoken yet forceful national Agenda leader, to change some of the language that seemed to me to be too precious. But Bria wasn't having any of it. She had originally written the first version of the Haggadah a decade earlier on rice paper with a group of women. She carried this one copy with her as she moved back and forth across the country and finally settled in Seattle. Bria had her favorite parts. And so in the answer to the child too young to ask, the pajamas remained. "We are thankful for the questions that children ask…for all the favorite relatives in the world; for trees, ducks, bunnies and raisins, peanut butter, clean pajamas, bicycles, dolls and bathtubs. For you, the young people here tonight; for all that you love and for your futures."

Esther moved the three-haggadot project along, inspiring all of us, and creating a network of collaborators. She met an Israeli artist in her elevator on West 30th Street, Amnon, son of the famous kibbutz artist, Ezra Danzinger. Amnon created the cover art for *The Shalom Seders*. The lovely blue-grey cover is adorned with his drawings of the Red Sea, people and rams in rich yellows and greens. Amnon also illustrated the Seder for the Children of Abraham. The Rainbow Seder is illuminated by drawings from The Prague Haggadah of 1526, bringing out its more religious themes. And A Haggadah of Liberation includes drawings and sketches by a variety of artists, emphasizing its idealistic and dream-like vision.

My final job as co-coordinator of the project (along with Jeffrey) was to visit the home of the wonderful short story writer, Grace Paley. Esther was friends with her, and she had agreed to write a preface to the volume. I went to pick up the preface at her small rent-controlled apartment in Greenwich Village. After climbing a few flights of stairs, I knocked on Grace's door. She seemed surprised to see me, but while I was there she sat down at her manual typewriter and banged out the words that introduced our haggadot to the world.

"…Down the hill under the Southern Boulevard El, families lived, people in lovely shades of light and darkest brown. My mother and sister explained that they were treated unkindly; they had in fact been slaves in another part of the country in another time.

Like us? I said.

Like us, my father said year after year at seders when he told the story in a rush of Hebrew, stopping occasionally to respect my grandmother's pained face, or to raise his wine glass to please the grownups. In this way I began to understand in my own time and place, that we had been slaves in Egypt and brought out of bondage for some reason. One of the reasons, clearly, was to tell the story again and again—that we had been strangers and slaves in Egypt and therefore knew what we were talking about when we cried out against pain and oppression. In fact we were obligated by knowledge to do so.

But this is only one page, one way to introduce these Haggadah makers, story tellers, who love history and tradition enough to live in it and therefore by definition be part of its change."

Agenda lasted for twelve years. A slew of single-issue progressive groups popping up in the Jewish community made it difficult for Agenda to compete and survive financially. Also, many of those tireless Agenda activists became parents, and looked for other ways to express their progressive Jewish ideals within the context of raising a family.

Adama Books also closed its doors. *The Shalom Seders*, now out of print, can be bought used on E-bay and other places.

Ronald Reagan is long gone. And exactly thirty-six years later we again woke up on a November morning feeling like shell-shocked zombies. A new, much more dangerous Pharaoh was now the leader of our country.

I reached Esther, now on to many other creative projects, and we talked about *The Shalom Seders*. Echoing what I have heard from many people, she said, "I still use it every Passover. It's full of life and hope.

A Museum of History Creates the Future:
The Contemporary Resonance of Ancient Ritual

Emily August

On April 4, 1969, the third night of Passover and first anniversary of Dr. Martin Luther King Jr.'s assassination, hundreds of people of varying backgrounds and faiths—black and white, Jewish and Christian—gathered in the basement of an African American church in Washington, D.C. They had come to participate in an unusual Passover seder, at which the traditional Exodus narrative was interwoven with texts that spoke to a contemporary struggle: Black America's fight for equal rights.

That landmark celebration is known today as the original Freedom Seder.

Rabbi Arthur Waskow, an organizer and leader of that historic event, had taken content from a *Haggadah* (the established text that guides the order of the seder) that he had been given as a young man when he came of age in the Jewish community as a *bar mitzvah*, and combined it with stirring writings by Dr. King, Mahatma Gandhi, Nat Turner, and others—seamlessly meshing ancient ritual and current events.

The *Haggadah* that Rabbi Waskow assembled for that momentous evening was subsequently published, and a first edition is on display at the National Museum of American Jewish History, located on historic Independence Mall in Philadelphia. The artifact sits in the museum's *Freedom Now* gallery, which tells the story of the Civil Rights Movement and Jewish activism during that period. The 1969 seder and its *Haggadah* have inspired hundreds of contemporary variations.

Including here, at the museum.

For the past seven years, the National Museum of American Jewish History has presented *Freedom Seder Revisited*, with curated, first-person storytelling and multi-disciplinary performances taking the place of a traditional service. Topics have included immigration, public education, personal reinvention, the environment, family, and the power of art to effect social change.

The museum's annual event began with a call for proposals in 2012 from PIFA, the Kimmel Center's biennial, citywide arts festival, which asked: *If you could go back in time, where would you go and why, and what would that look like as arts programming?* It was a challenging prompt for a history museum that covers more than 360 years of American Jewish life (Just one moment?). But as we considered notable milestones in the history we tell, we kept coming back to the idea of revisiting 1969's Freedom Seder. The event lived in the museum as a small moment in the larger narrative but resonated with us on many levels—providing a creative framework for telling the Passover story; making contemporary meaning of historical objects, texts, and events; teaching the next generation and encouraging them to ask questions; delving into the history of the Black/Jewish experience (represented in part by our special exhibition at that time, *Beyond Swastika and Jim Crow: Jewish Refugee Scholars at Historically Black Universities*); and inviting people of all backgrounds to the table, literally and figuratively.

That first year got off to a rocky start. The program was too long, we served the food too late, and we had to condense the allotted time for personal reflection and discussion to the attendees' disappointment. But in spite of all that, we knew the stars had aligned and we were on to something truly special. There was a palpable energy in the room. While I was on the sidelines wringing my hands about event logistics gone awry, there was something kind of magical happening.

As one participant described, "Yes the Seder is a ritual for Passover, a Jewish tradition, your organization took this to another level making this a ritual of freedom for all cultures not just one. Through the narratives we learned what it felt like to be an immigrant, to be a minority, to be part of the 1.5 generation, and through these narratives I received an understanding of what it really means to be American. The fact that you mixed so many cultures into the evening was very powerful and showed what the museum really stands for, freedom and equality. 'Until we are all free, we are none of us free.' To me NMAJH is not just a Jewish museum, but an American immigration story, one that can resonate in anybody."

The community partnerships initiated in that first year have blossomed and deepened into a significant portion of our attendees and table discussion leaders. Speakers have shared remarkably personal stories about enduring a deportation hearing; retracing the journey to the U.S. of a refugee grandfather who survived the Holocaust; and living as a "Dreamer," the cohort of undocumented residents brought to the U.S. as young children.

And, like most programming that touches challenging issues, we have weathered criticism about political bias.

For me personally, it's changed how I think about my own Passover observance. Even if my actual practice hasn't changed, the meaning of the holiday has. It's not just a "Bible Story" we read about each year; it feels genuinely connected to a tangible cultural lineage as well as the present day and my own life.

It also creates an opportunity in the room I don't always experience in "the real world" but want to: not feeling like differences divide us. We can be in the same room at the same table, and come to that table with different experiences, and perspectives, and just *be* different from one another, but appreciate and celebrate those differences, while coming together for a shared experience—it's a "peoplehood" and "humanity" moment in a world where those can seem absent. In fact, the museum was designated as a "Zone of Peace" by the Religious Leaders Council of Greater Philadelphia in great part because of Freedom Seder, an honor we accepted from the stage during *Freedom Seder Revisited 2015*.

It helps to break down barriers or misconceptions about Jews, Judaism, and especially and more tangibly the museum itself—people feel welcome here. As one notable WHYY radio producer who participated shared, "The Freedom Seder was an eye and heart opening experience for me. Sitting at a table with 3 students from Cheney University and one of their professors; a musician; a mother of three who follows Jewish traditions, and an African American cultural leader was both refreshing and totally comfortable. Questions about foods and tradition came naturally and nothing felt awkward. Conversations flowed with ease and a good spirit....I was very impressed and left with a sense of joy for having shared a great moment."

These comments fill me with great pride that I was able to be a part of creating something so important for the museum, and so meaningful for the participants.

Although we've settled into a framework for the event that works for us, the content therein is always changing, and there is plenty of room for growth. We're always trying to think creatively about what future Freedom Seders could look like, and how we might expand the online component, for example.

And there are always still challenges, too.

Because there are so many components of this event—a historical event, a holiday, a museum, contemporary issues, a meal, community partners, table leaders, discussion circles, not to mention the less tangible "feeling in the room"—it can be hard to describe and therefore hard to market. Fortunately, word of mouth kicked in quickly as far as attendance goes, but more challenging: it can make it hard to fundraise for because it's hard to explain just how wonderful and significant it is in just a short sentence or two. But we keep trying.

Even when our organization restructured and staff and budgets were significantly reduced, we held on as tightly as we could to this event. That meant scaling back event components such as the production, music, food, pre-event orientation sessions for community table leaders, and a more hands-off community partner engagement strategy. That same year our CEO, who usually had a significant role to play, was sick and couldn't make it—and she never missed a day of work. I pinch hit for her (fortunately I knew the script inside and out) and, despite a matzah ball soup-only meal, an emcee who was winging it, and technical difficulties (all of which gave us flashbacks to our very first event), we are currently—and gleefully—planning Freedom Seder Revisited 2020.

[Visit nmajh.org/freedomseder for videos from previous years' events.]

Feminist Seders

The Seder Sisters

Letty Cottin Pogrebin

An excerpt from
Deborah, Golda, and Me: Being Female and Jewish in America

Now, nobody *needs* three seders. God seems to think two are enough. Yet I have come to feel that the holiday is incomplete without the all-women ritual that I have attended on the third night of Passover every year since 1976.

Why is this night different from all other nights?

Because on this night, twenty to thirty women sit in a wide circle on pillows on the floor with a cloth spread like a table before us, and we ask the Four Questions of women. On this night, for a change, we speak of the Four Daughters, female archetypes yearning to know their past. And on this night, the goblet usually set aside for the prophet Elijah belongs to the prophet Miriam.

At the feminist seder, Miriam comes alive to me as a rebel (her name means "rebellion"), a leader and a visionary. A famous midrash says that when Pharaoh condemned Jewish babies to die and Miriam's father lost all hope for the future, it was Miriam, then seven years old, who dissuaded him from divorcing her mother Yocheved. It was Miriam who convinced her parents to stay together and continue having children. It was Miriam who rebelled against death and argued for life.

The result was the birth of Moses. Then it was Miriam who watched over her baby brother in the bullrushes and, when the Egyptian princess found him, it was Miriam who put forward Moses's own mother as his wet nurse. Years later, after the crossing of the Red Sea, it was Miriam who led the Hebrew women with timbrel and song, acts recognized as a sign of prophetic power. (Only three women in the Bible are given the title prophetess: Miriam, Deborah, and Huldah.) The traditional telling of the Passover story barely mentions Miriam. Our feminist Haggadah makes amends and gives the prophetess her due.

On this night, we use the Haggadah that Esther Broner wrote with Naomi Nimrod, who runs a parallel seder in Israel. Esther writes,

We were told that we were brought out of Egypt from the house of bondage, but we were still our fathers' daughters, obedient wives, and servers of our children, and were not yet ourselves.

On this night, we become ourselves. We speak with grammar of the feminine plural and invoke the *Shechina*, the feminine essence of the deity, whom you'll remember from the Western Wall. On this night, the ritual handwashing is not a solitary act but a rite of collective nurture. We pass a pitcher of water and a basin, and each woman washes the hands of the woman sitting beside her. On this night, one by one, we name our mothers and grandmothers, the women who cleaned, cooked, and served at family seders while the men reclined against their pillows retelling Jewish history—*his* story, the story of Jewish men.

On this night, we give *her* story equal time. We remember the five disobedient women to whom are owed the life of Moses and the destiny of the Jewish people: his sister Miriam; Shiphrah and Puah, the midwives who disobeyed the pharaoh's order to murder all first-born Jewish sons; Moses's mother Yocheved, who defied maternal desires and gave up her baby so that he might survive; and the pharaoh's daughter, a righteous Gentile who disobeyed her father's decree and adopted a Hebrew baby marked for murder. At our seder, we do not praise good girls and polite ladies; we honor rebellious women.

We also remember the unsung heroines of the rabbinic period: Rachel, who labored for twenty-four years so that her husband could study (what man has done that for what woman?). Beruriah, an esteemed teacher of Torah, whose husband Rabbi Meir insisted on proving that women are weak and thus tested her virtue by sending one of his students to seduce her, again and again and again, until she succumbed—and then killed herself. The daughter of Rabbi Gamliel, a wise woman who does not even have a name of her own. And Ima Shalom, another feisty intellect, descendent of Hillel, daughter of a scholar, wife of the head of the Sanhedrin (governing body), the man who left us such aphorisms as "It is better to burn the words of the Torah than to give them to women."

On the third night of Passover, the words *belong* to women.

Esther, our seder leader, wears her embroidered *kipah* and luminous spirituality with the grace of a high priestess. When she calls on us to read or when she explains the rituals, it is not in a commanding voice like my father's but in lyrical tones that ennoble every word.

Phyllis Chesler, the psychologist and author, also sits at the head of the table, cross-legged like a wise Buddha. Each year, her inventive rituals and the symbolic objects she brings for all to touch infuse our service with kabbalistic magic and mystical rightness.

Lilly Rivlin, a writer and filmmaker, adds sweet intensity and the power of a perfect quotation to illuminate our theme. One year she filmed the seder, and the resulting short feature, "Miriam's Daughters Now," was shown on public television.

Artists Bea Kreloff and Edith Isaac-Rose and journalist Michele Landsberg bring humor and candor to the proceedings, but more important, they contribute strong ideas and political content that ensure ours is not just a women's seder but a feminist one.

These six women and myself constitute the Seder Sisters, Seder Seven, Seder Makers, or Seder Mothers. Whatever we call ourselves, our job has been to bring the event into being, to plan the service, invite the guests, organize the potluck meal, and choose the seder theme.

Last year (1990), the theme was "Omission, Absence, and Silence." Under that heading, we asked participants to undo men's silencing of women and women's self-censorship. My assignment was to create a feminist midrash on Jephthah's Daughter, a character in the Book of Judges. Jephthah, a military general, promised God that in return for the defeat of the Ammonites, he would sacrifice the first thing that emerged from his house upon his return. The first to open the door and welcome him was his (nameless) daughter, whose perspective on the ensuing tale, unrecorded in the Bible, was the subject of my recitation.

"I am here to break the silence of Jephthah's Daughter," I said.

> *Now the questions begin. We ask God, Why did you allow an innocent girl to be sacrificed in your name? You stayed Abraham's hand and Isaac lived. Why did you save the son and let the daughter die? Why to this day have you forgotten all the daughters destroyed by their fathers, neglected, abused, exploited and violated by their fathers?*

The questions I posed to God, the Israelites, and Jephthah challenged us to reexperience a Torah event from the Daughter's point of view, and in so doing reframed the moral of the story.

Through the years, I've kept notes on our seder themes, menus, and guest lists, but my recollections would be dim without the supplementary details in Esther's as-yet-unpublished chronology, *The Telling*, an archival gem. Between the two of us, future historians will know the names of the women who have been part of our seder, who hail from both the secular women's movement and Jewish feminism. They will also know that we took in "the stranger"—non-Jewish women, white women and women of color—such as writers Kate Millett and Mary Gordon; Sonia Johnson, the Mormon woman who was excommunicated for her support of the Equal Rights Amendment; educators Amina Rahman and Betty Powell.

In 1976, we started small. At our first seder, thirteen of us sat in a circle at Phyllis Chesler's apartment and introduced ourselves as we would every year thereafter, by our matrilineage: "I am Letty, daughter of Cell, who was the daughter of Jenny." (Few of us could name a woman who predated our grandmothers.) Esther asked us who our *real* mothers are, who comforts and nurtures us now? One woman said Martha Graham, the dancer, mothered her goals; another credited her art teacher; I named my husband, Bert, realizing quite suddenly that his unconditional love had replaced my mother's.

Then we recited the Ten Plagues, *our* plagues, the afflictions of women: the plague of being unwanted daughters and taken-for-granted mothers, the plague of voices silenced and minds unused, the plagues of poverty, dependence, and discrimination, of rape and battery and sexual exploitation, of defamation and subordination and lost dreams. And we opened the door for the prophetess Miriam ...

The second year we brought our daughters with us, and they would attend every seder from then on. Esther's daughter Nahama, then seventeen, my twins Abigail and Robin, who were almost twelve, and another little girl named Maya Heiman went scurrying through the Broner loft with a feather and a candle, searching for chametz, which we burned together. In 1977, the mothers blessed the daughters. None of us could have known that a dozen years later, these young girls would bless us with a seder of their own.

My notes for the seder of 1978 remind me of how ambitious we were that year. We invited thirty-six women to fulfill our theme, which drew upon the ancient legend of the *lamed vavniks*. This legend holds that the world survives because of the deeds of thirty-six "just men" whose identity is God's secret. We asked each invitee to tell us about a "just woman" who might be a *lamed vavnik* for our age. They brought us stories of Ernestine Rose, Emma Goldman, Henrietta Szold, their mothers, aunts, and colleagues.

Also at this seder, we gave the *afikoman* a new meaning. "We spoke of that breaking of the matzah as a breaking in our own tradition, the hiding of our past from ourselves, the need to redeem it, to create a whole from the broken halves," remembers Esther. To ransom this stolen past would take many more seders and more than a silver dollar.

My 1979 seder list shows that Susan Brownmiller brought the sponge cake; Eve Merriam, gefilte fish; Gloria Steinem, kosher wine; and Bella Abzug, chicken. But I will always remember 1979 as the year of the veil. In response to the Ayatollah Khomeini's rise to power, Phyllis Chesler, our resident symbolist, brought us a *chador*, the head-and-body covering worn by Afghan women. The only opening in this heavy black garment was a small, tightly woven mesh window for the eyes. Each seder guest took a turn wearing the *chador*, felt the weight of its concealment, then each recalled those times when she was figuratively veiled, constricted, made carnal and ashamed. One woman put on the *chador* and found what we least expected: freedom. She said she felt liberated beneath the veil because men could not see her, touch her, evaluate and judge her. We wondered at women's dilemmas—to be hidden or harassed.

We began our 1980 seder by holding up our matzah and proclaiming: "This is the bread of affliction and poverty which our foremothers ate in Mitzraim (Egypt), and every place that has felt like Mitzraim."

The 1981 seder focused on our mentors, those who had influenced our development as women or as Jews. We brought photographs, artifacts, excerpts from their writings. We brought memories and gratitude. Our seventh seder was a numerological feast. Each woman came with her Sevens: the seven-branch candelabrum, Seventh Heaven, the seven seas, deadly sins, lively arts. Some brought the biblical sevens—the seventh day when God rested; the seven weeks between Passover (liberation) and Shavuot (revelation). The seventh year is the sabbatical year when slaves must be freed and the land must lie fallow; the Jubilee year comes after seven-times-seven years; Jacob labored seven years to win Rachel, and seven more after he found Leah in his bed; tefillin is bound seven times around the arm.

Phyllis remembered Joseph's dream. She brought us seven ears of corn to get us through the lean years, the Reagan years.

During the seder of 1983, she wrapped us in a "sacred *shmatte*," a rope of knotted lavender scarves that symbolized our bond, our covenant with each other. It would soon be taken to Israel where it would be wound around Jewish, Christian, and Muslim women in an interfaith peace ceremony. (Five years later, at our Bat Mitzvah seder, Phyllis proposed to burn the sacred *shmatte* as a sign of our coming of age. Horrified, I plucked it from the fireplace. Symbols of women's power are too rare to be destroyed, I said, even for the right reasons. The sacred *shmatte* is a part of feminist history. It is still with us.)

For our ninth seder and in honor of the nine months of gestation, we returned to the theme of mothers and daughters. We invited more mother-daughter pairs, talked about daughters leading the mothers as Miriam led the way for Yocheved. That year, Phyllis brought tablecloths and bedspreads and we raised a tent over our heads to shelter mothers and daughters from the sandstorms of sexism.

The tenth was our outreach seder. Black women came from the Black-Jewish group of which several of us had been part. Esther rewrote "Dayenu:" "If women bonding, like Naomi and Ruth, were the tradition and not the exception, dayenu." And Phyllis rewrote the Ten Commandments: "IV. Love and cherish your mother and all men who are good to her."

1986 was a hard year for the Seder Mothers. There were misunderstandings, quarrels, betrayals. Would the seder survive? Could women rise above their hurt feelings? It would and we did. The theme for this, our eleventh seder, was "conflict resolution." The symbol Phyllis brought for us to pass from hand to hand was a stone, hard and cold, like the angry heart.

During the following year, several of us experienced the death of someone close: Bella's husband, Martin; Esther's father; my friend Toby, who died of a brain tumor the year she turned fifty. So we dedicated our twelfth seder to "Loss and Continuity." As we wept, our daughters dipped their parsley into salt water and promised us a future.

In 1988, our thirteenth seder theme was "Coming of Age." Our Bat Mitzvah year was also the year Israel turned forty, entering middle age in the shadow of the *intifada*, the Palestinian uprising in the occupied territories. We worried about the Jewish soul. As a mark of our own maturity, the Seder Mothers decided we were ready to let go. Next year, the torch would pass to the daughters.

On April 23, 1989, the fourteenth annual feminist seder took place at the apartment that my daughters, Abigail and Robin, were then sharing on West 86th Street, three flights up. It felt strange to just show up with my pillow and a bottle of wine. After so many years encumbered by lists and chores, at last the Seder Mothers were carefree.

Everything had been taken care of by the daughters. Who could have imagined that those little girls tiptoeing around with their candles and feathers searching out *chametz* would so soon become these strong, self-assured, glowing young women who now welcomed us to their seder? Yet, here they were instructing us: this year a beaker of whisky would represent women's *chametz*, the stuff we have to get rid of before we can "pass over" into freedom. Along with our customary introductions ("I am Robin, daughter of Letty, daughter of Ceil, daughter of Jenny") each woman was to name her *chametz* and pour some whisky from the beaker into a large pan to get rid of it.

"My *chametz* is shyness," said one woman.

"My *chametz* is loneliness," said another.

And the list grew and the whisky flowed: Jealousy. Hurtful gossip. Obsession with body image. Passivity. Fear of failure. Addiction to pleasing men. When the pan was full, Robin put a match to it and set the liquid ablaze, burning the detritus of femininity.

Then we could begin. Laurie said kiddush in English, Michal, a young rabbinical student said it in Hebrew. Naomi asked the Four Questions from the Haggadah, then all the daughters posed questions to the "elders:" What do you want to pass on, and what don't you want us to inherit? Are you ready to let go, not just of the responsibility, but of the power? Will you let the daughters be Jews and feminists in their own way?

The young women worried that passing it on meant we were giving it up. They worried that they might not do justice to our legacy; that they would just glide along on the road we paved for them. They felt guilty about being feminists for themselves but not in the context of a movement. They wanted to know: Could they keep their mother's traditions and also change them? At what point does feminist orthodoxy become as oppressive as any other orthodoxy? Could we have an ongoing dialogue between the generations instead of a linear lesson? Mothers who are good role models also are a tough act to follow. We made them strong, now would we set them free?

Naomi broke the middle matzah for the *afikoman*: "What is broken with questions will be made whole when we have the answers."

A question was posed to everyone: Which one are you: Sarah, the self-abnegating wife, Miriam, the smart but unheralded daughter, or Deborah, the fearless leader? Which one are you?

Immediately, controversy raged: "Biblical models are too limiting." "My mother is a Sarah; I can't reject Sarah without rejecting *her*." "Why does a Deborah have to end up alone?" "We all have in us parts of all three women." "Let's synthesize them." "Let's create new paradigms." "Let's continue the seder," said Robin, and we poured the third cup of wine.

Michal talked about the traditional meaning of three of the symbols on the seder plate—matzah, *maror* (bitter herbs), and *pesach* (shank bone). Then we discussed women's equivalents. For the matzah, Nahama held sand, a reminder that we are still in our desert. For the shank bone Robin held a key, symbol of separation and connection—even independent daughters have the key to their mother's door. To symbolize women's bitter herbs, Abigail brought out a wire hanger (a reminder of death from illegal abortion) from which she had hung a toy soldier, a hair curler, a pot scrubber, a 59¢ coin (then the wage gap per dollar between women and men), a TV remote control (our enslavement to media), and pictures of Vice President Dan Quayle (a political adversary) and convicted murderer and batterer Joel Steinberg. The mothers stared. Those were our pharaohs. That was our Egypt. All this we do not pass on.

After communal hand washing, *charoset*, hard-boiled eggs, and a fine meal, it was time for closure. "We have broken the *afikoman* with the daughters' questions and now we choose to restore it with the mothers' answers," said Nahama. "We ask you to help us make it whole again."

But the mothers had no answers. And that, I believe, was our legacy. We said they must find their own answers. We told them to never stop asking questions. We told them that we do not have it all figured out; we only appear more secure because we made our revolution together, with passion and anger. That was our way; they would find theirs.

The truth is, I do have one answer for them: Just as Jews are instructed to remember slavery as if it had happened to each one of us, daughters should remember their mothers' oppression—that wire hanger with its grotesque symbols—as if it had happened to them. Because it could happen to them. Women's Exodus is not complete. Our Sinai is still to come.

The Wellspring: A Public Women's Seder

Rabbi Tamara Cohen

In the winter of 1994, not a full year after I had graduated Barnard College, by a mix of serendipity and good connections, I was hired to do data entry for a feminist seder being planned by a newly founded organization called Ma'yan: The Jewish Women's Project of the JCC on the Upper West Side. I remember little about my interview with Eve Landau and Barbara Dobkin, two friends from Westchester who seemed to me to be surprisingly warm and welcoming of me.

My liberal Jewish parents had still not fully warmed to the idea of my being a lesbian and the institutions of the Conservative movement that raised me were deciding that gays and lesbians had no place in their leadership. But Barbara and Eve didn't seem to care at all. They were funny and loving, they needed help planning a Seder, and they saw in me, with my recent degree in Women's Studies and my 12 years of day school education, an addition to their team they would embrace and nurture and elevate without hesitation.

Barbara had been hosting a feminist Seder in her own apartment and the guest list was getting longer than she could accommodate but she was clear that she didn't want to turn anyone away. She knew well of the invite-only feminist Seder of Esther Broner and Letty Cottin Pogrebin. This was a seder that dared to ask questions, on this night of many questions, like what would the seder look like if it featured four daughters instead of the classic four sons. Barbara loved and respected many of those women and their radical innovations; but the exclusivity of their seder, which was held in an Upper West Side apartment, was not what she believed was the ultimate way to hold a feminist seder.

Barbara wanted something that was open to anyone who wanted to come and she was willing (and able, as a major feminist philanthropist) to make this vision a reality. As soon as I learned about Barbara's vision and met her, I felt I had found a new home and purpose. I resonated deeply with the call, to paraphrase the words of the Haggadah, to "let all who are hungry for a feminist Passover experience come and eat, come and learn, come and dance, come and build community." And that's precisely what I was able to help make happen for close to 50,000 women and their loved ones, allies and friends, over the coming ten years.

I came to Ma'yan and to the project of co-creating large and inclusive communal feminist seders and a Haggadah to use at those seders, both very prepared for what I was about to help create and very much in need of the healing that the process of working on the Haggadah and seder was going to provide me. I grew up in a home where the Passover Seder was a yearly peak experience that my whole family poured significant energy and focus into creating. While my mother cooked and cleaned and put away and took out dishes, my father stacked up books of poetry and biblical commentary, and came up with themes and questions for each Seder.

The non-egalitarian nature of this Seder preparation was lost on no one, and yet it persisted. My father was an ideological feminist deeply committed to the independence and power of his three daughters and his wife, but he never became a true helper in the kitchen.

The ways in which this limited my mother's ability to celebrate the Festival of Freedom was something I carried with me right into the Ma'yan seders. I also carried my father's creativity, his model of leading a seder that was relevant, engaged in the political and social questions of our day, and one that always made space for every person at the table regardless of age or gender or anything else to participate and contribute. I carried his passion for using the seder to not only tell the story of the Exodus but to tell and explore many Jewish and non-Jewish stories about the complex and often painful journey of seeking liberation.

In 1989, five years before participating in my first Ma'yan seder, I co-organized a Jewish feminist conference at Barnard while also slowly beginning the process of coming out to myself and others as a lesbian. That process would have been difficult no matter what, given the strong heteronormative assumptions of my liberal suburban Jewish community and family and the larger society around us. But it was made all the more painful by the proximity to me of the Jewish Theological Seminary, the institution of higher learning of the Conservative Movement with which I still identified at the time, which was debating and then deciding against the ordination of gay and lesbian rabbis just as I was coming to terms with my own queer identity.

During my time at Barnard, I felt torn asunder at the prospect of all I was going to lose by being true to myself, my identity, and my desires. I also felt angry at a Jewish community that had given me the tools to create innovation but was now telling me I could not use those tools or further develop them because I was not fit to be a role model to young people because of my sexuality.

So, five year later, to have the story of the Exodus from Egypt—a primary metaphor of coming out of narrow places into freedom in Jewish tradition and beyond—and the practice of telling a story about liberation suddenly at the center of my life, through the job at Ma'yan, was an incredible gift and invitation.

When I reflect back on it now, I feel immense gratitude to the forces in my life and to the Source of All, that somehow I was given the opportunity to create a Haggadah and a Passover experience that would, over the course of the next decade, not only bring together thousands of Jewish women and their friends, family members and allies, to sing, learn about, and explore the powerful metaphors and relevant symbols of the seder, but would also bring me right back into the center of Jewish innovation and life and take me out of the exile I felt that the debate on gay ordination had forced me into.

Ma'yan held one seder attended by over 200 women in 1994. That first seder was led by Rabbi Joy Levitt and Cantor Nancy Abramson. For it, I think I only co-wrote one piece, a Dayenu prayer that allowed me to begin to reflect on what was enough for me in terms of Jewish connections and observance as opposed to what were the norms of many in my community. That seder happened to be held in the dining room of the Jewish Theological Seminary. This was a room I had come to as a Barnard student when I was among those speaking to faculty and rabbinical students about the gay ordination issue. This time I was back—not telling my personal story in the hope of influencing change, but taking part in a retelling of a communal story that highlighted for me just how difficult the journey to liberation could be.

After that year, Ma'yan began holding multiple seders in the weeks before Passover. We moved to a catering space in South Street Seaport and for three nights in a row sang and danced with hundreds of women and a few men. The seders were attended by many synagogues' Sisterhoods, Rosh Hodesh groups, and intergenerational gatherings of matriarchs, daughters and granddaughters. Some came drawn by Debbie Friedman's name and the desire to sing with her. Others came because they had heard this was something not to be missed. Many returned year after year.

The Haggadah evolved from the one first created by Rabbi Joy Levitt and a committee of volunteers to the final one, which I edited and which included numerous original songs the late pioneering singer- songwriter Debbie Friedman, z"l (may her memory be a blessing), several of which I co-authored after Debbie's and my experiences leading the seders. For example, we wrote "Gather Round" after the experience of being in a loud room with hundreds of women and not wanting to hush them in order to get folks' attention to begin. The Haggadah also drew on the one created by the American Jewish Congress Feminist Center in Los Angeles where Rabbi Sue Levi Elwell had worked before she came to Ma'yan.

The introduction to the 1997 edition of the Ma'yan Haggadah which was co-edited by me, Debbie Friedman, Rabbi Sue Levi Elwell and Ronnie M. Horn, explained that the Haggadah, which we named *The Journey Continues,* "was created to answer the need for an Exodus story told in its fullness, in the voices of women as well as the voices of men." [We were still quite binary in those days.]

It continues, "It incorporates questions posed by daughters as well as sons and includes symbols, stories, and midrashim that flow from women's reflections and analyses. Interweaving new and traditional texts, this is a document of an evolving Jewish tradition that is being transformed by women's perceptions and strengthened by women's songs."

While these statements reflect a feminist approach that is solidly focused on the category of women as there is some nuance in understanding that category, the introduction does go on to lean more towards a wider view of feminism when it states that "a vision of a better world in which freedom belongs to all people is reflected throughout the text."

Through the years of seders and the various editions of the Haggadah, I struggled with whether the seder and the Haggadah were taking participants far enough. I wondered, and often, we, the staff at Ma'yan debated, about the power of the seders. What could ritual do and what was beyond what ritual could do? What kind of change could we effect through these communal rituals? Could we connect people to organizations that would engage them in longer-term movements for feminist social change?

Was what we were doing enough? Was it *dayenu* to bring women, largely white upper middle class women from all over the New York area (and when Debbie Friedman and I travelled with the seder all over the country) together to learn women's history, talk about liberation, say the words racism and homophobia, and make connections between the Exodus and the treatment of Hagar by our foremother Sarah?

We continually added more to the seders. We put tzedakah boxes on the tables and raised money each year for different feminist causes and organizations. We added "Do Something" boxes highlighting various feminist initiatives in the Jewish community in the Haggadah. We honored activists with each of the 4 cups. We created a national competition to get artists to make Miriam Cups and stimulated the popularization of that ritual object. We sold 30,000 Haggadot to groups and individuals all over the country. We taught thousands of women about feminine God language and gave them the experience of using it.

And still we asked, as perhaps, the Haggadah instructs us to, is this dayenu? Is this enough? Is this a good use of time and money? Or perhaps to paraphrase Isaiah on Yom Kippur, we asked, *Is this the seder You desire?* In the end, with hindsight, I think the Ma'yan seders were incredibly powerful foundational and sustaining experiences for thousands of feminists. If I were to do them today, they might look somewhat different; they would be more trans-inclusive, they would likely be interfaith, they would be more much more centrally antiracist and reflective of the experiences and leadership and music of Jews of Color and Mizrachi and Sephardi women and queer and non-binary people. But I do believe that what we did in those years helped pave the way for many of the queer and feminist and progressive seders that happened in the years after the Ma'yan seders.

Perhaps the most powerful part of the seder for me was dancing to Miriam's song with hundreds of women of all ages, many with tambourines in their hands, through the huge ballroom. It was an experience of living midrash. I felt like I was reimagining the past with each step, and more than that; not only was I transforming my understanding of the past, but that collectively we were changing the past by dancing in the present. We were changing the memory of the past. It was that powerful.

Women: Enslaved or Liberated by the Seder?

Rabbi Shalom Schachter

Chag Sameach. May you have a joyful holy day!

Each year when Pesach comes, our circumstances are different—so we can identify a current reality that in some way oppresses either ourselves or others.

I want to identify one area of oppression that may not have been the subject of your *seder* discussions during the last two evenings—that is, the abuse of women in domestic relationships.

There is a myth that domestic abuse does not occur in the Jewish community. Unfortunately this is not the case. Israel's first Prime Minister is reported to have said, "When Israel has prostitutes and thieves, we'll be a state just like any other." In a similar vein, we are a community like any other, with our share of people engaging in anti-social behaviour, wife abuse being just one example.

The following are some statistics to clarify the prevalence of abuse in the Jewish community and society at large: Domestic violence in Jewish families occurs at about the same rate as it does in other religions—about 15 to 25 percent. The difference is that Jewish women take 7 to 15 years to leave abusive relationships versus 3 to 5 years for other women. In a study on domestic abuse in the British Jewish community, it was found that 26 percent of the 842 people surveyed had personally experienced domestic abuse, despite a third of the respondents admitting that they thought that abuse in the Jewish community was less prevalent than in other communities. In this particular study the number of Jewish women who were being abused was two percent higher than the national average!

In Canada... Out of the 83 police-reported intimate partner homicides in 2017, 67 of the victims—over 80 percent—were women. On any given night in Canada, 3,491 women and their 2,724 children sleep in shelters because it isn't safe at home.

In a moment I will set out a narrative for the four daughters from the *seder* ritual. For the men, however, I ask a more sensitive question. In the same way we are obliged to consider *b'chol dor vador* our own need for a *yitzi'yat mitzrayim*, we need to ask ourselves what part of that release is the need for us to liberate ourselves from the oppression we impose on women. How are we being coercive in our relationships with women?

One of the songs in the *Haggadah* is *Dayenu*. "It would have been enough for us." If we pay attention to the text however, *Dayenu* is really more of a question than a statement. If God had only taken us out of Egypt but not split the sea to enable us to escape Pharaoh and his army, would that really have been enough for us? The answer is clearly no.

So a *Dayenu* in a *seder* focusing on the need to end domestic violence would contain the following verses:

1. If he only stopped beating me, would that be *dayenu*?
2. If he only stopped threatening me, would that be *dayenu*?
3. If he only stopped using the children against me, would that be *dayenu*?
4. If he only stopped treating me as a sex object, would that be *dayenu*?
5. If he only stopped isolating me, would that be *dayenu*?
6. If he only allowed me to work, giving me sufficient money for family needs and access to family accounts, would that be *dayenu*?
7. If he had only begun to apologize and promise not to repeat his conduct, would that be *dayenu*?
8. If he had stopped imposing coercive control and asserting male privilege and instead, accepted me as a full partner—THAT could be *Dayenu*.

The four questions in such a *seder* could consist of the following:

1. Why even on this night, have I had to do all the household work including serving the food and cleaning up, so that the only item to be eaten remaining on the table when I can finally take a break, is the hard tasteless matzah?
2. Why even on this night when everyone else is celebrating, do I only experience bitterness?
3. Why even on this night do I only have salty tears and no access to the sweetness of *charoset*?
4. Why even on this night when everyone else is sitting and relaxing, am I limited, if I can eat at all, to grabbing a bite while on the run?

The narrative of the four daughters could be expressed as follows:

1. The *chachama*—the observant one—could ask, "How can I challenge my oppression? Won't my rabbis state that it is my fault and it is my

duty to better obey my husband?" That daughter can be responded to by pointing out the *halakhah* "ein maftirin." We do not exempt husbands in Jewish law from the prohibition on mistreatment of other human beings and we don't exempt rabbis from their responsibility to pursue a comprehensive *shalom bayit*—household peace—addressing the power and control dynamic in the house. We go back to the creation story where God said it is not good for a man to live alone and created *eizer k'negdo, a "counter-part."* The Rabbis teach: *zacha eizer, lo zacha k'negdo*; if the husband is worthy, he will merit a partner; if he is not worthy, he will have an opponent.

2. The *rasha*—the alienated one—could state, "There is no point in rebelling; the system is fixed and corrupt, and the authorities will always side with the husband." That daughter can be responded to with the phrase "*hakhei et shinav.*" We refute her claim by pointing out that we are all created in God's image, male and female we were created. It is not the architecture of Creation that is corrupt. The flaw comes from tyranny that some men enact, and the necessary answer—that is really built into the architecture of Creation, as Pesach itself proves—is to resist tyranny.

3. The *Tam*—the naïve one—will ask "How am I oppressed?— he isn't beating me." That daughter can be answered "*b'chozek yad hotzi'anu.*" It is not enough for the hand not to strike out; the hand has to be an instrument of liberation. The *yad* has to be connected to a "*z'ro'a netu'ya*"—an outstretched arm of sowing seeds of new possibility.

4. The *she'eino yoda'at lishol* is the one who is so overwhelmed by trauma that she cannot even begin to communicate the details of her oppression. The *Haggadah* identifies the proper response "*Aht P'tach la.*" You create the opening for her to find her voice with a range of supports including testifying for her in court, writing letters of support, etc.

In order for the seder to be an uplifting experience, there needs to be some *tikvah*—some hope for relief for redemption.

The four cups could be expressed as follows:

1. *V'hotzeiti*—I will take you out. The first step in your redemption is to remove yourself from the location of the abuse. There are women's shelters that can provide an immediate refuge for you and your children. Friends/family may be willing to step up and allow

you to stay in their home, which is much more hospitable than having to stay in a shelter.

2. *V'hitzalti*—I will save you. Once you are located in safer accommodation, you can be provided with the care and support you need, whether to heal the wounds of physical violence or to heal your soul with love and counseling.

3. *V'ga'alti*—I will redeem you. You will be provided with access to legal representation to pursue protections you need to live independently, whether restraining orders to bar the abuser from contacting you, or representation for divorce to enable you to start over, and for custody orders to protect your children.

4. *V'lakachti*—Literally, I will take you. The Hebrew letters of the source of this word are *Lamed Kuf Chet* which also means a lesson. You will have learnt a lesson in relearning how to be kind to yourself and have a positive self-image.

Most *haggadot* mention a fifth cup, the cup of Elijah or the cup of Miriam, *V'heiveiti*—I will bring you. This cup talks about a future redemption. This hope is reflected in the statement *L'shana Haba'a B'yerushala'yim*—next year in Jerusalem.

In this case, however, there is no need to wait for next year. There already is a helping hand ready to bring you towards your new promised land. There are centers to protect abused women with "doulas" who provide support and referrals for all client needs including food, shelter, accounting, and more.

This essay concludes with the guidance from the *Haggadah* on how the process of liberation starts.

1. V*a'afilu kulanu chachamim*—whether we are wise and have avoided oppressing others or being oppressed ourselves.

2. *Kulanu z'keinim*—whether we are worn out from being oppressed or from efforts to challenge oppression.

3. *Mitzvah aleynu l'sapeir bi'y'tzi'yat mizrayim*—it is a mitzvah to begin and to continue telling the story of oppression and to outline the path for escape.

4. *V'chol hamarbeh l'sapeir harei zeh m'shubach*—and the one who engages at length in this conversation is blessed.

Gay and Multi-Gender Seders

Mah Nishtanah?
Pesach Liberation and LGBTQ Coming Out

Rabbi Sharon Kleinbaum

Only when the Israelites come out of Egypt and pass through the Sea of Reeds, when they abandon the comfort and security of their familiar though oppressive lives, do they begin to experience the abiding presence of God. Upon leaving Egypt, they become the sacred community which is God's dominion.[1] *Pesach*, the night of their liberation, marks the beginning, not the end, of their journey. It is a long journey, a journey of unremitting crisis, a journey that often seems to be nothing more than an aimless wandering, a new exile without end—maybe even worse than their lives in Egypt. But it is also a spiritual journey, a journey of insight and understanding, of growth and revelation. The way of the Holy One is through the wilderness. Only weeks after leaving Egypt the former slaves are at Sinai, and their new identity as a free people is born.

Finding revelation in exile is a profoundly Jewish experience. It is not in the Promised Land, the land of milk and honey,[2] that the Torah is given to the people. It is in exile, in *galut*, that our identity as individuals and as a people is formed. The escape from physical persecution and oppression is ultimately not enough to form a spiritual identity; the physical liberation must be coupled with an existential struggle for genuine identity that is not defined by the fight against an oppressor. It is a journey of cosmic significance for the Israelites. In leaving the familiarity of slavery, they brave the desolation of the *midbar* (wilderness) for the promise of physical freedom, only to discover that Sinai still awaits them.

For LGBTQ Jews today, coming out is also a spiritual journey, not unlike the coming out of our ancestors that we celebrate at *Pesach*. Like Egypt, the closet is indeed a narrow place.[3] Only once we are in the open, in the wilderness of life, where we experience the welcome, indifference, or (God forbid) the hostility of family, friends, colleagues,, community, synagogues—that we, individually and collectively, discover ourselves and our relationship to God. Our true relationship to God is not defined by the oppression of the closet but by the lives we live once we come out.

---

[1] Psalm 114

[2] Deuteronomy 11:9

[3] The Hebrew name for Egypt, *Mitzrayim*, means "narrow places."

In every generation, the Haggadah tells us, we are bound to regard ourselves as if we personally had gone forth out of Egypt. The generation of the Exodus was not the first to experience the sequence of oppression, liberation, crisis, revelation, and growth; nor were they the last. We retell their story on *Pesach* not only to honor them with our remembrance but also because all of us—whatever our Jewish background or our path to a chosen Jewish identity, whether we are learned, ignorant, observant, secular; whatever our gender, sexual orientation or expression—have gone forth ourselves from so many Egypts and because so many more still wait for us in the wilderness.

As a Jew, a woman, a lesbian, and a rabbi, I find profound meaning in the Jewish holidays. To this lifelong activist, organizer, and leader of Jewish, feminist, LGBTQ+, racial and economic justice, and other causes, *Pesach* emerges as particularly special. I personally have known many Egypts and celebrated many moments of liberation. As a rabbi, I witness countless moments of liberation in the people around me. But I have learned that the initial exhilarating act of liberation is always, in fact, a beginning, never the culmination of the process.

My own story of emergence as a lesbian rabbi goes back nearly 40 years, and starts with the heroic "Mosaic" acts of courage of colleagues who came before me. I can place one first moment of liberation in 1985. In 1985, not one rabbinical student anywhere in the world was officially out to the faculty or administration of her or his seminary. Out rabbis were few and far between, and none of them were in pulpits. Then, in the spring of 1985, the Reconstructionist Rabbinical College adopted an admissions policy that stated simply, "RRC does not discriminate on the basis of sexual orientation."

The sense of relief was palpable. Lesbian faculty member Rabbi Linda Holtzman remembers it as "jubilation."[4] Only one problem remained: What now? What would this new freedom really mean in practice? Would lesbian and gay rabbis get jobs? Would donors to the RRC still donate? Would the college become a pariah, would the movement itself suffer? What would we have to do now? Since no one knew, in 1987 I formed a committee called "What Now?" to find answers and to help ensure that the liberation implicit in the college's new admissions policy did not remain on paper only.[5]

---

[4] Linda Holtzman, *Struggle, Change, and Celebration in Lesbian Rabbis: the First Generation*, (New Brunswick NJ: Rutgers University Press, 2001), 45.

[5] The committee included Rabbi Rebecca Alpert, Rabbi Jacob Staub, Rabbi Linda Holtzman, Rabbi Sharon Cohen (then a student), Rabbi Dan Kamesar (then a student), and myself (also then a student).

It did not. LGBTQ+ Jews have claimed and created their place in Judaism. It is an ongoing process and one that didn't happen in isolation. What began as the "gay synagogue movement"—itself a product of the post-Stonewall[6] gay liberation movement—was crucial, as was the support of prominent members of the wider Jewish community.[7] The evolution of the movement has not been linear or monolithic. Lesbian and gay synagogues sprang up all over the world. Some of them evolved into LGBTQ synagogues and continue to serve a unique function in the Jewish and queer worlds. Others did not evolve from their initial missions and became obsolete in a changing queer landscape. In 1985, a group of us gathered, via word of mouth: gay and lesbian rabbinical students, rabbis, cantorial students, cantors, educators—in a secret convening we called "aron hakodesh"—the Holy Closet. We were given a city to fly or drive to, and a phone number to call when we arrived; only then were we told where we were gathering. Many in that group came back from that gathering, strengthened and inspired to change the Jewish world for those who would follow.

In the meantime, mainstream synagogues have embraced their LGBTQ congregants, and strive to be welcoming. All of us, even those most progressive and whose evolution has taken them the farthest, acknowledge that for bi and trans Jews and for all Jews of Color, welcome and inclusion are still goals pursued more than goals achieved. It is inspiring to witness the strength of leadership emerging among trans, bi, non-binary Jews, and among Jews of Color, whose presence in Jewish life is as old as history yet has gone unpardonably unrecognized for too long. Trans people of Color are at great risk and are being murdered in our streets. The Orthodox community, also, has an important—if necessarily still low-profile—LGBTQ movement. CBST now has a Haredi Rabbi on staff as our scholar-in-residence, doing the urgent work of exploring LGBTQ issues from many angles within a halachic framework. Rabbi Mike Moskowitz is engaged in teaching and outreach in the Ultra-Orthodox and Modern Orthodox worlds that would have been simply fantasy when I started at CBST in

---

[6] The Stonewall riots were a series of spontaneous demonstrations of resistance by members of the gay and transgender community against a violent police raid that began in the early morning hours of June 28, 1969, at the Stonewall Inn in the Greenwich Village neighborhood of Manhattan, New York City. While neither the first nor only demonstrations of their kind, the Stonewall riots mark the beginning of the modern gay liberation movement in the minds of many Americans.

[7] Most prominently, Rabbi Hershel Matt z"l, Rabbi Alexander Schindler z"l, and Rabbi Arthur Green.

1992. ESHEL,[8] JQY,[9] openly gay Orthodox Rabbi Steve Greenberg, and others are openly organizing LGBTQ Jews and their families.

The non-Orthodox Movements—Reconstructionist Judaism, Reform, Renewal, and Conservative Judaism—have all adopted positions welcoming LGBTQ Jews officially. All ordain openly lesbian or gay people (more controversy remains around the recognition of bi and trans Jews). All allow their clergy to officiate at weddings for same-sex couples. Out LGBTQ rabbis get pulpit jobs and serve in leadership roles throughout the progressive Jewish world.

I am humbled and emotional when I think of the history that has led to this moment. When I began at Congregation Beth Simchat Torah (CBST) in 1992, we received a steady stream of telephone calls and emails pleading for help of all kinds: help with how to reconcile homosexuality with traditional Jewish law, help with coming out. Most urgently and poignantly, heartbreakingly, people begged for support in dealing with AIDS. At that time The Jewish Theological Seminary still rejected out lesbians and gays as candidates for ordination as rabbis. Marriage for lesbian and gay couples was still not recognized legally (this is, of course, not only a Jewish problem), a victory we have achieved since (and in which CBST played an important role); although we see under the current Trump Administration how fragile even that victory remains.

Hate crimes against LGBTQ people are still a tragic reality and antisemitism is resurging in American society. Liberation comprises more than release from slavery, more than leaving the closet. When we take the risk and step outside the narrow place, when we witness the persistent and newly emergent dangers of life in the wilderness, the pull to return to Egypt can become truly tempting. In the wilderness, the Israelite community grumbled against Moses and Aaron. The Israelites said to them, "If only we had died...in Egypt, when we sat by the fleshpots, at least we had our fill of bread! For you have brought us out into the wilderness to starve to death."[10]

This is not the only time the Israelites express their frustration. Later, they complain:

Did you bring us out of Egypt to kill us and our children

---

[8] Established officially in 2012, "Eshel's mission is to create a future for Orthodox lesbian, gay, bisexual, and transgender individuals, and their families."

[9] Incorporated in 2010, New York City-based Jewish Queer Youth (JQY) is a nonprofit organization supporting and empowering LGBTQ youth in the Jewish community that CBST hosts in its building.

[10] Exodus 16:3

and our livestock? If only we had meat to eat! We remember the fish that we used to eat fresh in Egypt, the cucumbers, the melons, the leeks, the onions and the garlic. Now our gullets are shriveled. There is nothing at all! Nothing but this manna to look to![11] When faced with the rigors of the wilderness and the uncertain promise of the Land, the people long to return to the comforts of familiar Egypt—even though it also means accepting oppression.

For LGBTQ Jews, the struggle to leave Egypt and enter the wilderness includes the internal, emotional strain of self-discovery and self-revelation; and it includes the enduring and horrifying risks of being visible and human in a society inclusive of those who embrace and celebrate their bigotry and inhumanity. We dreamed of a better and safer reality than this, but as in the biblical narrative, liberation did not mean safety. It brought new dangers along with a new identity. The journey towards freedom, the endless pursuit of justice, comes with great pain and exacts an enormous personal toll.

Egypt for the Israelites; the closet for LGBTQ Jews—each offers its sad compensations. We can understand those who felt more anxiety about the uncharted future than they did about the oppressive past. The invisibility and anonymity offered by Egypt crushed the soul, but it provided some measure of stability if it didn't suffocate the spirit or drive one to suicide. At least in Egypt your job was secure; slaves worked. Closeted, your marriage might be a lie, but your children would not be taken from you if your secret held. Closeted, you might get to be a board member of your synagogue. At least as a closeted Jew you could teach the stories of our people in a religious school and pretend that the problems of LGBTQ Jews didn't apply to you. At least in the closet you might not get beaten on the street or told you deserve AIDS or suffer a violent death for expressing your true gender, unlike the poor, pitiable victims out there. At least in Egypt there are leeks and onions. Liberation is exhausting, and we must have compassion for the nostalgia people felt.

The great tension of the experience of the wilderness is the tension between the impulse to go forward toward the Land and the understandable pull back to Egypt. There is both a willingness and an unwillingness to put Egypt firmly behind us. We want to come out, but we want to cling to our sense of security, even if it is illusory. And so the bulk of our Torah deals not with slavery nor with the Promised Land but rather with that trek, full of ambivalence and anxiety, through the wilderness. It is better to be

---

[11] Numbers 11:4-6

out of Egypt even if we are not yet in the Land. But while parts of each of us, individually and collectively, are out of Egypt, others remain. And we are—all of us—still far from the Land. But "*libi bamizrach*,"[12] the heart yearns for the East, the heart yearns to be in the East. The heart yearns for the Land. The heart yearns for full emancipation and enfranchisement, for true liberation. Despair is antithetical to Judaism, which teaches us that to yearn for and envision the Land even while living in the chaotic emptiness of the wilderness is no less than a divine commandment. Hope is not a luxury. Hope is more vital to survival than manna. That struggle to hold onto a vision and time to try to achieve it even while we wander in the wilderness has, for thousands of years, been the defining characteristic of an exiled people, homeless, always dreaming of coming home to the Land.

Moses' parting words to the Israelites 40 years after the first *Pesach* are words of vision and against despair. It is not an easy message to deliver from the edge of the wilderness. After all, as professor Arnold Eisen has pointed out:

> What has never been cannot be remembered and neither can it be described. All Moses has available is his language, and his own words will inevitably fall far short of the task assigned them because it is impossible to talk convincingly about a state of affairs which no one has ever experienced. What do wholeness and meaning look like? What will it be like to be really completely at home?[13]

The 16th century mystics, the Lurianic kabbalists, took this a step further, teaching that the exile would end only when a complete repair of the broken world was achieved. But ending exile and reaching the land is not enough. The vision that Moses imparts even while he is dying is clear. Access to, and tenure of, the Land is conditional. We must do more than reach the Land: we must do it with justice or else, as Torah warns us, the "Land will spew forth its inhabitants."[14] We must construct a moral, ethical code that affirms, challenges and even inconveniences us. When we have the privilege of freedom, we will have strangers to love and help. A stranger is someone whose story we see as "other" than our own and whose needs we see as secondary to our own. We will fear for our own security

---

[12] Title of a famous poem by Medieval Spanish Jewish poet Yehuda haLevi

[13] Arnold Eisen, *Galut: Modern Jewish Reflections on Homelessness and Homecoming,* (Bloomington IN: Indiana University Press, 1986), 21.

[14] Leviticus 18:5

and yet be obligated to establish and provide it for people whom we don't immediately recognize as "us." It will not be enough to cross the physical river Jordan. We must really leave Egypt and its soul-death behind. We must individually and collectively have the courage to live with a vision of Torah that both teaches us how to live in the wilderness and simultaneously pulls us further toward the Land. We will have to engage with the mitzvah of loving our fellow creatures as we love ourselves, which requires that we ourselves develop genuine pride in being who we truly are. With such a vision we may have the *zekhut*, the merit and privilege, to one day reach the Promised Land.

How do we get there? No matter where in the wilderness, no matter how close or how far we are from Egypt, we—all of us—must struggle to have a vision of the Land, a sophisticated and multi-dimensional view of liberation. If we can't envision a Land to dream of, with milk and honey for everyone, there will be no hope, the fatigue of the struggle will defeat us, and the pull to return to Egypt will be overwhelming. That pull will suffocate the very breath of our souls that ache to be in the East. *Libi bamizrach.* The time in the wilderness must be spent creating and living a vision of Torah, not consumed in hatred of the Egyptians, because that will stunt our growth and waste our time. Such a focus will not ultimately form a living Judaism that will sustain us spiritually, and God forbid it be our only bequest to the next generation. And not only the next generation of Jews we count as kin already. Pharaoh's last words to Moses and Aaron after telling them and the Israelites, finally, to be gone, are, "And may you bring a blessing on me also!"[15] We are responsible for fighting for our liberation and for creating a world in which we can transcend our anger and our history of oppression and bring blessings to all. Please God, may it be so.[16]

---

[15] Exodus 12:32

[16] This essay is a second adaptation of the keynote sermon given at the 12th International Conference of Gay and Lesbian Jews in San Francisco, May 24, 1991. In the 30 years since it was first written, the world has changed so much, and yet so much of my original thinking and framework feel current today. I could not have written this without the wisdom of Rabbis Sharon Cohen Anisfeld, Yoel Kahn, and Margaret Moers Wenig in 1991 and David Dunn Bauer in 2020. Rabbi Wenig's reactions to early drafts were insightful and helpful. Sections of this piece were first worked through in an extraordinary seminar taught by Rabbi Nancy Fuchs-Kreimer at the Reconstructionist Rabbinical College in the spring of 1990. I would also like to thank Andrew Goldfarb and David Rosen, Religious Action Center 1990-1991 legislative assistants, for their help.

The Song of Songs Seder:
A Night of Sacred Sexuality

Rabbi Robert dos Santos Teixeira, LCSW

The Freedom Seder, in more ways than one, gave birth to The Song of Songs Seder. I was nearly thirty-five when I attended my first seder,[1] and the host chose—from the thousands of haggadot in existence—The Freedom Seder. I can still remember the bold, black title against the bright red background.

Years later, at the height of Occupy Wall Street, I attended another Freedom Seder, at Judson Memorial Church in New York City. Reb Arthur, who led the seder, shared a teaching that stuck to me the way mortar sticks to brick: "The ingredients for charoset," he said, "are found in the Song of Songs, and this simple fact, if we think about it, can change how we understand our relationship with the Divine."[2]

As the original Freedom Seder was emerging—in the months following Dr. King's assassination—Chandra Mohan Jain, a young Indian teacher (who, years later, would call himself Osho) was making his public debut. His talks, *From Sex to Superconsciousness*, focused on the oppression and liberation of sexuality.

"Everything is nectar," he said. "It is man alone who has transformed this full cup of nectar into poison. And the major culprits are the so-called teachers, the so-called holy men and saints, the politicians.... Religion and culture pour poison against sex into the mind of man."

This work—a cogent assessment of humanity's sexual health—stayed with me. It illumined the *Sex-Is-Holy-Sex-Is-Dirty* divide, which is one of the oldest and widest fault lines cutting through the human family.

We find evidence of this divide in every faith tradition, including Judaism, where we encounter it numerous times in the Talmud, in reference to the

---

[1] As a descendant of Portuguese Marranos, it took me a while to find my way "back" to Judaism.

[2] At the first public celebration of *The Song of Songs Seder*, which took place at West End Synagogue, in New York City, on 29 April 2016, Reb Arthur repeated his teaching on charoset and the Song of Songs. That evening, teachings on Sacred Love were shared by Reb Arthur and Rabbi Phyllis Berman and additional teachings by Mr. Joshua Greenberg and Rabbi Robert dos Santos Teixeira.

Song of Songs. This book, which revolves around the play of two lovers, is by far the most erotic in the Bible, and Jews are enjoined to read it during the Festival of Passover.

According to the Talmud, the Song of Songs was actually set aside to be buried because of its X-rated content (Avot De-Rabbi Nathan 1:4). At length, the rabbis debated whether to include it in the Bible. In their deliberations, they used the curious phrase "renders unclean the hands."[3] Holy books, in their view, were "too hot to handle" on account of their intrinsic holiness. Handling them, then, renders unclean the hands, that is, makes one more or less untouchable, until specific rituals of purification can be carried out.

> Rabbi Judah says: The Song of Songs renders unclean the hands, but there is a dispute about Ecclesiastes. Rabbi Jose says: Ecclesiastes does not render unclean the hands, but there is a dispute about the Song of Songs.... Rabbi Simeon ben Azzai said: I received a tradition from the seventy-two elders...that the Song of Songs and Ecclesiastes render unclean the hands. Rabbi Akiba said: Far be it! No man in Israel disputed about the Song of Songs [by saying] that it does not render unclean the hands. For the whole world is not as worthy as the day on which the Song of Songs was given to Israel; for all the writings are holy but the Song of Songs is the Holy of Holies.
>
> (Babylonian Talmud, Yadayim 73a)

Go Akiba, go!

Including the Song of Songs in the sacred canon of scripture came with a price, however: The story was allegorized, that is, interpreted as a love affair between the Lord and the community of Israel, and in the process, it was desexualized. For example, in Rashi's eyes, the breasts of the female lover should be understood as the two staves (handles) of the ark, Moses and Aaron, the two Tablets of the Law, the king and the high priest, or the synagogue and the study hall, anything, anything but breasts.

Throughout the centuries, Jewish mystics—subscribing to the dictum "as below, so above"—clung to a more ancient understanding of the Song of Songs. The mysterious Kabbalist Joseph of Hamadan—a contemporary of Moses de Leon, who redacted the Zohar, the central work of Kabbalah—regarded the male and female characters in the Song of Songs as the masculine and feminine faces of divinity, as the heavenly Bridegroom and

---

[3] Martin Sicker, *An Introduction to Judaic Thought and Rabbinic Literature* (Westport, CT: Greenwood Publishing Group, 2007), 10-13.

Bride, celestial reflections of their earthly counterparts.

In his *Sefer Tashak,* Joseph of Hamadan writes of the Bride, whom he refers to as the Matrona (the Great Married Mother):

> King Solomon, may peace be upon him, said in his wisdom, "I am a wall, my breasts are like towers" (Song of Songs 8:10), this alludes to the breasts of the Matrona that are like towers, and from these holy apples of the Matrona the righteous in the Garden of Eden and the holy angels are nourished.... From these breasts of the Matrona the upper and lower beings are sustained, and the holy angels and souls of the righteous draw forth from there honey and milk. Thus it is written, "Honey and milk are under your tongue." (Song of Songs 4:11)[4]

We humans were fascinated by sex long before Solomon and the Shulamite began chasing each other. We have always been caught up in it, and we always will be.

Unfortunately, our faith traditions have not kept up with our interest, or perhaps I should say, kept it up. For millennia, religious establishments have been busy severing us at the waist and brainwashing us into believing that sexuality is confined to dirty old Earth and has nothing to do with the Supernal Light.

The Song of Songs Seder: A Night of Sacred Sexuality is a response to this Pharaoh! It can be celebrated on the eve of the Intermediate Sabbath of Passover (when many Jewish communities chant the Song of Songs), or it can be celebrated on the third, fourth, fifth, sixth, or seventh nights of the festival. Participants, gathered around a table, enter the Garden for the Wedding Banquet of the Heavenly Bridegroom and Bride.

The seder, which unfolds according to a fourteen-step Haggadah, includes themed variations on familiar components. Four cups of milk and honey, for example, replace the four cups of wine, the Love Story (the Song of Songs) swaps places with the Exodus Story, Four Wedding Guests stand in for the Four Sons, and the King's Cup for King Solomon and the Queen's Cup for the Queen of Sheba take the place of Elijah's and Miriam's. The excerpts that appear below should offer a taste of the banquet's richness.

The host, introducing the seder plate, says:

---

[4] J. Zwelling (translator), *Joseph Hamadan's Sefer Tashak: Critical Text Edition with Introduction* (J. Zwelling, 1975), 323.

The Song of Songs Seder Plate, like every seder plate, contains six foods, one for each point of the Sacred Hexagram. This shape, known since antiquity as the Seal of Solomon, is imbued with Love. First and foremost, it symbolizes the seamless unity of Divinity, indeed, of all things. The upward-pointing triangle represents the Divine Masculine and the downward-pointing triangle the Divine Feminine. HE and SHE are ecstatic Oneness, filling all creation and flowing into and through every human relationship, opposite- and same-gendered.

Guests, taking turns, introduce the foods:

… The Pomegranate, mentioned more than any other fruit in the Song of Songs, symbolizes fertility and conjugal love par excellence. The Shank Bone symbolizes the Divine Masculine, in particular, the Cosmic Phallus or Lingam, the upward-pointing triangle of the hexagram. The Egg symbolizes the Divine Feminine, in particular, the Cosmic Vulva or Yoni, the downward-pointing triangle of the hexagram…

While keeping one foot in the Garden, guests step into the Egypt of Sexual Oppression and come face to face with the Ten Plagues Inflicted on Sacred Sexuality:

The Tenth Plague: Death of the Firstborn (Sexual Violence)

Countless fathers and mothers cry out in pain over the Death of the Firstborn, that is, the deaths of their children, who were victims of sexual violence. Rape, hate crimes based on gender identity and sexual orientation, and state-sponsored sexual terrorism are forms of sexual violence. Homosexual sex between consenting adults punishable by death is an example of state-sponsored sexual terrorism. (Homosexuality is a capital crime in twelve countries: Afghanistan, Brunei, Iran, Mauritania, Nigeria, Pakistan, Qatar, Saudi Arabia, Somalia, Sudan, the United Arab Emirates, and Yemen. Armed groups, such as the Islamic State, while operating within the borders of Iraq and other countries, have executed people for homosexuality.)

Guests go on to eat the famous Hillel Sandwich; afterward, they prepare the Selfless Love Sandwich, consisting of charoset,—that is, Love Paste—and pomegranate seeds.

In sum, *The Song of Songs Seder*, first and foremost, offers a much-needed sacred context for celebrating, discussing, and exploring human sexuality, while at the same time offering much more. Someone once asked me, "Why did you choose the title, '*The Song of Songs Seder: A Night of Sacred Sexuality?*'" I must have had a puzzled look on my face because the person followed up with another question, "Why did you choose the words 'A Night of Sacred Sexuality?'" My answer then and now is the *raison d'être* for the seder.

To celebrate the seder is to celebrate the reality of sacred sexuality. Non-personality, I tell my students, cannot give birth to personality; non-gender cannot give birth to gender; non-sexual desire cannot give birth to sexual desire; and non-ecstasy cannot give birth to ecstasy.

"As below, so above."

To celebrate the seder is to step into a world, a Garden, where "God"—echoing Joseph of Hamadan—is thoroughly male, thoroughly female, and thoroughly sexual. God, you see, has accepted, is accepting, will always accept the invitation, "Eat, lovers, and drink: Drink deep of love!" (Song of Songs 5:1), and the implications for us (as a result of this acceptance) are many and far-reaching.

There is a lot to see in that Garden: If we see the Light shining through God, we can see it shining through ourselves. If we see the Light shining through God's body, we can see it shining through our own, every part. If we see the Light shining through God making love, we can see it shining through ourselves while we make love. And if we see the Light shining there at that moment, we can see it shining everywhere at every moment, and the TRUE NATURE OF THIS WORLD and WHO THE WORLD IS can be revealed.

At the end of the seder, the wedding banquet guests—having reached Nirtzah, the Fourteenth Step—conclude *The Song of Songs Seder: A Night of Sacred Sexuality* with these words:

> *HE and SHE are ONE, in Bliss, forever and ever! "Love is fierce as death, Passion is mighty as Sheol; its darts are darts of fire, a blazing flame. Vast floods cannot quench love, nor rivers drown it! (Song of Songs 8:6-7)*
> *L'shanah Haba'ah BaGan!*
> *Next Year in the Garden!*

Song of Songs Seder
Celebrating Queer Sexuality

Susala Kay[1]

JeWitch Collective's (JWC[2]) "Song of Songs *Seder* Celebrating Queer Sexuality" (Queer *Seder*) is inspired by "The Song of Songs *Seder*: A Night of Sacred Sexuality"[3] by Rabbi Robert dos Santos Teixeira LCSW.

Teixeira's ritual was a radical transformation within Jewish liturgy. A rabbi had written, led, and published a ritual about sacred sexuality in a mainstream Jewish context. Its focus on pharaonic forces made sense on the one hand since it was a Passover *seder* which was all about rebellion, escape, and liberation. On the other hand, I intuitively knew that I needed to queer it. I envisioned a flamboyant edgy ritual situated at the intersection of traditional Judaism and JeWitchery.

Queering the ritual de-centered heteronormativity and other majority cultural norms. It subverted the power structure of what and who are deemed worthy of praise, challenged the status quo and used quotes from traditional texts to provide a new theological experience. The goal was to open new pathways of understanding and truly be an act of *tikkun olam*.

Queering it was a multi-year odyssey. It has grown into a collective project that is still evolving and became an annual event. Synagogues and other Jewish organizations across denominations partnered with queer organizations to make it a community-wide event. In 2019, the Queer Cultural Center commissioned JWC to transform the haggadah[4] I authored into a ritual performance that was a part of the 21st National Queer Arts Festival.

Participating in unabashedly Queer activist Neo-pagan rituals produced in the San Francisco Bay Area by the Reclaiming Collective has inspired

[1] The author wishes to thank Devin Pastika, Nancy Kates, and Jonathan Furst for their input and support during the writing of this.

[2] Visit: www.jewitch.org to learn more about JeWitch Collective and what it means to be a JeWitch

[3] "The Song of Songs Seder: A Night of Sacred Sexuality" (2014) is available in its entirety at: https://ritualwell.org/sites/default/files/The%20Song%20of%20Songs%20Seder.pdf. It is also discussed on pages 54-58 of this volume.

[4] That haggadah had been adapted from Teixeira's and was entitled "Song of Songs Seder: Celebrating Queer Sacred Sexuality."

JWC to create deeply embodied rituals that employ audacious costumery and brazen sexual expression as ritual technologies to fuel "the life-changing, world-renewing work of magic, the art of changing consciousness at will.[5]" *Chutzpadik* Jewish feminists' writings have influenced this project. Joan Nestle, the legendary lesbian writer and historian, expresses the paramount role eros plays in *tikkun olam*. She said:

> ... as a lesbian (and) as a Jew, ... much of what I call history others will not. ... Erotic writing is as much a documentary as any biographical display.[6] ... Being a sexual people is (Queers') gift to the world .... We, who love this way, are poetry and history, action and theory, flesh and spirit."[7]

The Queer *Seder* employs explicitly sexual and erotic language and descriptions because eros is a generative and powerful life force that has sustained the LGBTQ community. Drawing on it empowers us.

The Ritual[8]

Entering the Song of Songs garden, you cross the threshold at the gate of Urban *Adamah*, an urban Jewish community farm in Berkeley, California. You arrive at one of the sensual stations, called "G-spots." This G-spot uses sound to cleanse toxic patriarchy. Percussive sounds that disrupt the energy surround you, clearing negative vibes.

You make your way toward the G-Spot of Abundant Blessings. Here, you pick a blessing for dancers to bestow upon you. "Do you feel comfortable with respectful touch or being touched by a *tallit*?" they ask. After answering, Blessers envelop you with sounds, whispering the requested blessing in your ear and chanting it as they dance around you with swirling hands and a flowing *tallit*.

You and other participants linger to watch and listen:

---

[5] Reclaiming Collective's definition of magic can be found at: https://reclaiming.org/principles-of-unity/.

[6] From the Preface to the 1st edition of *A Restricted Country*, 1986.

[7] From "Flamboyance and fortitude: An introduction." In J. Nestle (Ed.), *The Persistent Desire: A Femme-Butch Reader* (pp. 13-22). Boston: Alyson. Queen, C. A. (1994).

[8] Go to: https://www.jweekly.com/2019/06/12/magic-sex-and-blessings-at-an-unconventional-seder-in-berkeley/ to read an article about the event and see photos.

May the schmutz of life be washed away.

May you roll in spice beds and your lover inhale your fragrance.

May meshugas in your life lift like morning dew.

Sister Lilith of the Valley[9], her gold lamé glistening in the sunlight, is heard saying "HONEY, I would like DIS-respectful touch!" Peals of laughter ring out as the chants continue:

May you lie among your lovers' lilies and immerse yourself in their perfume.

May your lips and tongue explore petals and stalks until love pleases.

You wonder what lies ahead, realizing that the actual *seder* has yet to begin.

You make your way toward the G-Spot of Delicious Delights, where The Daughters of Jerusalem are. One asks "would you like one of these juicy ripe plump fruits, so deliciously described in the "Song of Songs? I'm happy to feed you if that is your desire." Another Daughter of Jerusalem, Sister Norma Lee Chaste, in full drag, offers to drizzle wine or honey into your mouth.

The shofar sounds beckoning you to join a procession led by singers and other musicians chanting a *Sephardic* melody of "Song of Songs." You join them and dance under a *tallit* into the sacred tent where the *seder* takes place on *Pesach Sheni*, a second Passover and holiday of second chances. You learn that this is an ancient holiday, carved out for those deemed "ritually impure" and those who could not attend the first *seder* after the liberation from Egypt because they were away on a journey. Its very existence illustrates how Jewish tradition creates customs to welcome the marginalized. Queer Jews, in Israel, claiming it as their own, have declared *Pesach Sheni* a Day of Religious Tolerance,[10] a time to engage in dialogue with orthodox communities about feeling stigmatized, unwelcomed, and far from home.

---

[9] Sister Lilith of the Valley is a Jewish Sister of Perpetual Indulgence playing a Daughter of Jerusalem, a character in "Song of Songs," at the event. For more about the Sisters of Perpetual Indulgence see: https://www.thesisters.org

[10] See https://awiderbridge.org/tomorrow-pesach-sheni-religious-tolerance-day-in-israel/

In the tent, you look around and notice the diversity of the community and its leaders. The *Ohlone* people who were the first to live in Berkeley and still inhabit the land are acknowledged. A rosy-cheeked rabbi and his husband, who is wearing a garment traditionally worn for special occasions within his Yoruba community in Nigeria, describe Queers as a people who journey spiritually and physically, reminding us that we are known for resilience and overcoming obstacles.

The ritual foods are introduced. First you find out about the challah:

> This challah represents the roundness of breasts, bellies, and buns ... As we share it, we embrace families of choice, the beauty of round bodies, polyamorous relationships, as well as a spectrum of genders and sexualities within our communities. Chapter seven verse two of "Song of Songs" (says) "your navel is perfectly formed like a goblet filled with spiced wine. Between your thighs lies a mound of wheat encircled with lilies."

A *Mizrachi* feminized blessing is led, you are fed and feed the *challah* to others savoring all of this.

Next the egg is explained:

> "The egg symbolizes the Divine Feminine, in particular, the Cosmic Vulva or Yoni referred to in *Kabbalah*"[11] ... Song of Songs chapter five verses four to six are quite explicit: "My beloved thrust his hand through the latch-opening; My heart beat wildly. I rose to open to my love, my fingers wet with myrrh, sweet flowing myrrh, on the handles of the bolt. I opened for my beloved" ...

The next reader tells you that:

> ... *Marror* represents the bitterness that can be inter-twined with erotic energy; when love is unrequited, when shame and/or trauma blocks an ability to embrace sexual-ity. It also reminds us of the hotness that can come from safely, sanely and consensually playing with power and pain; whether it's the sting of complete surrender, the hot

[11] This is a quote from Rabbi Robert Teixeira's "The Song of Songs Seder: A Night of Sacred Sexuality, page 52 of the present volume.

scratches from a wild date, or wrestling and tumbling with a rough lover. Chapter two verse two of "Song of Songs" references the bitterness: "Love can be painful, "like a lily among thorns" You are invited to ingest some horseradish, letting yourself feel the rush of it – connecting with and finding pleasure in the sting of pain.

To end the Queer Seder, the group conjures a magic spell based on Allen Ginsberg's poem "Excerpts from Footnote to Howl," which you learn is probably inspired by the *Kedushah*[12] in *Yotzer Ohr*[13]. In this poem, Ginsberg, the renowned out Jewish[14] gay Beat poet, celebrates cocks and assholes as holy.

Rising up and down on your toes,[15] chanting "Holy, Holy, Holy" over and over, you begin to feel empowered as the energy in the room increases. A cone of power[16] builds. Spontaneously, others call out verses from the poem and other meaningful phrases. The intensity builds and you join others in gathering all the energy fueled by this JeWitchy experience of feeling deeply in your body, the sacredness and power of Queer sexuality. All at once, everyone focuses and sends this magical, primal life-force energy out to all who need it, knowing that the essence of queerness can help transform the world.

---

[12] For an explanation of this prayer see: https://en.wikipedia.org/wiki/Kedushah_(prayer)

[13] The first of two blessings that precede the Sh'ma in Jewish morning religious services

[14] To read about a recording from 1969 of Ginsberg speaking at a Hillel where he reflected about his spirituality and faith as well as his thoughts about "the power of "hypnotically repeated chants" of the rabbinical tradition and specifically the "spiritualized voice" of Rabbi Shlomo Carlebach" go to: https://www.yiddishbookcenter.org/language-literature-culture/vault/man-out-time-allen-ginsberg-montreal.

[15] "It's an ancient custom to spring up and down on one's heels while saying these verses ...to enact our striving upwards towards holiness like angels each time we pronounce the word "holy" (this quote is from "Bouncing in the Kedushah" by Rabbi Julian Sinclair published on March 19, 2015 in The Jewish Chronicle. The entire article can be viewed at: https://www.thejc.com/judaism/jewish-ways/bouncing-in-the-kedushah-1.65724).

[16] For an explanation of what a cone of power is go to: https://www.learnreligions.com/the-cone-of-power-2561490

Tikkun Olam

Experiencing the *seder*, in and of itself, was a healing experience for many participants. Lorelai Kude, a straight attendee, went directly home from the Queer *Seder* and penned an article[17] about her experience of the event. The following excerpts illustrate some of the ways she found it healing.

> (I arrived at the Queer *Seder* as) someone who has never really found a demographically appropriate connection to where the Queer community intersects with the Jewish community, I hoped this was a chance to forge that connection. ... Walls ... have been my experience in Berkeley – until the "Song of Songs *Seder*." ...

> ... For the first time since coming to Berkeley almost six years ago, I found bridges instead of walls ... "I am as light and free as a gazelle!" I cried out loud to the garden, ... A gazelle with a second chance, every day.

> ... Flashes of my own "long journey" rose unbidden to my mind, clouding my eyes with tears more than once during the *Seder*. ...

Lorelai mentioned other's healing journeys as well.

> ... As the *Seder* neared the end, (a) diminutive, older woman ... spoke to me ... "I just came out a couple of months ago," she said in a soft voice, her eyes shining with pride. "I'm 81 years old." ... (Lorelai replied) "That's a long, long journey to become yourself indeed." We smiled into each other's eyes, sharing a moment of intimate light.

This woman's pride in coming out exemplifies what Joan Nestle says

> the freedom to be sexually expressive, the freedom to be different, is a freedom for all of us. ... In our difference we must

---

[17] Kude, Lorelai. *Walls and Bridges: A Bridge-Builder's Experience of the "Song of Songs Seder Celebrating Queer Sexuality"* (May 2019) Published in The Aquarian Minyan's Newsletter.

join together.[18] ... (because to do so is powerfully healing.)

Like Lorelai, another *seder* participant who identifies as a straight observant Jew seemed moved by the event. Her email said:

> I wanted to thank you and all the organizers for the *Seder*. The inclusiveness, expansiveness, respect, and generosity woven into the entire ritual moved me and changed me. Thank You.
>
> Warmly,
> Aliza

The Queer *Seder* seems to have succeeded at highlighting the gifts that Queers and Queer culture bring to society, and how these influence the larger world.

Future of the Queer Seder

The Queer Seder had become a JeWitch Collective tradition until the pandemic. Our hope is that it will be adopted by others and have a life of its own. We would be very honored to help other communities make this happen.

---

[18] From the documentary about Joan Nestle's life "Hand on the Pulse," which was made by Joyce Warshow.

Israel-Palestine Seders

The Seder of the Children of Abraham

Rabbi Brian Walt, Rabbi Mordechai Liebling and Catherine Essoyan

> *We come to this seder as Jews committed to Jewish survival and to the survival of the State of Israel.... We as Jews acknowledge that we are deeply affected by the historic pain and suffering of our people. At this point in our history we feel that it is crucial for our survival to hear not only our own pain and vision but the pain of the Palestinians, the people with whom we so urgently need to effect reconciliation. We admit that it will be hard for us to hear of their anguish and suffering, yet it is in fact in our own self-interest to open ourselves to listen, however hard it may be. Listening to their story in no way negates our own—our claim and our vision remain legitimate, central to our identity and survival.*

This quote is from the introduction to *The Seder of the Children of Abraham,* the first-ever Pesach Haggadah focused on the Israeli Palestinian conflict, that the three of us, Mordechai Liebling, Brian Walt, and Catherine (Cat) Essoyan, wrote in 1983—along with Rabbi Devorah Bartnoff z'l of blessed memory.

Looking at this quote, some 37 years later, we are struck by our beliefs that informed the writing of the Haggadah. Our strong conviction about Zionism and the need for a Jewish state are particularly striking, as is our passionate commitment to hearing the voice of the Palestinians. The most radical piece of our Haggadah was including the Palestinian voice alongside the Israeli Jewish voice in every part of the Haggadah. Other haggadot included references to Israel; several even included the singing of Hatikvah at the end of the seder. Ours was the first Haggadah that told the story of the Israeli Palestinian conflict from both sides. It was the first dual-narrative Haggadah.

In the 37 years since then, much has changed in Israel/Palestine and in our own lives and understanding. We have all learned a lot about the conflict, including many historical realities that we didn't understand back then. We still believe that it is essential for Jews to hear the Palestinian narrative and to understand their struggle for justice. Yet, if we were to write a Haggadah now, it would look very different from the one we wrote in 1983. In this essay we will examine:

1. The beliefs and values that informed the Children of Abraham Haggadah
2. Changes in the context and our perspectives since 1983
3. Lessons we draw

Part 1:
The beliefs and values that informed
the Children of Abraham Haggadah

The beliefs and values that informed the 1983 Children of Abraham Haggadah reflect our lives at that time. Mordechai, Devorah and I were rabbinical students at the Reconstructionist Rabbinical College. Catherine Essoyan (Cat), who is not Jewish, had lived in Lebanon from age 10 to 18 and has a master's degree in Middle Eastern studies and conflict resolution. In 1983, when we wrote the Haggadah, she was on the staff of the American Friends Service Committee working on issues of the Middle East, Lebanon, the Occupied Palestinian Territory, and Israel. From 1984-87, she ran a Quaker legal aid center in East Jerusalem for Palestinians on the West Bank.

Three of us were liberal Zionists. We supported Israel as a Jewish state, yet we also fully acknowledged that the creation of Israel had caused great suffering to the Palestinian people. Brian and Devorah were particularly connected to Israel and Zionism; Mordechai less so. Cat was deeply committed to a solution for both Palestinians and Israelis and to nonviolence as an approach to peacemaking. We all believed that both peoples had a claim to the land and that both claims needed to be fulfilled. We supported a historic compromise based on mutual recognition and a two-state solution. We were also members of New Jewish Agenda, a national Jewish organization devoted to social justice, that followed the demise of Breira ("There is a choice!"), the first Jewish organization to challenge the unquestioning support of the American Jewish community for Israel. The Haggadah was printed by New Jewish Agenda in *The Shalom Seders*, a collection of three alternative freedom haggadot.

At the time, our beliefs put the three of us who were Jewish on the progressive edge of the American Jewish community that devoted a massive amount of resources to unequivocal support for Israel—and to silencing anyone who was sympathetic to the suffering of the Palestinian people and their right to an independent state of their own. This censorship was national in scope, but the Philadelphia Federation and other mainstream Jewish organizations in Philadelphia were particularly intolerant of any dissent. We knew and feared that our activism on the issue of Israel/Palestine could affect our professional lives as rabbis in our community. And, indeed it did.

We also wrote this Haggadah in the context of a class on the Jewish holiday cycle taught by Rabbi Arthur Waskow at the Reconstructionist Rabbinical College. Arthur was a prominent Jewish teacher who also supported justice for the Palestinians. The assignment in the class was to create a new ritual for a Jewish holiday. Our Haggadah was the fulfillment of that assignment.

The structure of the Children of Abraham Haggadah was quite traditional, even though its content was not. Every section of the traditional Haggadah was included and every section was related to the conflict. The four cups of wine were dedicated to different values that were essential ingredients in solving the conflict: security, trust, hope, and peace.

For example, for the first cup, we quoted the Talmud:

> "A person who does not own a piece of land is not a secure person."
> And we might add in the land of one's heritage.
> We raise the first cup in acknowledgement of the legitimate desires of each people to lead a secure life—a life free from fear—secure in the knowledge that they have a land from which they cannot be driven.

The four questions were questions about the conflict.
For example, the third question:

> On all other nights we don't dip herbs at all; on this night we dip them twice to honor two peoples, the Palestinians and Israelis who must and will together find the path to mutual respect and coexistence.

The ten plagues were instances of horrific violence inflicted by Israelis and Palestinians on one another: Deir Yassin, Maalot, Kfar Kassem, Hebron, Sabra and Shatila.

The *maror* (bitter herb) symbolized the bitterness and bloodshed between the two peoples.

The name of the Haggadah, *The Seder of the Children of Abraham*, reflected our commitment to presenting a dual narrative about the Israeli-Palestinian conflict. With quotes from Torah and the Quran. we highlighted the story of the two brothers—Isaac, one of the patriarchs of the Jewish people; and Ishmael, the patriarch of the Muslim people. We wrote:

> In Jewish tradition Isaac is the son who is bound to be sacrificed. In Muslim tradition it is Ishmael. In our generation, both peoples, the Israeli and the Palestinian, have faced the possibility of extermination, our only alternative is in fact mutual recognition. The urgent challenge of our time is to learn to dwell "face to face" as brothers and sisters.

We were also very moved by a teaching that we learned from Arthur Waskow. He pointed out that when Abraham died, the Torah records that the two estranged brothers come together to bury their father.

Shortly after the publication of the Haggadah, Jewish feminists pointed out to Arthur that we had ignored Sarah and Hagar. This was clearly a mistake that was corrected when Arthur wrote a revised version a few years later that included the matriarchal line.

The dual narrative character of the Haggadah was most evident in the maggid (telling the story) section, by far the longest and most important section of our Haggadah. We told the history of the Israeli-Palestinian conflict mostly through selections from first-hand accounts by contemporary Israelis and Palestinians. We hoped that this section would educate readers about both narratives—particularly the Palestinian narrative—about which most American Jews knew very little.

About the maggid, this historical section of the Haggadah, we wrote,

> These threads of history are not offered as an authoritative, objective historical account but rather as a way of gaining an understanding of our commonalities and finding a way to move towards peace. Therefore our history will focus on the commonalities shared by both peoples: our common love for the land, our common experience of exile and our common oppression. We also acknowledge the tragic, destructive killing that we have inflicted on one another. We will focus special attention on those Israelis and Palestinians who have had the courage to envision a new reality, a reality of peace,

sharing and mutual respect.

The process of choosing passages written by Palestinians was very challenging. Whose voices would we include in the narrative? At the time, the Israeli and American governments refused to even recognize the Palestinian Liberation Organization (PLO). Would we include people who were associated with the PLO? Would we include Palestinians who had engaged in violence?

Telling the history through the voices of Palestinian leaders alongside those of Jewish Israelis was probably the most radical part of the Haggadah and the most challenging for us personally. The readings of those passages were some of the most powerful moments at the public seder we held at Society Hill Synagogue in Philadelphia in 1983. (It was hard to find a Jewish venue that would host the seder and the synagogue bravely hosted us out of a commitment to free speech, even though they didn't agree with the goals of the seder.) Including Palestinian voices was a direct challenge to the complete censorship of these voices and of this history in the Jewish community. And it was those passages that our opponents in the Jewish community highlighted when they attacked the Haggadah.

One such passage was from Raymonda Tawil describing her friendship with a Jewish girl, Dvorah, whose family occupied the house of Tawil's aunt who fled to Lebanon during the fighting.

When she told her Jewish friend, Dvorah, that her house belonged to her aunt, she was shocked.

> *"Take your doll," she exclaimed. "Let's be friends!" She explained that her family had received this house from the government on arriving in Israel. "We came from Poland; we were also refugees.... Later she showed me the Auschwitz number tattooed on her mother's arm. "I'm very sorry we took over your aunt's home," she said, "But try to understand—if we hadn't come here we would have all ended up in the gas ovens."*
>
> *I bore no resentment against Dvorah or her parents. I sensed that they, too, felt the injustice of occupying someone else's home. "Soon the Arab refugees will be allowed to return to their homes, they reassured me, and our government will build new houses for us and then Jews and Arabs will live in peace." They were as naive as I: neither they nor I knew the true intentions of their government. My aunt was never permitted to return, and Dvorah's family remained in that house for twenty-five years.*

Composing this telling of both stories side by side was a challenging and transformative experience for us on a personal level. The three Jews were deeply connected to Israel—two of us were passionate Zionists—and like the overwhelming number of American Jews, Israel was a critical part of our Jewish identity. Our Judaism was integrally connected to Zionism. We had internalized the Israeli story of the conflict that denied the history and suffering of the Palestinians and presented an incomplete and false narrative about the founding of Israel. The realities we were learning about Palestinian history contradicted deep beliefs from childhood. Unlearning what we had learned was painful and evoked a profound sense of loss.

We knew very little about the history of Palestinians. We knew about the Occupation; but we knew little if anything about the *Nakba* (the catastrophe), the term Palestinians use to refer to the 1948 war and expulsion of the majority of Palestinian inhabitants from what was to become the State of Israel. Nakba was not a term we used. We may even have been inclined to dismiss stories of expulsion and massacres by Jewish Forces as lies. Yet we knew that our knowledge about Palestinian history and suffering was extremely limited and that we had lots to learn. On a personal level, the process of writing the Haggadah was a process of learning about this history. It was intense.

We all remember one night working on the Haggadah when the three Jews involved in this project all complained of intense psycho-somatic symptoms. We each imagined that we were about to have a heart attack, to get cancer or have a breakdown. Cat was just dumbfounded; we were all bemused and could laugh at ourselves together.

Undoubtedly, one source of anxiety was our fear of composing a Haggadah that would be condemned by Jews and Jewish communal institutions. However, it was much deeper than that. It was about our personal confrontation with the reality that the creation of Israel involved the expulsion of the Palestinians. How were we, as Jews and rabbis, to integrate this truth into our understanding of our own faith? We believed that the essence of Judaism is about the inherent dignity and equality of all people. We believed that we were the descendants of slaves who wrote a sacred text that insisted that we should never oppress anyone else. What we as Jews and rabbis were learning about Israeli actions against Palestinians challenged the very foundation of our Judaism, our Jewish identity, and our support for Zionism.

In addition to telling both narratives side by side, a second goal of the Haggadah was to support Israelis and Palestinians who were taking actions towards peace and to inspire American Jews (and Arab Americans) to challenge "it's either us or them" perspectives in our respective communities. We especially wanted to highlight folk on both sides who took risks to advocate a compromise between the two peoples. For this reason, we dedicated the Haggadah to Issam Sartawi and Emile Gruenzweig, a Palestinian and an Israeli Jew, who were both murdered because of their advocacy promoting compromise. Their lives were a source of hope and inspiration for all of us.

Towards the end of the seder, Cat introduced the third cup of wine, the cup of hope, that celebrated actions by Israelis and Palestinians that moved the communities towards one another. In her remarks, she highlighted a private meeting between Israelis and Palestinians at Harvard that included members of the PLO and Knesset, who reached substantial agreement on different ways to end the conflict. She also pointed to twin opinion columns that had just appeared in the *New York Times* by Knesset member Yossi Sarid and Harvard professor Walid Khalidi, in support of mutual recognition and a two-state solution.

The cup of hope ended with a quote from Nissim D. Gaon, the president of the World Sephardi Federation, in his call for mutual recognition. "It is high time that we bore in mind the fact that we all are the Children of Abraham, whether through Isaac or Ishmael. May this call for fraternity not remain unanswered."

Part 2:
Changes in The Context and Our Perspectives Since 1983

So much has changed since we wrote the Haggadah, in the conflict and in our own lives and perspectives. In some ways, it was a much more hopeful time in 1983. So much blood has been shed since then, so many lives destroyed, and a solution seems so far away. In this section, we will highlight six important changes and end by examining how the work we did in 1983 would need to be revised in the light of how the changes have shaped our current understanding.

1. A One-State Reality has Replaced the Two-State Solution
This may be the most important change. In 1984, the two-state solution was an idea that was gaining support among liberals and progressives even though it was still rejected at that time by the PLO, Israel, the United States, and by the mainstream American Jewish community. Following the first intifada, in 1988, the PLO recognized the State of Israel and

implicitly accepted a two-state solution. Increasing numbers of people around the world came to see this as a solution to the tragic, protracted conflict between the two peoples.

Unfortunately, Israel's settlement policy and the siege on Gaza, coupled with the unquestioning support of successive U.S. governments, have all but destroyed this hope. At the time of writing this article, the Trump administration launched its "peace plan" that excluded Palestinians and allows Israel to annex even more territory on the West Bank. Today there are some 600,000 settlers on the West Bank and in East Jerusalem. Settlements and a network of highways have deliberately been built in a way that makes a viable Palestinian state on the West Bank and Gaza almost impossible. As settlement construction increased during the 1990s, scholars warned that the window was closing on the possibility of a two-state solution. Since then, for far too many years, scholars and analysts argued that it was "five minutes to midnight" for the two-state solution. The Palestinians have also contributed to the failure of peace efforts, though we need to keep in mind the huge power imbalance. Even now, almost two decades later, there are still some who insist that a two-state solution remains a real possibility; but most analysts believe that it is dead.

Ian Lustick, political scientist and longtime Middle East expert, recently published *Paradigm Lost*, a book that describes how the two-state paradigm is no longer a possibility. Today, he argues there is a One State Reality with Israel controlling Israel, Gaza, and the West Bank. He suggests that we must start with the truth of this reality when envisioning how to build a better future, rather than embracing the illusion of a two-state solution. He believes that accepting this truth could open up a number of possibilities that would ensure justice, equality, freedom, and safety for both peoples.

2. Palestinian Agency and Legitimacy

When we wrote the Haggadah, Palestinians were rarely given a voice in public discourse about Israel/Palestine and they were generally not accorded respect and credibility in the United States. As a result, most Americans knew very little about Palestinian history other than *hasbara*, the official Israeli narrative. This is partly why writing the Haggadah was shocking and eye-opening, especially for the three of us who are Jewish. It was an important step in opening our eyes to the Palestinian narrative. In the past thirty-seven years, the voices of Palestinians, the history of the Palestinian people, and their current reality have increasingly become critical ethical and political issues that are discussed in American political and cultural life.

Another big change is that the Boycott, Divestment and Sanctions movement (BDS), a global nonviolent resistance movement initiated by Palestinian civil society, has placed the Palestinian demand for equality, freedom and justice in the public realm, creating debate on the Palestinian issue in many universities and local communities. Although the BDS movement does not speak to the issue of one state or two states, it has fundamentally changed the public discussion of the conflict by making justice, freedom and equality for Palestinians a primary, non-negotiable goal of any solution. It has also given the Palestinians greater agency.

3. A New Understanding of the Origins of the Conflict

In addition, new historians in Israel and Palestinian scholars have fundamentally changed the way in which we understand the origins of the conflict, particularly what happened in 1948. These historians have documented the Nakba in which about 700-800,000 Palestinians, constituting the overwhelming majority of Palestinians who lived within what is now Israel, were expelled or fled beyond the borders and were not allowed to return after the war. These new historians documented massacres, expulsions, and looting by Jewish forces. They also made a strong case that this depopulation of the territory on which Israel was created was a coordinated plan (Tochnit Dalet) of the Zionist forces who understood that for a Jewish state to exist, it needed to expel as many Palestinians as possible. This is also why these Palestinian refugees were not allowed to return to their homes after the war. Furthermore, scholars have demonstrated that even earlier, in the 1920s and 1930s, Zionist leaders developed different plans for "transfer" of the Palestinian population to enable a Jewish state to come into existence.

4. Decoupling Judaism and Zionism

A very significant change within the Jewish community is the growing number of committed Jews, especially young Jews, who define themselves as non- or anti-Zionist. Before the Holocaust, the majority of European and American Jewry opposed Zionism. From the time of the Second World War through the 1967 war, more and more Jews around the world began to see Zionism as an integral part of their understanding of Judaism. In the 1950s and 1960s, Zionism and Judaism were fused together. One could argue that in some liberal Jewish communities, Zionism became the central faith of Judaism. Our Haggadah reflected this Judaism that was part of our own Zionist and Jewish education in the 1960s. This education was reflected in our framing of the history of the conflict and also in the Israeli songs and poetry that were included in the text. When we wrote the Haggadah, Brian, Devorah, and Mordechai were Zionists. Brian and Mordechai no longer consider themselves Zionists and are still committed to justice, equality, freedom, security, and safety for all those who dwell in Israel/Palestine.

5. Heightened Awareness of White Privilege and Racism

Over the past decade, many whites in the United States—including many white Jews—have come to understand that racism in America has been a systemic and structural part of American society from its founding. This systemic racism privileges all white people over people of color in many different ways.

With this understanding, it is very easy to see how this is true of Jews in Israel as well. The discrimination and oppression of Palestinians in Israel is also systemic and structural; all Jews in Israel enjoy ethnic privilege just like whites in America enjoy racial privilege. This ethnic privilege is extended to Jews all over the world, who can immigrate to Israel and will receive many benefits, while Palestinians are routinely denied equal rights in Israel. Furthermore, even among Israeli Jews, white Ashkenazi Jews also have privileges over Sephardi and Ethiopian Jews, and essentially over all peoples not of European origin.

6. New Progressive Jewish Organizations

When we wrote the Haggadah in 1983, New Jewish Agenda was the only national Jewish organization that worked on Israel/Palestine. Today there are four national Jewish organizations that do this work in different ways:

- T'ruah, a national organization of rabbis, educates rabbis about the human rights violations against Palestinians and encourages them to speak out;
- If Not Now, an organization of young people working to end the Occupation and transform the American Jewish community;
- J Street: an organization that is pro-Israel and pro-peace and supports a two-state solution;
- Jewish Voice for Peace, a national organization of Jews who stand in solidarity with the Palestinian people's demand for equality, justice, and freedom. JVP is an anti-Zionist organization and supports the Palestinian call for BDS.

Jewish Voice for Peace and J Street are large organizations with significant budgets, staff, and outreach. JVP is the only organization that offers a home for Jews who are non- or anti-Zionists and for Jews who support BDS.

All four organizations offer some resources every Pesach for their members. JVP produces a Haggadah every year that includes many of the values that we have outlined in this article.

Part 3:
Lessons We Draw

The changes outlined above have affected all of us in our thinking about the conflict and raised important questions about the Haggadah we created then. We turn now to some critical reflections on the values that guided our work then and what we might do very differently today. As we look back on our Haggadah, we are struck by several questions related to the way we used the Exodus story as a frame for addressing the Israeli-Palestinian conflict.

Writing a Haggadah that draws on the Biblical narrative and the story of the Exodus is powerful. But it also inadvertently implies that the Israeli-Palestinian conflict is a religious conflict. While Israel/Palestine is definitely a place with deep religious significance for Jews, Christians, Muslims and many others, the Israeli-Palestinian conflict is a conflict between two nationalisms. Highlighting the religious element of the conflict distorts the fact that Zionism and Palestinian nationalism are not primarily religious in nature. Framing the conflict in this way is not accurate and may make any resolution even more difficult.

In the Torah and in Rabbinic Judaism, the Exodus story is integrally connected to the Conquest of the Land. God takes the Israelites out of slavery and brings them to the Land of Canaan where, according to the Torah, they dispossess several other peoples. Both events—the Exodus and the Conquest—are a fulfillment of God's covenant with Abraham and his descendants.

While historians doubt that the Exodus or the Conquest of the Land ever took place as described in the Book of Joshua, in the Torah and in Jewish mythology the Exodus and the Conquest are linked: The liberation of the Jewish people is tied to the dispossession of other peoples. They are both part of the covenant between God and the Jewish people. While the Exodus story has inspired many movements for liberation, we have to delink the freedom of the Jewish people from the Conquest of Canaan. Having experienced oppression should never justify oppressing others.

In the Exodus story, it is clear that Pharaoh and the Egyptians who enslaved the Israelites are the oppressors and that the Israelites are the victims who deserve freedom. In the Haggadah we wrote, we skirted the critical issue of oppressor and victim by framing Pharaoh as the **"fear, violence and hatred between the Israelis and Palestinians."**

For example, we reinterpreted the passage from the Haggadah, "this year we are slaves, next year may we all be blessed with peace." We wrote:

> As long as we are imprisoned in our own fears, not recog-
> nizing the rights of others, we are slaves. As long as Israel is an
> occupier operating from her fears she cannot be healthy and
> is a slave. As long as Palestinians are not willing to recognize
> the rights of a Jewish homeland in Israel, they too are im-
> prisoned in the slavery of fear. Next year may we recognize
> the needs of the other and be free.

We presented a dual narrative as if the two sides were equally culpable for the conflict and equally eager to resolve it. In our telling of the story, both sides were victims and oppressors and the nature of the oppression was the psychological reality of fear. While it is true that Jews were victims in Europe, in the context of the conflict between the Jews and the Palestinians, the Jews were and currently are the oppressor wielding enormous power over the Palestinians for the past seventy years. Ignoring this power imbalance, as we did in the 1983 Haggadah, is wrong and immoral.

Liberal Jews in the United States identify with the struggle of People of Color and Native Americans for justice. Any Haggadah that addressed these issues would never think about portraying the conflict between White settlers and People of Color as an issue of mutual violence and hatred. It would be seen as obscene. Many Jews today see the Palestinian issue through the same lens as we see the issue of racism in America. Israel is a nation state that officially privileges Jewish lives over Palestinian lives in the same way America privileges white lives over the lives of people of color. Our Haggadah framed the conflict as a story of mutual mistrust that was comfortable for Jews for whom accepting that Israel is an oppressive and unjust—maybe even racist—state, was just too uncomfortable.

It is profoundly challenging for Jews to acknowledge that although we were victims in the past, now we are the oppressors of another people. Judaism is a faith community that places the lesson of the Exodus story that is dedicated to freedom, justice, and equality for everyone at the center of our faith. Judaism integrates faith and the pursuit of justice for all. This is the foundation of Judaism for most liberal and many traditionally observant Jews. We would argue that for Jews, working for justice, freedom, and equality for the Palestinians is an expression of our aspiration as Jews to be true to the call of our faith. Justice, freedom, and equality for all is also the only path that offers the possibility of long-term security and safety for Israeli Jews.

Moreover, of all the many social justice issues that American Jews care about, we have the most impact as a community on the issue of Israel/Palestine. Indeed there are many other social justice struggles that are urgent and more consequential for larger numbers of people, and we should be engaged in them, *but there is no other struggle over which our particular community has more impact and for which we as a community bear direct responsibility.* It is inconsistent as Jews to be liberal or progressive on every social justice issue except Palestine. Some of us may feel called to work on other issues for a variety of very good reasons, and that is perfectly understandable. For example, many Jews have made the environmental crisis their primary social justice work. The environmental crisis is by definition greater than any, maybe even than all, other specific social justice struggles. However, it makes no sense for Jews to be actively engaged in many important struggles for justice but to completely ignore—or worse, to be on the wrong side of—*the one issue on which our community has the greatest impact.*

Doing this work is very difficult in several ways. We mentioned earlier how difficult it was for Brian, Devorah, and Mordechai, given our own education as Jewish children growing up in the first two decades of Israel, to confront the story of the suffering of the Palestinians. This is still true for many young Jews today. For example, Jewish college students who grew up in Jewish families and attended day schools, went to Jewish summer camps and/or on Birthright or other trips to Israel, will still learn little if anything about the reality of living as a Palestinian under occupation of the West Bank or under the Israeli siege in Gaza. In fact, Hillel International and Birthright make every effort to prevent Jewish students from having any exposure to Palestinians and Palestinian life.

Then they may find themselves at colleges where the history of the Israeli-Palestinian conflict is taught in a way that totally contradicts what they have learned in their schools, camps, or trips to Israel. They also may encounter students in Students for Justice in Palestine, some of whom are themselves Jewish, who support the BDS movement and advocate for justice for Palestinians. Some Jewish students perceive both what they learn in their college courses and the activism on their campuses as antisemitic and they are encouraged to do so by a well-funded international campaign by Israel and mainstream Jewish organizations to portray any support for BDS as antisemitic.

We acknowledge and lament that there are real instances of antisemitism on college campuses. Just as all white people have unconsciously learned racism, all non-Jews have learned antisemitism. Criticism of Israeli government policies and practices or support for BDS is clearly not *ipso facto* antisemitism; each alleged incident needs to be examined. And the Jewish students who feel uncomfortable or even targeted when they encounter the Palestinian narrative or advocacy need compassionate support from other Jews who love Judaism and are dedicated to justice for all, including, and maybe especially, Palestinians.

It is not only students who face this challenge. The international campaign against BDS led by Israel and the American Jewish community has weaponized antisemitism as a way of silencing, even criminalizing advocacy of justice, freedom, and equality for Palestinians. They have expanded the definition of antisemitism to include criticism of Israel. This campaign effectively supports and enables Israeli oppression of Palestinians by denying the Palestinians their right to struggle for equality, freedom, and justice. Every oppressed people has the right to resist oppression. To imply that the Palestinian people don't have this right is racist.

Conclusion

While we are proud of the work we did in 1983-84 to open the discussion in the Jewish community about the oppression of the Palestinians, today we would write a very different Haggadah.

A new Haggadah would:

- point out that the story of the Exodus and the story of the Conquest of Canaan must be decoupled. Exodus must be about liberation for all, not liberation at the expense of others.

- emphasize that the Israeli Palestinian conflict is a conflict between two nationalisms. It is not essentially a religious conflict.

- acknowledge the power differential between Israelis and Palestinians, identifying Israel as the oppressor and the Palestinians as the victims in this conflict.

- affirm solidarity with the struggle of the Palestinians for equality, justice, and freedom as a Jewish commitment.

- encourage Jews to take responsibility and atone for the oppression of the Palestinian people.

- celebrate a Judaism that unequivocally stands with Palestinians in their struggle and works toward a future where all Palestinians and Israelis are equal in the eyes of the law, and have the freedom to enjoy their rights as equals in a country where all are safe.

- offer compassionate support for Jews struggling to integrate the history of Israel and Palestine into their own Jewish identity.

Lastly, in 1984, when we wrote the Haggadah, there were four of us. Sadly, Rabbi Devorah Bartnoff, our dear friend and colleague, died in 1997. She was a very passionate and devoted Zionist with a deep connection to Israel. We dedicate this article to her. We know that she would also be as heartbroken as we are by the direction Israel has taken in the last 37 years, and shaken by what we didn't understand when we wrote the Haggadah.

Devorah loved Israeli music. In memory of her, we end this article with some of the lyrics of Israeli singer/songwriter Chava Alberstein's version of Had Gadya (One Little Goat), one of the songs at the end of the Passover Seder that addresses the cycle of oppression. The traditional song tells the story of a goat that my father bought for two zuzim. The cat eats the goat, the dog bites the cat, the stick hits the dog, the fire burns the stick, the water quenches the fire, the ox drinks the water, the slaughterer slaughters the ox, the Angel of Death kills the slaughterer, and God kills the Angel of Death.

Chava Alberstein then adds the following verses:

> And why all of a sudden are you singing Had Gadya,
> Spring has not come yet, Passover hasn't arrived.
> What makes you different? What has changed?
> I myself have changed this year.
> On all other nights, on all other nights
> I have asked only the four questions,
> But on this night I have another one:
> Till when will the cycle of hatred continue
> The pursuer and the pursued, the beater and the beaten,
> When will all this madness end?

And what makes you different? What has changed?
I'm changed, I'm changed this year.
Once I was a sheep, a happy kid,
Today I am a tiger; a voracious wolf
I was a dove
I was a lamb
These days I don't know who I am.

The question that Alberstein poses is the question that underlies the Haggadah we wrote in 1983 and it is the question that Jews face today. Who are we? Are we a faith community dedicated to freedom, justice, and equality for all human beings, including Palestinians living under Israeli rule; or are we a people that oppresses, humiliates, and denies freedom to another people?

Devorah would have agreed that this is the question that faces all Jews who take Judaism seriously in our time. It remains an urgent spiritual and moral question that confronts all Jews now.

Next year may all be free!

A Freedom Seder in Hebron

A. Daniel Roth

When I think about Passover, I remember the cold evenings and late nights of Toronto's early spring months. I see my family and our friends around a long table in whichever neighborhood home was hosting that year. We were gathering, as we do in every generation, to tell the story of our people finding liberation in becoming a people.

We were there to examine our ideals and ethics through classic parables read throughout the world, and new additions that one of us had decided to include that year. In my memory, the kids would spill swiped wine on the already beaten up Haggadot while the parents were out in the backyard striking a match to begin what they called "The Burning Bush" ceremony before we began the Seder.

I can hear the hysterical laughter echoing in the dining room. I can feel the heaviness of too much gefilte fish and too many deviled eggs. I remember the annual arguments over the meaning of this or that portion of the Exodus story, the off-key singing of our entire clan, and the warmth in that room.

Our celebrations of a hard-won collective freedom weren't just warm. They were radical, critical, and feminist. Our table always included Miriam's Cup filled with water and an orange on our Seder plate. There was no *Wicked Child* in our Haggadah. This character was recast as the *Rebellious Child*. Defiance and independence were celebrated.

Those values were emphasized in our Seder as we marked the Warsaw Ghetto Uprising, which began on the eve of Passover. We would tell of the revolt and read the final letter written by their leader, Mordecai Anielewicz, a member of the Hashomer Hatzair youth movement, where I grew up too. Sitting around our secular-humanistic table we emphasized the connections between the ancient oppressions that we escaped and celebrated each year, and this more recent example of Jewish resistance, a piece of collective history with a personal connection to our community.

Discussion of self-determination, justice, and equality were common in our home, community, and education. I remember learning how to organize my peers in a letter-writing campaign at some point at Cherrywood, the alternative elementary school I went to. I grew up on stories of my parents' activism, learning about my mom's high school sweetheart,

Andy Goodman, and the racists who killed him when he went down to Mississippi as part of the Freedom Summer campaign of 1964. When I was a kid I remember once asking my mom about some story or another from her hippy days. She looked at me sternly and said, "I was not a hippy. I was a radical."

My Jewishness and the ongoing work of social change that I take part in are inextricably tied up with one another in my identity, and I am not alone. The idea that culture and community inform and enrich activism and action for a better world is at the core of the idea of the Freedom Seder, and it formed the common tapestry for the group of activists who organized the Freedom Seder in Hebron, in the occupied West Bank, in the spring of 2018.

One of the unique and most important elements of the Freedom Seder in Hebron was that it was organized by Jews and Palestinians together. Palestinian nonviolent activists from Youth Against Settlements and the Hebron Freedom Fund, all living under occupation in Hebron, one of the most violent and stark examples of the reality of the occupation, and Jews—folks from around the world, including Israelis —from All That's Left: Anti-Occupation Collective.

Though we had been engaged in organizing anti-occupation actions, events, and education together for a number of years, it's not a given that this kind of thing could have taken place. Differences in opinion on politics and tactics, as well as fears about how this event might affect one's image, all could have easily stopped this Seder from happening. But none of those things stopped us. Our aim was both to build and strengthen the movement by creating this space together, and to honor the work that has been done so far in the long march to freedom.

The Freedom Seder that we held took place in the heart of the occupation. Youth Against Settlements hosted us at their community center, which sits in the shadow of the Tel Rumeida Settlement. The event brought together more than one hundred people, including Palestinians living under occupation, Israeli members of the Knesset, Jews from around the world, and others in a space surrounded by violence and oppression, with armed soldiers and settlers on all sides.

It's because of determined nonviolent resistance and organizing that they've been able to hold on to that incredible space with an almost unbelievable view of the old city of Hebron, Shuhada Street directly below and off limits to Palestinians, and the Ibrahimi Mosque/Tomb of the Patriarchs in full view, filled with prayer and bloodshed.

Against this backdrop, the Freedom Seder in Hebron happened

because of trust and relationships. It happened because of years of joint actions and solidarity work which built trust and deepened the friendships that we were drawing on to create a space where we could share our cultures and traditions, and connect them at their roots to the cause we are all pursuing: ending the occupation, and freedom for all people. It happened because our relationships were built on the shoulders of the previous relationships that our partners in the struggle, from groups like Breaking the Silence and Ta'ayush, had built over the years.

The Freedom Seder happened because we had a long history of examples to draw upon that connect who we are and where we come from to what we do in the world. For us, the thread from the first Freedom Seder in Washington, D.C. to the Freedom Seder in Hebron, an ocean away and nearly five decades later, was explicit. This is how we opened the Seder in front of that extraordinary gathering of people from Palestine, Israel, and around the world:

> On April 4th, 1969—one year after the assassination of Dr. Martin Luther King Jr.—hundreds of people from a variety of backgrounds gathered in a church in Washington, D.C. to celebrate the Jewish tradition of Passover in the first "Freedom Seder," which wove the ancient Jewish story of liberation from bondage with contemporary struggles for civil rights and against the war raging in Vietnam. "Seder" means "order" or "agenda." Tonight we make our agenda clear: Tonight, fifty years after the first settlers began the process of dispossession of Palestinian land and homes under occupation in Hebron, we stand together here and now to reaffirm the commitment to liberation in every generation and for all peoples.

There is a long tradition of Jewish ritual in justice work and members of All That's Left: Anti-Occupation Collective have built upon that in recent years, even if it isn't the most common practice in this land. We've rooted a number of anti-occupation actions and events in our Jewish traditions: The Global Shabbat Against Demolitions in 2016 drew attention to the threat of home demolitions for villages like Susiya in the South Hebron Hills; Global Sukkot Against Demolitions continued this tradition with its built-in themes of shelter and home, supporting villages like Al Araqib in the Negev and Khan Al Ahmar in the occupied West Bank; and Purim Against Kahanism exemplified an alternative to supremacy and violence in the streets of Jerusalem.

Passover lends itself especially well to the project of weaving our culture and identities in with our movement work. The ancient story of the Exodus from slavery to freedom is not isolated in the past. It informs and inspires our actions here and now. For me, participation in our culture is about examining where we come from, to inform and inspire how we act as individuals and as a collective in the world today. The values of equality, justice, and freedom that we read, discuss, and sing about around the Seder table are central to the Jewish story, and they are also human values. They have the power to break down the barriers and blur the lines between the particular and the universal, and for a growing number of us, it is impossible to disconnect the violence and dispossession of the occupation from the values that we celebrate every spring.

In Hebron, the aim was to connect the culture and ritual of Passover to the ongoing struggle to end the occupation and to build equality, but it wasn't an easy process. Anyone who has ever engaged in a process of building a Jewish event in a collective way knows that each organizer brings their histories and norms and readings to the table. Now imagine engaging in that creative process with folks who primarily know annual Jewish celebrations in Hebron as the times when their freedom of movement is restricted even more than the usual that the Israeli military dictatorship they live under allows. Connecting along those fragile lines required listening deeply, deconstructing ideas and traditions that we come from, and rebuilding them in this context.

At the outset of the evening the lead Palestinian organizer from Youth Against Settlements ensured that everyone understood where we were. He reminded us that even though we were all sitting together in the same plastic chairs, eating the same chicken, rice, and vegetables, and reading the Haggadah that we compiled and wrote in Arabic, Hebrew, and English in turns, equality, justice, and freedom were not realities for him or any of the other Palestinians there that evening. His opening ended with a reminder that none of us are free until all of us are free.

We read poetry by Mahmoud Darwish and Marge Piercy. We centered the biblical civil disobedience of the midwives Shifra and Puah who saved Moses' life at a time when the Pharaoh's hate and violence became policy, and we recognized that the resistance that would come later was only possible because of their bravery. We worked together to face the violence all around us and the half century of occupation in the ritual we built, as we created space for Jewish and Palestinian life and stories to merge in order to hold up multiple voices in one space. One example can be seen in our version of The Four Questions:

> Every year the youngest person present at the Seder asks
> the *The Four Questions*, which each ask in different ways,
> "Why is this night different from all other nights?"
>
> Tonight is different from all other nights, for four reasons:
>
> 1. On all other nights we eat bread; tonight we eat this
>   unleavened *matzah* instead. Why? To remember
>   oppression in the world and all forms of injustice (our duty
>   for every generation, to remember).
>
> 2. On all other nights we eat all kinds of vegetables, tonight
>   we eat the bitter herb *maror*. Why? We refuse to look
>   away from the bitterness of the occupation and we
>   commit ourselves to ending this injustice.
>
> 3. Tonight we dip parsley in salt water. Why? To mourn
>   the dead here in Hebron, the lives that have been taken as
>   this injustice persists.
>
> 4. Most nights we don't sit at ease at dinner. Tonight,
>   we rest for a moment, in celebration that we are here
>   together.

The Hebron Freedom Seder was possible because we came together, as our whole selves, in defiance of the occupation. It was possible because we are part of a larger movement, which is built on courageous friendships and the core value that we are all equal. That particular evening was possible, in large part, because of the deep understanding that our traditions, rituals, and cultures are alive, and ours to shape and employ in creating a world that reflects the values that we celebrate every year. We did exactly that in our Freedom Seder in Hebron—defying the powers that be in that place by creating, for an evening, a world in which a community built on friendship, trust, and a commitment to the equality of all human beings was present, active, and alive.

Campus Freedom Seders: Freedom For Who, Exactly?

Jess Schwalb

(An earlier version of this essay was published in New Voices Magazine in April 2019.)

Lift your head from the Haggadah. Where is Pharaoh's army today? This inquiry motivated Rabbi Arthur Waskow to create the first Freedom Seder in 1969, and remains a potent call to action for Jewish communities celebrating Passover today. After Dr. Martin Luther King Jr.'s assassination in April 1968, Waskow saw the police and military occupation of Black neighborhoods in Washington, D.C. and in other cities nationwide as an uncanny parallel to Pharoah's cruelty in the Passover story. The next year, Rabbi Waskow hosted the first Freedom Seder in D.C. with a group of Black and Jewish activists and wrote a new Haggadah connecting the biblical Jewish Exodus from slavery to the history of U.S. racism and slavery. This Seder was a revelation, as Waskow told *New Voices*, "I realized that the seder was in the streets; the streets were the seder."

Social justice-related Passover content today seems ubiquitous; haggadot about queer liberation, environmental equity, and racial justice likely graced many of our Seder tables this weekend. But Rabbi Waskow, a Philadelphia-based radical faith leader, explains that this was not always the case. Though most Jewish organizations now embrace modern-day takes on Passover, Waskow explained that many Jewish leaders initially disapproved of the Freedom Seder: "They said to me, 'There already exists a Haggadah!'"

Waskow remembers that when he hosted the first-ever college campus Freedom Seder at Cornell University in 1970, over 2,000 people crowded into the school's fieldhouse to break matzah—but Cornell's Jewish institutions did not officially sponsor the event. The 1970 campus Freedom Seder was a preview for campus Jewish organizations' reluctance to connect the story of Passover with the fight for freedom in our own time. In particular, major Jewish institutions frequently rescind relationships with other marginalized groups over disagreements about the Israeli-Palestinian conflict.

In this context, the Freedom Seder seems a useful parable for understanding the most pressing questions facing Jewish life on campus. In attempting to discuss Passover's contemporary relevance, many Jewish groups on campus prefer to ignore, or minimize, the Israeli-Palestinian conflict. These groups often express their disappointment and discomfort when other communities express solidarity with the Palestinian cause, but choose to engage selectively in actually discussing the Israeli-Palestinian conflict. Hillel and some J Street U chapters have refused to host events with most pro-Palestinian student organizations on the basis of reductive redlines. Discussion of the Boycott, Divestment, and Sanctions (BDS) movement, let alone partnership with an organization in support of BDS, is off the table.

In effect, major Jewish institutions are preventing Jewish students from building relationships and coalitions necessary to fight the common enemy of white supremacy. The history of the Freedom Seder at my own Northwestern University proves that instead of engaging in difficult conversation about Israel-Palestine, campus Jewish organizations often choose to defend their pro-Israel stance at all costs and reject coalition in favor of political redlines. The contentious history of the Freedom Seder on campus should remind Jewish institutions to recommit to justice and solidarity on this and every Passover.

In 1971, *The Daily Northwestern* offered a brief advertisement for Waskow's *Freedom Seder Haggadah*: "You saw it condemned by the Jewish Establishment. Now you can buy the "Freedom Seder" at Hillel." (They enticed cash-strapped students with a "Special Price.") Despite having been "condemned" by the Jewish establishment some decades earlier, the first Freedom Seder at Northwestern occurred in 2003 as a collaboration between Hillel and For Members Only (FMO), the black student union. Though the event was not actually held on Passover (attendees ate leavened bread), the program referenced the Jewish holiday as a framework for discussing historic Black-Jewish coalition during the Black freedom struggle of the 1950s and 1960s. A version of this event continued on campus between 2003 and 2014.

In 2015, the Freedom Seder at NU ceased abruptly. Northwestern's Associated Student Government successfully passed a resolution to divest from companies profiting from human rights violations in Israel and Palestine in February. When I arrived on campus the following September as a first-year student, I was told that hosting a Freedom Seder was now impossible because the divestment campaign had fractured Jewish institutions from affinity spaces and activist groups led by students of color. FMO, the former cosponsor of the Freedom Seder, joined the NUDivest coalition, The group formed to oppose divestment, NU Coalition for

Peace, was largely made up of students in the Hillel-affiliated J Street U and Wildcats for Israel as well as members of AEPi. In this moment, as in many others, Hillel International's national guidelines put Jewish students in a bind—they could no longer publicly partner with groups who supported divestment without violating Hillel's standards of partnership, which prohibits Hillel from hosting speakers or cosponsoring events with groups that support BDS.

The divestment campaign both explicitly and implicitly drew lines in the sand between Jewish and Black groups at NU, extending beyond differences over Israel-Palestine activism. Since the resolution passed in 2015, I have rarely, if ever, seen a Jewish group on campus sponsor or host an event with FMO. Nor have Jewish groups acknowledged the extent to which we have stepped back from building coalitions with communities of color as a result of disagreement over Israel-Palestine. In 2016, a private prison divestment campaign called Unshackle NU received no campus Jewish institutional support or endorsement.

This spring, a group of students and I attempted to revitalize the Freedom Seder on campus. Our group felt it was impossible to host a Freedom Seder that ignored the Israeli-Palestinian conflict—in a practical sense, how would we purport to rebuild the relationships between Black and Jewish groups on campus without acknowledging the reason (i.e., divestment) for such strained relationships? But major Jewish institutions on our campus were not so willing. At first Hillel and J Street U were willing to cosponsor a liberation seder in the tradition of Freedom Seders past. Yet when we began to compile a Haggadah that described the need to fight white supremacy through collective liberation and coalition, when our group insisted we discuss Palestinian liberation as a part of the Seder, and when we proposed to include non- and anti-Zionist perspectives in our event, Hillel and J Street U rescinded their official support for the Freedom Seder.

Even if these Jewish groups had wanted to cosponsor the Seder, national policy guidelines restricted them from partnering with the major arm of Palestinian student organizing on campus, the pro-BDS Students for Justice in Palestine. National J Street U leadership explained that they would not cosponsor events with SJP, for reasons which seem to be nebulously justified in the group's official policy. (Other campuses have hosted events between J Street and SJP in the past, such as Bryn Mawr.)

More explicitly, Hillel International's standards of partnership prohibit campus chapters from hosting events with groups that support divestment, effectively shutting down official spaces for dialogue between

Jewish and pro-Palestinian students. These standards also preclude Hillel from working with campus groups that "exhibit a pattern of disruptive behavior towards campus events or guest speakers or foster an atmosphere of incivility." This not-so-coded language preventing Hillel from working with "disruptive" students means that activists in our group, whether a part of SJP or FMO, would likely not be allowed to be an official part of the Seder if Hillel were a sponsor.

Thus, despite years bemoaning the lack of Black-Jewish partnership on campus, when an opportunity arose to bring our communities together with pro-Palestinian students, Jewish groups such as Hillel and J Street U opted out from the event. Facing the possibility that no Jewish group would officially sponsor the Freedom Seder, we created a separate, independent group called Jewish Progressive Alliance and urged Jewish students to attend the Seder regardless of the reticence of major centers of Jewish life on campus.

Many Jewish organizations have expressed outrage at Black solidarity with the Palestinian cause over the past year, notably in response to campus divestment resolutions, the Women's March leadership rhetoric about Israel, and Representative Ilhan Omar's critiques of AIPAC. These repeated cycles of Jewish chastising of people of color for their Israel politics has only deepened divides in our already-fractured coalitions. This year's Freedom Seder aimed to be a space to speak to such intercommunal frustrations and to address the barriers to solidarity between Black, Jewish, and Palestinian activists. It was a Seder that particularly highlighted the work and words of Black Jews, who Jewish groups often ignore in conversations about solidarity and coalition. But on my campus and beyond, Hillel's restrictive national standards of partnership prevented this major organ of Jewish student life from sponsoring a Seder which brought together Black, Jewish, and Palestinian students to actually discuss what liberation and freedom mean to our (sometimes overlapping) communities.

Campus Jewish institutions would do well to take a page from Rabbi Waskow's Haggadah. His Freedom Seder reminded us that the liberation of the Jewish people requires solidarity with non-Jewish communities and a deep commitment to their liberation as well. The very history of the Freedom Seder and its initial rebuke by Jewish institutions challenges us to speak to, not avoid, that which divides our communities. That Jewish institutions have once again chosen to remove themselves from this year's Freedom Seder at NU was both deeply sad and worrying. In a time of rising white supremacy and of escalating antisemitic and Islamophobic violence egged on by our president, I fear the consequence of Jewish groups walking away from progressive coalitions because of redlines around Israel-Palestine.

More than 250 students gathered for the first Freedom Seder on NU's campus in 4 years. Despite Northwestern Hillel's unwillingness to cosponsor the event, several members of its staff attended the Seder in April. We sang songs of mourning and of liberation, discussed potential pathways to freedom and the limits of nationalism, and began the slow process of building relationships with new allies. The songs and discussions, certainly imperfect and always with room for improvement, were unlike any campus activist space I had attended. We used the Pesach story in order to tell and retell our own stories of liberation, to connect ourselves to the past and to forge new relationships for the future.

The Freedom Seder's legacy reminds us that there is no shortage of Pharaohs in our time. In attempting to revive the Seder at Northwestern, it became clear to me that we cannot avoid conversations about the Israeli-Palestinian conflict when we discuss freedom and liberation, particularly when our Jewish communities envision freedom from antisemitism and from white supremacy. Campus Jewish organizations must support young Jews' desire to build coalitions with other marginalized groups and to speak directly about our seemingly insurmountable political differences. These groups ought to reject the notion that divisions between Jewish, Black, and Palestinian freedom struggles are too great to overcome. This year, Northwestern students created a Freedom Seder that demanded collective, not partial nor selective, liberation. I hope next year the Jewish institutions that purport to speak for young Jews will join us.

Rabbi Arthur Waskow's comment:

Of course I feel great joy in hearing that my work across the decades, continuing from 50 years ago, continues to stir creative and transformative thought today. I mostly agree with Jess Schwalb, with some reservations and important nuances.

Most important: After I talked with other people in and near the Northwestern University scene, it became clear to me that the local campus Hillel was itself forced into *Mitzrayim* (that's the Hebrew name for ancient slave-holding Egypt, with the underlying meaning of a "dual" noun for a doubled reality—the "Doubly Tight and Narrow Place"). In English we might say *caught between a rock and a hard place*, or *Between the Devil and the Deep Blue Sea.*)

It is Hillel International that imposes on local Hillels the strict prohibition of working with or sharing space with any organization that supports

BDS directed against Israel, or even a more focused BDS directed against the Israeli Occupation of what could become a State of Palestine at peace with Israel.

This prohibition puts local Hillel staff in a terrible quandary. If they violate the policy ukase in order to pursue the kind of dialogue that Schwalb is urging, they are likely to be fired, and staff that is hostile to dialogue and to the exploration by students of a creative Judaism is likely to be hired in their places. If they obey the ukase, they may feel their Jewish spiritual and ethical commitments shattered, and may be scorned by the students they hope to offer a liberating Judaism.

What to do? If the Freedom Seder itself could speak, it might suggest that local Hillel staffs connect with others on other campuses to create an independent network that could challenge Hillel International.

More easily said than done. In the meantime, quiet acts of independence that ripple into the future. Jess Schwalb mentions that some Hillel staff took part in the Freedom Seder that Hillel would not house. Where local Hillels dance beyond the rigid boundaries, creating fringes of possibility rather than walls or fences, those like Schwalb who seek a broader dialogue should be clearer about who is imposing walls and fences.

And the wider Jewish community should pay attention to the dangers of erecting walls and to the need for fringes of interconnection. Attempts by Hillel International and others to forbid events that encourage dialogue among Jewish, Black, Muslim, and pro-Palestinian groups on and off campus are worse than mistaken—they are acts of idolatry. They make the Government and/or the State of Israel into an idol that cannot be criticized or confronted.

The Talmud tells a story, a parable: Some ancient rabbis went searching for the Yetzer Hara, the Evil Impulse, for Idolatry, intending to kill it and thus wipe out idolatry. They found it hiding in the Holy of Holies. The teaching: there is a danger that even, or especially, the most sacred place or practice can be made into an idol.

What distinguishes what is sacred from what is an idol? Carving out any piece of the Great Flow of Life, the Interbreathing Spirit of the world, from that great flow of Truth and bowing down to that one piece as if it were the whole Great Flow—that is idolatry. The most important way of "bowing down" is forbidding and punishing criticism. Today some Jewish institutions have done that to the State of Israel, by forbidding any connection with those who support nonviolent efforts to change or criticize it.

And BDS itself should not become an idol, impervious as a stone statue to doubt or criticism or amendment. Should we discuss BDS, debate about it, for or against it or choose a new path that is not growing from the Binary Yes/No? Sure! (I have.) Should we forbid discussion and co-operation with those who support it? Idolatry.

Most Jewish institutions don't forbid working with the Roman Catholic Church on issues like immigration where we mostly agree, though its thought and actions on abortion and birth control are repugnant to most Jews. What makes the difference? Clearly, one involves Israel and the other doesn't. The signal that idolatry's afoot.

When I wrote the first Freedom Seder, I replaced the debate in the traditional Haggadah over whether there had been 10, 50, or 500 plagues with a debate between violence and nonviolence as a path to freedom. That issue in 1969 was just as fraught, the debate just as intense, and the consequences just as important as any debate over BDS today.

In the same spirit, today I welcome the creation of a new version of a Freedom Seder that will discuss the issues roused by the conflict between Israel and Palestine, alongside many other Seders that the first Freedom Seder stirred into being.

At The Shalom Center, we ourselves in 2019 created a new #Freedom-Seder50 that was celebrated in a mosque (!!) and was led by Rev. William Barber and Ana Mara Archila, among others. (https://theshalomcenter.org/freedomseder50). God forbid that the Freedom Seder, which came into being as a resistance to American racism and Jewish religious rigidities, should itself be frozen into an idol!

Earth and Refugee Seders

Earthy Teachings of Pesach

Rabbi Arthur Waskow & Rabbi Jeff Sultar

As the Passover Haggadah says, "In every generation, one rises up to destroy us." And then, "In every generation, every human being must go forth to freedom."

Today, the greatest danger of destructive plagues comes from the global climate crisis and the top-down, unaccountable power structures that are pushing us ever closer to the edge of climate disaster.

So it makes sense to focus on the elements of Passover that call us to free and heal Earth and our society from that danger.

Searching for "Chameitz"—What is Chameitz in Our Lives Today?

The tradition teaches that before Passover begins, we rid our houses of *chameitz* in any form. Chameitz, literally, is anything made out of wheat, spelt, barley, rye and oats, that has been mixed with water and allowed to ferment for more than eighteen minutes. It is food that has swelled up.

Chasidic teachers, though, saw chameitz metaphorically, as the swelling up of excess in our own lives.

What is metaphorical chameitz in our own day? What is the excess in our lives that we need to rid ourselves of, or that we can at least tone down, to keep it in proper proportion and perspective?

Chameitz, first of all, can be carbon dioxide. It is the one single element most responsible for the global climate crisis. It is the element that we must immediately reduce spewing into the atmosphere.

Chameitz can be seen as overconsumption. Is one lesson of Passover this year that we should simplify our lives?

More specifically, is coal-fired electricity a kind of eco-chameitz? Is our addiction to the overuse of oil, coal and gasoline an eco-chameitz?

Seen this way, what then do we need to do in order to sweep eco-chameitz from our lives?

Some answers:

- Switch our households and institutions to wind or solar power and other renewable sources of energy; support legislation that supports this switch, as well; get an energy audit; change all lightbulbs to CFLs (compact fluorescent lamps) or LEDs.

- Drive less; purchase fuel-efficient and hybrid cars; support public transportation; shop online.

- Make green renovations and new buildings. Support legislation mandating such measures.

Making these changes is, of course, not easy. Chameitz looks better and it tastes better. Being more puffed-up in size, it tends to attract people and get more attention. And it's not even completely bad, as it's permissible to enjoy chameitz 51 other weeks of the year. What's not all right is to be a slave to it. More about that later.

Shabbat HaGadol: The Great Sabbath

The Shabbat just prior to Passover is called Shabbat HaGadol.

Shabbat HaGadol gets its name from the haftarah, the prophetic portion, that is traditionally read on this day. The context of the haftarah is dramatic: its 25 lines represent the final words of the final prophet, Malachi.

He writes, speaking on behalf of YHWH:

> Behold! I will send you Elijah the Prophet before the coming of that great and awesome day of YHWH, so that he will turn the hearts of the parents to the children and the hearts of the children to the parents, lest I come and strike the Earth with utter destruction. (Malachi 3:23-24)

This call from 2,500 years ago that the generations must work together to heal the earth from the danger of utter destruction comes alive with new force in our generation. When we invoke Elijah the Prophet on Shabbat HaGadol and during our Passover seders, we must make sure that we are giving voice to our own commitment to take actions in our own day to move this world closer to redemption—in our own lives; in our synagogues, offices, and institutions; and by working for changes in public policy.

This is what we mean when we sing of Elijah the Prophet coming to us: Elijah is not a person who comes and changes our world, but is rather the name we give to the change that we ourselves bring about through our determined and inspired action.

Sing:

Eliyahu hanavi, Eliyahu hatishbi
Eliyahu, Eliyahu, Eliyahu hagiladi
Bimherah veyameynu yavo eleynu
Im mashiach ben David, im mashiach ben David
(Elijah the Prophet, come speedily to us,
hailing messianic days.)

Passover Seder

Early in the Seder, we dip green vegetables—parsley, mint—into salt water—the oceans where all life was nourished. We can pause to celebrate the Source of Life that is now endangered, and to pledge our help to heal the green and the blue that enrich our planet, lest the salt water become tears as the green plants wither.

Four Questions for Today:

We can sing the first line, and then continue as a wordless melody: *Mah nishtanah halailah hazeh mikol haleilot?*

[Translation: Why is this night different from all other nights?]

Why is this blight different from all other blights?

1. For other blights we can be concerned only for ourselves; why for this blight must we be concerned for others?

Because the climate crisis affects everyone on Planet Earth, since the atmosphere does not respect the political boundaries that nations erect between themselves.

2. For other blights, we might not really know what's happening; why for this blight are we so sure?

Because there is a scientific consensus that human action is leading to global climate temperatures increasing; can we muster up the will to do something about it?

3. For other blights, the problem might seem too hard or too distant for us to do anything about it; why for this blight is it possible for us to make a difference?

Because each one of us contributes daily to the crisis—each one of us uses energy, each one of us causes carbon dioxide to be released into the air.

And therefore each one of us can daily make a positive change to address the crisis.

4. For other blights, it can seem impossible to get the attention of politicians; how can we do so for this blight?

Our "children" of the Malachi outcry are turning their hearts to their elders in politically powerful ways: sit-ins in Congressional offices, sit-downs on major city streets, strikes from work and school.

Avadim Hayinu—Once We Were Slaves:
Passover as a Call for Ecological Justice:

Later in our seder we read, "In every generation, we are obliged to regard ourselves as though we ourselves had actually gone out from Egypt." We are to remember the experience of being slaves, of being disenfranchised, of being the ones with the least power, with the least resources, with the least number of people looking out for our welfare and our well-being. We are to remember the experience of being dis-valued because we had no power, because we couldn't *do* for ourselves or others, rather than *be*—in our inherent value as human beings.

Degradation of Earth in the United States and elsewhere most severely harms those people who are already the ones with the least power. All one needs to do is think of the aftermath of Hurricane Katrina. Or look at asthma rates in lower-income neighborhoods, or exposure rates to toxic waste. Similarly, the global climate crisis most severely harms people in those countries that also have the least.

While we in the United States will be forced—and may be able—to make gradual changes to adapt to a changing climate, people in other countries will face refugee crises and fierce wars over shifting agricultural and water distribution patterns.

And so, on this Passover, we remember *avadim hayinu*, that we were slaves.

> *Avadim hayinu, hayinu, atah beney chorin, beney chorin*
> *Avadim hayinu atah atah beney chorin.*
> (Translation: Once we were slaves, but now we are free).

We remember that we were slaves, doing so in order to remember that our obligation is to help set everyone free. And we don't just sing the words. We commit ourselves to making sure that the moral voice continues to be spoken, ensuring that concern for environmental justice continues to be a part of any public policy.

For example, the Green New Deal proposals include legislation about environmental justice. On Seder night, we can commit ourselves that during the week of Passover we will write one letter to the editor of our local newspaper urging stronger action by Congress to prevent global climate disaster.

Plagues: Then and Now

In the Exodus story, nearly all but the final two plagues were Earthborn in nature. We can see this clearly from the teaching of Rabbi Yehuda Halevi, a twelfth-century Spanish physician and poet, who explained that the first eight plagues could be divided in a way that made their environmental basis clear: two came from water (blood, frogs from the Nile); two came from earth (lice and wild animals); two were infections carried by the air (plague and boils); and two were carried by the air to do physical damage (hailstorms and locusts).

In our own day, we face a daunting array of environmental plagues as well.

[Everyone fills the next glass with wine or grape juice. Leader lifts up kiddush cup and invites everyone else to do likewise. As each plague is said out loud, a drop of wine/grape juice is poured out, or drops are removed by dipping finger into cup.]

Leader asks: What are the Earthborn plagues that are befalling us in our own day?

Answers might include:

- undrinkable water in rivers
- frogs dying
- Great Lakes drying
- glaciers melting
- polar bears drowning
- seacoasts rising
- droughts increasing
- extreme weather conditions increasing
- temperatures rising

- unhealthy air quality
- changing bird migration
- melting of permafrost
- spread of infectious diseases like Covid-19
- famine
- animal and plant extinction

Rabban Gamliel and the Three Elements of Any Passover Seder

Rabban Gamliel used to say: Whoever does not explain the following three things at the Passover festival has not fulfilled their duty, namely: the Passover sacrifice, Matzah, and Maror.

1. Passover Sacrifice:

[Point to the shank bone, beet, or Paschal yam, pass it around]:

This shank bone/Paschal yam that we put on our seder plate represents idolatry. The ancient Egyptians worshiped the lamb. And so to sacrifice a lamb right under the Egyptians' noses was an act of defiance, one of the first ways that the ancient Israelites began to throw off the shackles of slavery. The shank bone/Paschal yam in our own day represents saying and doing what is right, in defiance of what the Pharaohs in our own day tell us to say and do.

Who are the Pharaohs in our own day? Who tells us what to do—not because it's right, but because they tell us to? [Invite responses from people gathered there].

How about those in our own government, who for so long denied that there even was a global climate crisis, even while they provided subsidies to the oil industry in Texas and Saudi Arabia?

Or the top officials of the Environmental Protection Agency, which this past December denied California and 18 other states the ability to set greenhouse gas emission standards stricter than federal levels?

How about Senators and Representatives who serve those who pay the most money, at the expense of those who pay the most dearly for shortsighted and self-serving policies?

How about the leaders of the oil and automobile industries, who enrich themselves at the expense of planet Earth? Who devise ever more ingenious ways to entice us to waste more resources, to deplete more energy reserves, and to burn more carbon into the air, while their own pockets deepen and the global climate worsens?

The hearts of Pharaohs too often, as in the Exodus story, become hardened.

So that an overwhelming scientific consensus about rising climate temperatures can be ignored. So that a unanimous recommendation by EPA legal and policy advisers can be ignored, as in the case of the denial of California's request to enact stricter carbon emission standards.

But we can't just look outside of ourselves, blaming others. Who buys gas-guzzling cars? Who allows politicians to get away with serving the interests of Big Business in the present at the expense of our shared future? Who allows Congress to subsidize the coal industry while allowing alternative sources of renewable energy to be underfunded?

In the Maggid section of our seder, we read another reason, other than slavery, for our need for redemption: *Mit'chila ovdei avodah zara* (Translation: In the beginning, our ancestors were worshipers of idols.) Not only the Egyptians worshiped idols. We did, too!

At Passover, we mark the need for liberation not just from external Pharaohs, but from internal ones as well. Passover is a time to ask not just four questions, but hard questions: In what ways are we addicted to oil? To over-consumption? To having the newest and the latest and the most advanced? To comfort and convenience that takes a toll and levies a cost that doesn't get tallied up until some later year, off in some distant murky future? To a lifestyle made possible by the hands of and/or adversely affecting people half a world away, out of sight and too often out of mind?

2. Matzah

[Distribute pieces of matzah to everyone present; leader holds up piece.]

We began the Maggid section of the Seder by holding up a piece of matzah and saying, "This is the bread of affliction." It represents where our spirits are flat. It represents what happens when we are beaten down, pressed down, and see ourselves as powerless.

But just as matzah literally has two physical sides, so too does it have two sides spiritually. From one perspective it is the bread of affliction; but, when turned over, when seen from the other side, it is also the bread of liberation, of freedom, of power to change our worlds for the better.

How do we make this transformation, from being pressed down to rising up?

Before we can transform our matzah from the bread of affliction into the bread of liberation, we must face squarely the challenge before us.

Matzah as a Call to Action

We don't actually get to eat a piece of matzah until after the Maggid/Telling section of the Seder. As we approach being able to take that first bite each year, let's take a moment to examine a key question: How does the bread of affliction transform into the bread of freedom?

Chameitz can only be made from ingredients that can also become matzah. The only difference between matzah and chameitz is what we do with those ingredients. Making chameitz is easy; all you have to do is mix the ingredients together and then do...nothing! The source of the substance forbidden during Passover is simply waiting and not doing anything.

Inaction.

Making matzah, on the other hand, is difficult. It takes great determination, swift action, and constantly working toward the goal. When this great effort is made, when we don't let obstacles stand in our way, when we take each step that needs to be taken, with our eyes always on the prize, then the bread of affliction transforms into the bread of liberation.

3. Maror

Maror means bitter herbs. It represents the pain of our slavery in Egypt. It represents the harm of our actions today.

Throughout the recent past, here is the legacy that has set back the cause of global climate health:

[As someone says each action aloud, everyone else can sing the refrain, "Let my people go."]

1. Denied California the Clean Air Act waiver, thus blocking 18 other states from enacting the stricter greenhouse gas emissions standards as well.
[Sing: "Let my people go."]

2. Interfered with climate change science, revising NASA and other agency documents to remove language regarding climate change, and engaged in a systematic effort to mislead policy makers and the public about the dangers of global warming.
[Sing: "Let my people go."]

3. Advocated for more nuclear power plants.
[Sing: "Let my people go."]

4. Opened public land in the Rocky Mountains and Alaska to oil and gas drilling.
[Sing: "Let my people go."]

5. Declared carbon dioxide not to be a pollutant.
[Sing: "Let my people go."]

6. Weakened regulations governing air pollution.
[Sing: "Let my people go."]

7. Rejected the Paris Accord, withdrawing the United States from the global warming treaty.
[Sing: "Let my people go."]

Second Seder: Counting Toward Sinai

During the seder on the second night of Passover, we begin counting the 49 days that link freedom from slavery to freedom to enter into a relationship of responsibility and purpose. Our tradition recognizes that big changes don't happen overnight, but rather take careful planning and preparation.

Pulling our world back from the brink of the global climate crisis will require many small and large steps. No single step alone will solve the problem. But we can ensure, with each step, that we are at least moving in the right direction.

Just as our tradition gives us a 49-day period to spiritually prepare ourselves to stand at Sinai, the second seder is a good time to begin making a plan for what steps each individual, family, and community will take toward addressing the crisis we face.

One Day of Passover is Often Earth Day!

In many years, Passover converges with Earth Day, or comes very close. And it does so at a time when the global climate crisis can no longer be ignored, calling for us to take bold action.

Let's make our voices heard at Congressional offices, visiting our Senators and Representatives to say that the Green New Deal matters greatly to us, and that we insist that it become the law of the land.

And let's do so in a way that is not only a protest, but also a celebration, a reaffirmation, of our power to free ourselves from limitations both external and internal. At Passover, we invoke Elijah the Prophet as the harbinger of a world redeemed through the actions that we take.

Seventh Day of Passover: Crossing the Sea

Traditionally, the seventh day of Passover is associated with the Israelites crossing through the Sea of Reeds to escape the pursuing Egyptian army.

In a midrash from the Babylonian Talmud (Sotah 36), Rabbi Yehuda described how "Each tribe said: 'I am not going into the water first.'"

During the endless debates, Nachshon from the tribe of Judah jumped into the sea. He was on the point of drowning when God suddenly divided the waters.

In other words, the miracle of the splitting of the sea wasn't simply a divine intervention. And it wasn't brought about by one strong central leader. Rather, one single person, a member of the crowd, took action that was so bold and so inspired and so filled with faith that the miracle then was activated.

What a powerful counterbalance to all the words associated with Passover!

Time to stop talking; time to do!

My People Were Refugees:
The Writing of the HIAS Haggadah

Rabbi Rachel Grant Meyer

> *The ones who understand...*
> *They see that the Jewish refugee story never really ends; our role in the story shifts. Together, they take actions big and small. While they know they cannot complete the work, they do not desist from trying to make a difference. "We used to help refugees because they were Jewish," they say. "But now we help refugees because we are Jewish."*
>
> —The HIAS Haggadah

There could be no more apt a holiday tradition through which to explore the contemporary global refugee and asylum crisis than the Passover Seder. The Passover story is the Jewish people's original refugee story. It is the story that reminds us that we, too, have stood in the shoes of refugees and asylum seekers in search of safety and liberty. It was with this belief in mind that the HIAS Community Engagement team undertook the process of writing a Haggadah focused on educating the American Jewish community about the current refugee and asylum crisis, forging connections between the Jewish people's ancient story as a refugee people and the experiences of today's refugees and asylum seekers. The epigraph that opens this chapter encapsulates the pedagogical theory behind our Haggadah: to help American Jews see that, although Jews no longer represent a majority percentage of today's refugees, our refugee story does not end; rather, our role in the story shifts to one in which we help refugees and asylum seekers not because *they* are Jewish but because *we* are.

In 1881, the organization today known as HIAS was founded as the Hebrew Immigrant Aid Society to assist Jews fleeing violent antisemitism in Russia and Eastern Europe. From a storefront on the Lower East Side of New York City, early HIAS staff provided essential services like temporary housing, kosher food, clothing, and job training to thousands of Jews arriving in the United States. Shortly after our founding, in 1904, HIAS established an office on Ellis Island to provide translation services, guide newly arrived Jewish immigrants through medical screenings, intervene against deportations with the Boards of Special Inquiry, obtain bonds to guarantee employable status, and lend money for landing fees. Beginning in the 1890s and continuing through the major waves of Jewish immigration to the United States until the 1920s, Ellis Island was also the site of a Passover Seder each year for the Jewish immigrants who had not yet been approved to enter the United States, a ritual HIAS was instrumental in conducting. From our beginnings, the rites and rituals of Passover held a special place in HIAS's history.

For the next 120 years, HIAS assisted millions of Jewish refugees fleeing violence and persecution, helping them to find safety in the United States. At the turn of the 21st century, as the number of Jewish refugees dramatically reduced, HIAS turned our attention to helping all refugees regardless of faith or ethnicity. Today, we work across the globe, including around the United States, to assist refugees and asylum seekers in realizing their legal rights and rebuilding their lives and to advocate for their right to do so. With the shift in the religious and ethnic identities of the majority of our beneficiaries, it became critically important to build a robust grassroots constituency of American Jews supporting this work, advocating for the rights of refugees and asylum seekers and taking direct action to help meet their needs, grounded in the Jewish imperative to welcome, love, and protect the refugee. HIAS's Community Engagement department was formed in the early 2010s to facilitate that process. Our department's mission is to educate, organize, and mobilize the American Jewish community in support of and in solidarity with refugees and asylum seekers.

Part of our educational strategy involves looking at Jewish holidays and rituals through the lens of the current refugee and asylum crisis. As stated earlier, there could be no more fitting a holiday and ritual for such an exploration than Passover and the Passover Seder. While the HIAS Haggadah itself provides the opportunity to reimagine each of the ritual moments in the Passover Seder—such as a discussion of the violence refugees face today in concert with the recitation of the original ten plagues of the Haggadah or an alternate set of four questions to contemplate connections between the ancient story, our family stories, and the stories of today's refugees and asylum seekers—the real goal is to inspire those who use it to rise up from their tables to take action with and on behalf of today's refugees and asylum seekers. The HIAS Haggadah was written with the belief that transforming our ancient rituals and translating them to map onto today's most critical social issues is what helps us continue to be in conversation with our ancient texts and to breathe new life into our age-old rituals.

Over the course of four years, as HIAS's Rabbi-in-Residence, I undertook the process of writing new blessings, questions, and readings for each major piece of the Passover Seder. When we were just beginning this work in 2016, we elected to rewrite just a few pieces of the Passover Seder to give our supporters a taste of what bringing the contemporary refugee and asylum crisis into their Passover rituals might look like. By 2019, we had produced Haggadah supplements that covered more than two thirds of the Haggadah; so, it made sense to complete the entire Haggadah. While the HIAS Haggadah is not exhaustive of the original text, it does provide an opportunity to reimagine each individual ritual through the lens of refugee and asylum issues.

We also felt that it was important to include photographs and illustrations to accompany those words. In 2018, we collaborated with artist Hillel Smith to create evocative illustrations to accompany each piece of the HIAS Haggadah. These illustrations are themselves a commentary on the original Haggadah text, creating visual connections between the Seder ritual and refugee issues. The *Karpas* (green vegetable) section of the Seder, for instance, contains a reading reflecting on the connection between the salty tears cried by those who have made the journey from persecution to freedom throughout time, the dangerous and salty waters on which they often make those journeys, and our hope for their redemption as represented by the green vegetable we use to dip in the salt water. This reading is accompanied by an illustration of a human being crying tears that flow into a river on which a boat of people search for a safe place to call home, viscerally conjuring the reading's themes in a powerful visual representation.

From its inception through its completion, the HIAS Haggadah has been met with enthusiastic reception from the American Jewish movement for refugees and asylum seekers, including former Jewish refugees as well as the family members of Jewish refugees. Igor Chubaryov is a Jewish refugee who fled persecution in Russia with his family, arrived in the United States in March 1989 with HIAS's assistance, and began working for HIAS in November 1989. Today, Igor serves as a program manager for HIAS New York, helping newly arrived refugees integrate into their new communities in New York City. In Russia, Igor's town did not have a synagogue or kosher food stores. The closest place to buy matzah for Passover was Moscow, which was 400 miles away. Yet, Igor's mother always made a wonderful Passover dinner, and he received his first Haggadah in Hebrew and Russian from Lev Furman, a long-time Jewish activist and refusenik—one of Igor's most valued possessions to this day.

Reflecting on the HIAS Haggadah, Igor shared that he continues to remember the lessons of the Haggadah as they inform his work today. The words "*avadim hayinu b'Mitzrayim*—we were slaves in Egypt" from the Haggadah remind him that the Jewish people should never forget what we overcame in getting our freedom, nor should we forget that there are still people who are fighting for that same freedom today. For Igor, the words of the HIAS Haggadah deeply resonate with his own lived experience and his commitment to enabling today's refugees to find the refuge that he was able to find decades ago. From Igor to Dr. Ruth Westheimer—herself a Holocaust survivor—to the thousands of Jews around the world who have downloaded the HIAS Haggadah from the HIAS website or purchased a print edition, the message of the HIAS Haggadah rings true. The HIAS Haggadah has been featured in dozens of articles about various modern Haggadot and Haggadah supplements, and it has also been used as the basis for communal refugee Seders in the United States and around the world, as well as at many personal home Seders.

In this moment when more people are displaced than at any time in modern recorded history and in which the number of people displaced by violence and persecution continues to grow precipitously from year to year, the HIAS Haggadah remains a relevant and timely resource. Like the original Passover Haggadah, the HIAS Haggadah is a living document, meant to continue the conversation between the ancient Israelites who wandered in search of safety, those who themselves or whose families have found refuge in new lands, and those who still yearn to be free. The HIAS Haggadah ends with these words: "Just as our own people now eat the bread of liberation, we pray that today's refugees and asylum seekers will fulfill their dreams of rebuilding their lives in safety and freedom in the year to come. Blessed are all those who yearn to be free. Blessed are we who commit ourselves to their freedom. Blessed are You, Adonai Our God, source of strength and liberation." These words articulate both the purpose of the Haggadah itself and our collective hope for today's refugees: that we may all locate ourselves in this ancient story of breaking free from oppression in order to renew our commitment to stand with those who seek to do the same today.

Discovering the Ecological Imperative of Passover

The Backstory of
The Promise of the Land: A Passover Haggadah

Rabbi Ellen Bernstein[1]

My outlook on life had always been ecological. I found my way back to Judaism in my twenties when I began studying Torah with a friend and discovered so many earthy connections that I became hooked. Still, it took quite a while for me to come to truly appreciate Passover, Judaism's signature holiday. The central theme of Passover, the idea of a triumphal God whisking the Israelites out of Egypt to freedom on a tongue of dry land through the Red Sea, never spoke to me. But I was charmed by all the foods on the seder plate. My favorite step of the ritual was the *karpas*, **the green vegetable that heralds the beginning of spring. I loved the modesty of the matzah. And the gnarly horseradish root captured my curiosity; it was raw and wild like a visitor from middle earth.**

While I could appreciate the story of Passover through the foods, the seder itself felt like a labyrinth, and I had a hard time finding my way around. Every year I found a new section of the Haggadah to wonder about. Why does it repeat the same story over and over? Why should we care about the rabbis of B'nei Brak? What was the long midrash riffing on "My father was an Aramean" all about? The traditional seder is not a straight-through narrative. It can feel repetitive, opaque, and confusing. It is an ancient ritual with layers of commentary added over centuries. I realized if I were ever to understand the Haggadah I would need to approach it like an archaeologist in an archaeological dig.

The Earthy Foods of the Seder

The most obvious and accessible strata of the Passover seder includes the foods on the seder plate. Food, besides nourishing us and delighting us, links us back to the earth. Passover is first and foremost a celebration of the simplest, most elemental food: matzah—just wheat and water. The holiday is even called "*hag ha-matzot*," holiday of matzah. Nothing reminds us of earth like matzah. In the context of Passover, the humble matzah is

---

[1] Thanks to Rabba Kaya Stern Kaufman for offering valuable feedback on this piece.

the opposite of puffed-up bread. At Passover time, bread is symbolic of the additives, the excesses that enslave us, while matzah, in its elemental simplicity, sets us free.

The other foods on the seder plate flesh out the earthy story of Passover. The greens and the bitter herbs represent spring, the shank bone reminds us of the sacrificial sheep, the lettuce points to our agrarian way of life. The foods on the seder plate are the subject of the four questions that open the story section, and the subject of Rabbi Gamliel's discussion that closes the story section. Four glasses of wine commemorate the grapes, and we honor the land and our food in the many blessings.

The very first seder I ever led—long before I had ever thought much about Judaism—relied entirely on the symbolic foods of the seder. I was in the Grand Canyon on a backpacking trip with a group of geology students, and it was Passover. I had brought along a few pieces of matzah and a couple of apples, nuts and raisins for a makeshift charoset. I suggested to the group that since it was Passover and we were in the desert, it would be auspicious to celebrate; and they—none of them Jewish—were all game.

I sent them out into the desert to collect the ingredients for the seder plate: bones for the shank bone, herbs for maror, and greens for karpas. Everyone went out with a mission and returned hours later with their symbolic plants and skeletal remains. We found a beautiful spot where the red canyon wall formed an overhang. As the sun set, we gathered together for a lentil feast, and there cradled in the most awe-inspiring river canyon, with the full moon rising overhead, we sat through the night telling stories of the Israelites' and our own journeys of moving from deprivation to liberation.

Backpacking in the desert has always felt like a most appropriate way to celebrate Passover. The simplicity of the holiday calls on us to let go of our attachment to everything that weighs us down. Backpacking, like Passover, is a celebration of minimalism. We take only what we need to survive and enjoy all gifts that come with just "being:" being in nature, being in community, being in beauty. The (incredible) lightness of being is the path to freedom.

Simplicity can be a political statement. From an ecological perspective it could change everything. Recently the *New York Times* reported that if everyone in the country ate more simply and lower down on the food chain (fruits and vegetables), and scaled down their meat-eating by just one-quarter, we would reduce our greenhouse gas emissions by one percent and free up about twenty-three million acres of high-quality land, an area roughly the size of Indiana—not to mention that everyone would be the healthier for it.[2]

Spiritual Slavery

Digging down a layer below the emblematic foods on the seder table is the theme of spiritual slavery, an idea with ecological roots.

Most of us associate the slavery of Passover with the hard labor and wretched conditions that the Israelites suffered under Pharaoh in Egypt. But the slavery of the Passover Haggadah is not just physical. It is also a more insidious kind of slavery, a spiritual slavery. We enslave ourselves. The eleventh-century rabbi and philosopher Maimonides said that the dramatic story of the Exodus, replete with an evil king/pharaoh, miraculous plagues, and a rag-tag band of Israelites rushing through the Red Sea, is the story we tell our children to engage them, so they can grasp the broad strokes of the holiday. But the story that we adults need to grapple with is the story of our own self-inflicted spiritual slavery.

The concept of "spiritual slavery" at the heart of the traditional seder is another way of teaching the ecological value of right livelihood. Spiritual slavery is the slavery that we unknowingly cultivate when we elevate some idea or value like money, power, status, technology, an ideology, and revere it too much—when we make of it an idol. In every generation one of the greatest threats to our freedom is the threat that we will lose our selves to the gospel of affluence and status. From ancient times to today, the ruling culture from Mesopotamia to Egypt to Europe to America, has been a culture of hyper-materialism and accumulation, of exploiting the earth and people, creating wealth for the few. Rabbi Jonathan Sachs z"l (of blessed memory) reminds us, "Affluence, no less than slavery, can make us forget who we are and why." Passover teaches that excess is a distraction and an illusion and can enslave us, and that freedom comes when we relieve ourselves of the burden of too much.

The climate crisis is a reflection of our spiritual slavery. We have grown too attached to our things at the expense of nature and our relationship with her. The consequences of our consumer-oriented lives are profound: an ocean of plastic, an overheated sky, ruptures in the earth's physical and biological processes, and questions about the future of life on our planet.

Our environmental predicament reflects both the breakdown of our relationship with nature and the disconnection between mind and body. We humans yearn to be connected, to have a sense of belonging to something larger than ourselves. But we've so accommodated to the world of things that we don't know we've lost touch with the simple gifts of nature.

[2] https://nytimes.com/2019/08/21/climate/what-if-we-all-ate-a-bit-less-meat.html

One of the tragedies of modern times is that the economic, political, and cultural structures that inform our lives devalue the natural world and its web of relationships, and foster an illusion that we are independent, separate from the rest of the living world.

The Passover seder begins with the brokenness of our lives as symbolized by the broken matzah of *yachatz* (an early step in the seder) and ends in wholeness, as symbolized by the finding of the *afikomen*. True freedom rests in renewing a sense of wholeness in the world and wholeness in ourselves. The seder is a celebration of our freedom and it is also ultimately a *tikkun*, a kind of repair.

Land as Freedom: The Promise of the Land

It would take me many years of study and reflection before I could unpack the oldest strata of the seder. Its roots were entirely entangled in the earth, invisible to most of us. And before I could even begin to think about the Haggadah's deepest connections to the earth, I would need to learn more about the meaning of earth in Torah.

I had already been on a lifelong journey exploring the ecological roots of Judaism. In the early days of the Jewish environmental movement, many of us scoured the (Hebrew) Bible and other Jewish texts, identifying particular verses or ideas as ecological. But I always thought there must be something more. I had hoped to find an ecological through-line in the Bible, connecting all the disparate nuggets of ecological wisdom.

I had long been curious about the concept of land in the Bible. As in English, the Hebrew for earth and land are somewhat synonymous. The Hebrew *eretz* and *adamah* are associated with both earth and land. In the field of ecology, "land" is a fundamental concept, and a land ethic is foundational for environmental ethics. Aldo Leopold, known as the first eco-philosopher and writing in the 1940s, defined *land* as an interdependent ecosystem of soils, waters, air, plants, animals, and us. The land is a living organism—a community—of which we are a part. The land or earth is our habitat and we are its inhabitants. Leopold argued that the lack of a land ethic in our culture is the root cause of our environmental problems today.

I realized that *land* might be the ecological clue I was looking for. Repeated stories of landedness and landlessness, the promise of a land to call our own, and the desert saga of trekking across a desert wilderness, spoke of the centrality of land in Torah. I did a quick word search and found that the word *eretz* (earth/land) occurs over two thousand times in the Hebrew Bible, and the word *adamah* (land/soil) appears about two hundred times. I believed I was on to something.

In Torah, we had a sacred agreement with God and the land. The land would never be ours to own. We would only inherit the land as temporary residents if we honored our covenant with God by living good, wholesome, and righteous lives (Lev 25:23). If we behaved unethically or irresponsibly toward each other, the land, or God, our negativity would generate an energetic pollution that would contaminate the land; the land was that sensitive. The land could dry up, swallow us up or vomit us out; it was not guaranteed. I was intrigued by how the Torah's idea of the interdependence of people, land, and God mirrored nature's cycles and feedback loops.

But in contemporary times, the word *land* (in a Jewish or Torah context) often brings to mind the modern-day state of Israel. Those who read the Torah literally view the physical land of Israel as God's *unconditional* gift to the Jews alone. They consider the land of Israel as the legacy and destiny of the Jewish people. Others consider literal approaches to the idea of *land* in Torah immoral and disturbing, and they may end up dismissing the Bible altogether. Today the concept of the *land* of Israel has been so fraught politically and religiously that people tend to avoid even considering the ecological meaning of the word *land*. When people understand *land* as territory, to be fought over and acquired and owned, or a commodity to be bought and sold, their view of *land* invariably becomes economic or political. This anthropocentric and political perspective mars the deeper ecological and spiritual meaning of *land*.

Of course, many people don't even notice land in Torah the same way that most of us don't notice the earth beneath our feet. We associate land and soil with dirt—something to rid ourselves of—never recognizing it as the ground of our being.

Given the hiddenness of land in Torah (or rather, our inability to see it) and given the many layers and intricacies of the traditional Haggadah, it took me many years before I realized that the biblical passage, "My father was a wandering Aramean," around which the whole Passover Haggadah revolves, was also grounded in the land. Many modern haggadot drop this section entirely because it is shrouded in a *midrash* (a rabbinic teaching), and unless you are extremely knowledgeable about Jewish tradition, it can be very confusing. *But even the traditional haggadot which include "My father was a wandering Aramean" do not include the whole passage. They drop the last two lines which concern our relationship to land.*

The biblical passage "My father was a wandering Aramean" passage boils the Exodus story down io a few verses (Deut. 26:5-10). The verses go like this: *My ancestors were wanderers. They went down to Egypt. They suffered terribly at the hands of the Egyptians. They cried out to God. God heard their cries and led them out of Egypt with signs and wonders.* These are the verses that we commonly see in a Conservative or Orthodox Haggadah today.

However, there are two more verses to this passage that the rabbis cut before the passage ever made its way into the traditional Haggadah.[3] The two verses continue: "*And God gave us a land. And we brought back the first fruits of that land to God.*" Without these two verses, the punchline to the whole story of the Jewish people is lost. Why did God free us from Egypt in the first place? God freed us so that God could give us a land and we could bring the first fruits of the land back to God. The missing verses insist on a reciprocal relationship between God, the people, and the land. In a mythical, universal reading of the Torah, our bringing the fruits—our generosity, our practice of right relationship—completes the cycle of God's giving to us. We return our gifts to God and to the land, and our giving back ensures the healthy productive life of the land. As long as we keep giving back, the cycle will be unbroken. The land-God-people cycle is attuned to the very cycles of nature.

The missing verses also teach that freedom means something entirely different than the freedom *from* our evil oppressors (brought to us by a victorious God). Freedom means having a land in which to raise our own food and have agency over our own lives. Freedom means living according to nature's cycles of giving and receiving and giving back. Our freedom depends on a land that is free from exploitation so that it can continue to flourish and produce its fruits in perpetuity.

Not long after I had been grappling with these ideas, the publisher Behrman House approached me to write a Passover Haggadah from an ecological perspective. The timing of this was perfect. I would not even have considered the idea of an ecological Haggadah without the confidence I gained from recognizing that the original idea for Passover and the experience of freedom was rooted in our relationship with the land.

Over the next couple of years, I developed *The Promise of the Land: A Passover Haggadah* around the biblical verses that were left behind so long ago. I returned them to their central place in the Haggadah, highlighting the significance of land and our relationship to her in our tradition. *The Promise of the Land* Haggadah strives to awaken participants to the universal, spiritual, and life-giving meaning of *land* and suggests that true freedom depends on a relationship with the earth.

Communicating the Ecological Message

---

[3] The instructions for celebrating Passover include drinking 4 cups of wine, discussing the symbolic foods of the seder plate, reciting Hallel and other blessings, and reading the *Entire* passage that begins "My father was a wandering Aramean."

Given my own struggles understanding the traditional Haggadah, in creating one myself, in addition to clarifying the ecological dimensions of the holiday, I wanted to develop a commentary that could help people who are not Torah scholars—or even particularly knowledgeable about Judaism—navigate the Haggadah and be comfortable participating in a seder.

The Difficulties of Language

Some people have wondered why *The Promise of the Land: A Passover Haggadah* doesn't use explicit environmental language in its title or subtitle. I deliberately chose language that I hoped would speak to all comers. My goal was to reach a wide audience, not just people who identify as environmentalists. I feared that if we subtitled the Haggadah "a *Green* Haggadah," for example, we would scare off many that I hoped to reach. Terms like "climate change," "global warming," and "environmentalism" are charged and can evoke adverse reactions among conservatives, who tend to associate the language of "environmentalism" with northern elites.

The language of "environment," "climate change," and" global warming" can also be problematic for avowed nature lovers because such language does not convey the story of our rich relationship with the whole natural world. The word "environment" reduces the spicy scents and saturated colors, the patterns, textures, rhythms and songs of the natural world into an abstraction. Abstract language tends to distance us from the natural world and all of its riotous diversity and glory. When so many people feel frightened by or hopeless about the climate crisis or suffer from "green fatigue," we need to be sensitive and careful about how we package our message so that many can hear it.

I chose the word *land* to convey the ecological nature of the Haggadah because the Torah speaks ecologically through the land. Farmers and everyone who lives close to the earth understand its ecological significance. And while the use of the word, *land* poses its own potential problems, *The Promise of the Land* strives to dispel a political orientation towards land which can contribute to a kind of land blindness. *The Promise of the Land* invites us to revisit and reinterpret the meaning of a "promised land."

Hiddur ha-Mitzvah / The Beauty of the Mitzvah

I wanted to create a Haggadah that would convey the beauty of the natural world and inspire people to care. For many, the experience of beauty can be religious—religious without the sometimes heavy-handed religious language. I hoped my words could capture the poetry I heard in the text and in the land.

I have always believed that the beauty of the natural world can touch hearts and inspire wide audiences to protect our earthy home. Scientific rigor or ethical arguments should not be the only strategy by which we try to influence people to respond to the climate crisis, especially those who are on the other side of the political divide and whose opinions are already formed. "Facts don't change our minds," wrote Elizabeth Kolbert in a compelling *New Yorker* cover story. It is widely known that emotions can trump reason in peoples' decision making.

The beauty of the natural world offers a way to tap into the emotions. I am speaking of beauty as a spiritual experience: beauty as wholeness. Beauty can express a sense of intimacy with the world, a sense of nearness. Beauty can move people and elevate them in unexpected ways. It can provide hope and inspiration in a time when many people are despairing and exhausted from climate distress.

It was important to me that the Haggadah have a spacious and elegant feel, so that it could reflect the elegance and simplicity of the natural world. The art functions as a visual midrash, inviting people to take the time to linger on each page, and to reflect on the words and pictures. The art and design also helped weave together the many seemingly disparate pieces of the Haggadah, making it accessible and easy to follow. Through the process of creating the Haggadah, I came to appreciate how attending to the balance of the verbal and the visual is its own kind of *tikkun olam*, the repair of a broken world.

My ultimate goal was to speak a universal ecological language of text and image to reach across the divides—from the traditionalist uncle who is eager to celebrate Passover as he has always loved it, to the teenagers struggling to make sense of their own Jewish identity, to the secular person who is queasy about religious ritual, to the newcomer who had never made sense of the anatomy of the Haggadah, to the partners, spouses, and friends who are not Jewish and feeling timid about participating. I hoped to create a Haggadah that was whole and welcoming enough to make space for friends and families who may hold very different beliefs to share the holiday together, while reflecting on the freedom that comes when we embrace our ultimate heritage—the earth—and our connection to her.

New Symbols: Friends and Families

Kos Miryam Ritual of 1987
and Kos Miryam for Pesach

Stephanie Loo, M.Ed. and
Rabbinic Pastor Matia Rania Angelou

Introduction: The Feminist Context of Kos Miryam

Kos Miryam is one twentieth century Jewish feminist response to the relative absence of women from traditional Jewish texts, and the textual silence about specifically female experiences, concerns, ideas, and feelings. The development of Kos Miryam also exemplifies how contemporary Jewish women work cooperatively to create and practice new rituals.

Biblical hints, archeological findings, and evidence collected by folklorists and anthropologists show that throughout the ages women in Jewish communities created customs, rituals, and language to support, guide, comfort, and celebrate one another throughout all the stages of their life journeys—but what became of that precious heritage?

Because women were excluded from text study, writing, and publishing for much of Jewish history, and because women's ideas and activities were of minor concern to male writers, the written record is pitifully sparse. The wisdom of Jewish women was preserved and transmitted not through texts, but through *minhag*/custom and oral tradition. Unfortunately, those means of transmission are particularly vulnerable to the discontinuities, dislocations, and destruction of Jewish families and communities throughout history—and thus our whole community lost a huge amount of female wisdom. The loss of female elements, creating a lack of balance in Jewish culture, was harmful not only for women, but for our whole people.

Following the onset of second-wave feminism in the United States in the 1960s, many Jewish women found the courage to undertake a variety of strategies to recover or reconstruct elements of this lost legacy, or to create new elements to fill the gaps. They studied traditional Jewish texts for ideas and hints about women's lives, customs, and rituals, and then used imagination to expand upon these hints.

Some of us, trusting our intuition and emotions, drawing from wisdom gained through our own life experiences, and working in community with one another, also turned for guidance to an *inner* source: the spring of living waters that arises inside each of us, a perennial and inexhaustible source of nourishment, strength, and inspiration.

Sources and Forerunners

In the midrash we hear that after the Exodus from Egypt, the Israelites in the desert complained of thirst. Because of the righteousness of the prophet Miriam, God gave the Israelites a miraculous well filled with pure, healing waters. This well, known as Miriam's Well, traveled with the people during their years of wandering in the desert until, upon Miriam's death, the well dried up (Talmud, Taanit 9a / Midrash, Bamidbar Rabbah).

The first time Matia encountered the idea of drinking water in connection with Miriam was in Penina Adelman's book *Miriam's Well: Rituals for Jewish Women Around the Year* (Biblio Press, 1986, p. 11). Matia also learned about an ancient women's custom of drawing and drinking water from a well at motzei Shabbat because it is said that after Shabbat all the wells of the world are connected to Miriam's Well. "Therefore, they are accustomed to draw water every Saturday night, since perhaps they will chance upon the well of Miriam and be healed" (Eliyahu Kitov, *The Book of Our Heritage*).

The Boston Area Rosh Hodesh (New Moon-th) Group and the Original Kos Miryam

In the mid-1980s, scholar and storyteller Penina Adelman, and singer/songwriter Maia Brumberg settled in the Greater Boston area after several years' study in Israel. Their arrival raised feminist consciousness and energized many Jewish women. Matia and Stephanie were fortunate to participate for several years in a dynamic Rosh Hodesh group started by Penina and Maia. Janet Zimmern, Joyce Rosen Friedman, and Gail Liebhaber also contributed immeasurably to the group. When the group met, different women would take turns leading singing, chanting, study, or discussions; many members of the group improvised, playing off each other.

At one session, Joyce led the group in a guided meditation. She asked us to imagine taking a walk outdoors and coming upon Miriam's Well. There we could drink from the waters or immerse ourselves in them as a source of strength, healing, and renewal.

At this time, Stephanie had given birth to a son who was a very demanding infant, and she was raising him with limited support from other adults. Although usually unable to connect to visualization exercises, on this occasion Stephanie...

> *imagined finding a pool in the woods. On its banks she met Miryam herself, wearing a pair of red leather sandals. Miryam helped Stephanie immerse in and drink from the pool. Then she*

gave the red sandals to Stephanie, told her she was walking in the right direction, and encouraged her to keep going.

Inspired by this vision, Stephanie created the original Kos Miryam ritual: a kiddush (words of holy connection) recited over water, used alongside the traditional kiddush over wine to welcome Shabbat on Friday nights. The ritual comprises four elements:

1. A ritual object, the cup or *Kos*
2. Water, or *mayyim hayyim*
3. **Ritual words** spoken by the leader, some of which are repeated by the company
4. A **sung version** of the response

Kos: For the cup, Stephanie originally used the crystal goblet she and her husband had drunk from under the chuppah at their wedding. She made this choice because she felt that ideally the cup should be a virtually invisible container for the water.

Mayyim hayyim: Stephanie filled the cup with sparkling seltzer water to represent the living waters of Miriam's well. Plain water or spring water is also acceptable.

Ritual words: The accompanying words came into Stephanie's head fully formed. They are not exactly a *brachah*/blessing but rather an assertion that the healing waters of Miriam's well are still accessible to us today.

Song: To complete the Kos Miryam ritual, all can sing the song "Hazak, hazak v'nit'hazek" to the melody written by Faith Rogow (©1990).

KOS MIRYAM[1]
Leader holds up glass kiddush cup filled with sparkling water.

Leader:
ZOT KOS MIRYAM, KOS MAYIM HAYIM;
HAZAK HAZAK V'NIT'HAZEYK!
(This is the cup of Miriam, the cup of living waters;
strength, strength, and let us be strengthened!)
Company:

---

[1] © Stephanie Loo 1987 and Kol Isha. PO Box 132, Wayland, MA 01778.

May be used, but not sold, by notifying Kol Isha in writing. Please include this copyright on all copies.

HAZAK HAZAK V'NIT'HAZEYK!
(Strength, strength, and let us be strengthened!)
Everyone drinks from the cup in turn.

After Stephanie shared this new custom with the Rosh Hodesh group, Matia developed an expanded version of Kos Miryam for erev Shabbat. Seeing Shabbat herself as a well in which we can refresh and purify ourselves after a long work week, she asks everyone present to share an inspirational thought, something that helps them to renew themselves. After reciting the Kos Miryam formula, she adds: "Blessed are You, Shekhinah, Source of life, who gives us living waters" and "Blessed are You, Yah our God, Majestic Spirit of the Universe, by whose word everything is created." (This second blessing is *she-hakol,* the traditional blessing said before drinking water.) Her family welcomes Shabbat by remembering the prophet Miriam, while ending it at Havdalah (the ceremony that marks the end of Shabbat) by remembering Elijah.

Matia realized that Kos Miryam is a living ceremony which can be adapted to any holiday or occasion. Because it is so compact and unspecific, people can interpolate Kos Miryam into rituals for other Jewish holidays (such as Rosh Hodesh), life-cycle events (such as Bat/Bar Mitzvah celebrations), or personal milestones and transitions. One way to do this is to create an introductory text (inviting one's intention)—a kavannah—to tie it to the specific occasion, as illustrated by the Kos Miryam ceremony written for Pesach.

Kos Miryam for Pesach
Because Miriam plays such a prominent role in the Exodus narrative and because water is integral to the story, the Passover seder is a natural place to include Kos Miryam. In 1990, Matia undertook that project in collaboration with Janet Berkenfield, who had recently written some beautiful meditations and Psalm translations for *Siddur Birkat Shalom,* the egalitarian prayer book produced by the Havurat Shalom Siddur Project. Matia uses this version of Kos Miryam at the beginning of her seder to set the tone for the evening. (Others use Kos Miryam before or after Kos Eliyahu toward the end of the seder.)

Using Kos Miryam on the Passover seder table has caught on in the past few decades as a way to honor the women in the Torah, particularly in the Exodus narrative. While we are happy that people are using and finding meaning in Kos Miryam, the Passover Haggadah doesn't mention either Miriam or her brothers Moshe or Aharon by name. The Torah tells us that God alone brought us out of Egypt into freedom through miracles and wonders. And yet, our Sages tell us that the entire Exodus was in the merit of the righteous women of Miriam's generation (Rav Avira, Sota 11b). Perhaps this is a reason that Kos Miryam for Pesach has become popular, especially at women's seders.

KOS MIRYAM FOR PASSOVER[2]

We begin our seder with Kos Miryam, Miriam's Cup, symbolically filled with *mayyim hayyim*, living waters from Miriam's Well. Elijah's Cup, of which we speak at the end of the seder, represents our future redemption, when peace will fill the world. Miriam's Cup represents our past redemption, when our people were brought out of Egypt and delivered from slavery.

Miriam's Well was said to hold Divine power to heal, sustain, and renew. It became a special source of transformation for a people leaving slavery to form a new identity. Throughout our journey as a people, we have sought to rediscover these living waters for ourselves. With this cup of clear spring water, we remember God's gift of living waters from Miriam's Well.

Tonight at our seder, we continue this journey. Just as the Holy One delivered Miriam and her people, just as they were sustained in the desert and transformed into a new people, so may we be delivered, sustained and transformed on our own journey to a stronger sense of ourselves as individuals and as one community. May the living waters of Miriam's Well nourish us and give us inspiration as we embark on our journey through the Haggadah.

(lift cup)
Reader: *Zot Kos Miryam, Kos Mayyim Hayyim.*
Zakheir l'tzi-at Mitzrayim.
This is the Cup of Miriam, the Cup of Living Waters.
Let us remember going out from Egypt.

All: These are the living waters, God's gift to Miriam, which gave new life to Israel as we struggled with ourselves in the wilderness.
Blessed are You God, Who brings us from the narrows into the wil-

---

[2] © 1990 Kol Isha (Matia Rania Angelou, Janet Berkenfield, Stephanie Loo)
May be used, but not sold, by notifying Kol Isha in writing at PO Box 132, Wayland, MA, 01778. Please include this copyright on all copies.

derness, sustains us with endless possibilities, and enables us to reach a new place.

(blessing for drinking water)
Barukh Atta Yah, Eloheinu Melekh ha-Olam, she-ha-kol n'hi-ye bi-d'varo

Blessed are You, Yah our God, Majestic Spirit of the Universe, by Whose word everything is created. (drink)

Kos Miryam is for Everyone

Although the most common use of Kos Miryam has been at Passover seders, this is not its only purpose, nor is it meant to be solely about or for women. Just as Kos Eliyahu is not for use by men only, Kos Miryam was never meant to be a ceremony for women alone. Kos Miryam emerged in a feminist context, but feminism itself is for the benefit of all. Kos Miryam and Miriam's Well are universal symbols for all humankind.

Our original focus on the *mayyim hayyim* seems to have been over-shadowed by women's desire to honor Miriam. Kos Miryam is fulfilling a necessary purpose for women as they find their voice in relation to Jewish practice. Hopefully, one day the full potential and spirituality of the living waters will be recognized, and Kos Miryam will not be seen solely as "a women's custom" but will be used throughout the Jewish community as a way to bring feminist consciousness into our ritual.

In Gratitude

Kos Miryam could only have emerged in the Rosh Hodesh group in which Matia and Stephanie participated in the late 1980s. Every member of the group helped nurture the creative environment that nourished Kos Miryam. Thank you to founding mothers Penina Adelman and Maia Brumberg Kraus, and to Joyce, Janet, and Gail. Thank you to anthropologist Susan Sered (part of Stephanie's current Rosh Hodesh group) for contributing to this article. May the memory of poet Janet Berkenfield be for a blessing.

Why an Orange?

Susannah Heschel

How many of us remember the horrors of the 1980s, when a rare form of cancer—Kaposi's sarcoma—soon became a signal in the gay community of a new and terrible disease? The newspapers called it a "gay plague," and it killed hundreds and thousands of men in a relentless, painful progression of infection that spread rapidly through the gay community. Ultimately called AIDS, it relentlessly attacked the immune system, leaving people open to a host of infectious diseases.

The 1980s were the years of the Ronald Reagan presidency, and despite desperate pleas, Reagan refused to appropriate emergency funding for medical research to stop the epidemic. He and his cronies, especially his right-wing religious supporters, called the plague a punishment for being gay.

Hysteria blossomed: gay people were shunned, those suffering from AIDS were isolated, blamed for their illness, and often died alone, rejected by their families. Extraordinary talent was lost as young gay men were murdered by the relentless disease, and everyone in the gay community lost friends and colleagues and found themselves constantly attending funeral services, in mourning, terror, and rage.

In the early 1980s, the Hillel Foundation invited me to speak on a panel at Oberlin College. While on campus, I came across a Haggadah that had been written by some Oberlin students to express feminist concerns. One ritual they devised was placing a crust of bread on the Seder plate as a sign of solidarity with Jewish lesbians, a statement of defiance against a rebbetzin's pronouncement that, "There's as much room for a lesbian in Judaism as there is for a crust of bread on the seder plate."

At the next Passover, I placed an orange on our family's Seder plate. During the first part of the Seder, I asked everyone to take a segment of the orange, make the blessing over fruit, and eat it as a gesture of solidarity with Jewish lesbians and gay men, and others who are marginalized within the Jewish community.

Bread on the Seder plate brings an end to Pesach—it renders everything *chametz*. And it suggests that being lesbian is being transgressive, violating Judaism. I felt that an orange was suggestive of something else: the fruitfulness for all Jews when lesbians and gay men are contributing and active members of Jewish life. In addition, each orange segment had a few seeds that had to be spit out—a gesture of spitting out, repudiating the homophobia of Judaism.

In the 1980s, solidarity with gay men and lesbians was radical and even shocking to many people who attended lectures I gave on feminist issues at synagogues and Jewish centers. At my own Seder, everyone would eat a segment of the orange, recognizing that all the segments stick together, that an orange is always full and juicy, never missing a segment, and we would spit out the orange seeds in repudiation of homophobia.

Perhaps the gesture was too shocking for some to bear, which is why a rumor began circulating that putting an orange on the Seder plate was symbolizing women's right to be on the bimah. Indeed, a story circulated that after I lectured in Miami Beach, a man stood up and admonished me, saying that a woman belongs on the bimah like an orange on the Seder plate—thus erasing the homophobia and putting my idea into the mouth of a man. It was also ridiculous—women were already on the bimah, ordained as rabbis and cantors—so this new story also had no political meaning.

Nothing happened in Miami Beach, of course, but the rumor made it clear how far we had to go; homophobia was relentless. Indeed, my custom had fallen victim to a folktale process in which my original intention was subverted. My idea of the orange was attributed to a man, and my goal of affirming lesbians and gay men was erased.

For years, I have known about women whose scientific discoveries were attributed to men, or who had to publish their work under a male pseudonym. That it happened to me makes me realize all the more how important it is to recognize how deep and strong patriarchy remains, and how important it is for us to celebrate the contributions of gay and lesbian Jews, and all those who need to be liberated from marginality to centrality. And Passover is the right moment to ensure freedom for all Jews.

Back then, debates were still taking place: could a gay man or lesbian become a rabbi? People hid their identity out of fear. I was a graduate student at U Penn in the 1980s, and many of my friends were gay and lesbian rabbinical students, some bisexual, some intersexed, and some who identified as queer or transgender. They were imagining how they might shape their work as rabbis in a new and inspiring way, drawing on their sexual identity and addressing the fear that was rampant in the gay community.

In the early 2000s, a young woman took me aside after a lecture and poured out her heart: she had been adopted by a Jewish family but was harassed in the Jewish community for not "looking Jewish" (whatever that means!). She asked me to include her and all Jews who "look different" in the symbol of the orange, which I did. Marginality in a Jewish community that claims inclusivity is particularly painful, as it denies the reality that so many Jews are excluded. I witnessed this when my mother became a widow, and when I became an orphan, and I have seen the treatment of black and Asian Jews, especially of children attending Jewish day schools, where suspicion and, at times, mockery undermined their own Jewish identity.

If being gay was viewed as a curse in the 1980s, being suspected of being gay was part of the disciplinary toolkit of compulsory heterosexuality. Forcing people into heterosexual relationships against their will and human nature was a form of terror. Appalling human suffering resulted and continues to affect far too many people. Homophobia remains a persistent plague. Lives are at stake: too many young people, including a former student of mine, are plunged into despair by the homophobia and cruel rejection of their sexual identity by their communities and even, at times, by their own families; some, including my student, commit suicide.

I'm gratified that so much has changed since the 1980s, and I am delighted to have officiated at several weddings of gay friends. Still, the current political climate should not leave us feeling secure, and we certainly have much left to accomplish. The orange represents for me not only inclusivity, but also expresses the fruitful vitality offered by gay and lesbian perspectives and experiences.

So much of Judaism comes to us from male-only study houses where a homosocial environment no doubt gave rise to homoerotic and even homosexual love; we should celebrate that experience, just as so many Jewish texts tell us to rejoice and celebrate our sexual expressions of love and care for others. From those expressions come the rabbinic, kabbalistic, and philosophic traditions that constitute the many faceted Judaism that we love.

The Freedom Plate on the Seder Table

Martha Hausman

Introducing the Freedom Plate into the Seder was my first act of Jewish empowerment, of taking my Jewish practice into my own hands. Since then, it has become the most important feature of our family's Passover Seder each year.

It was 1992 and Jewish life in the United States was opening up—to me anyway. Innovative movements and organizations like Jewish Renewal, *Tikkun Magazine* and Peace Now were becoming active and visible. I was 30 and, after a Conservative-movement upbringing and a fairly secular young-adult life, I was finding my own Jewish practice through a chavurah community. (*Chavurah* is the Hebrew word for a fellowship for Jewish prayer, learning, and action, in which leadership is shared by the members rather than held by "the rabbi" or a rabbi-like person.)

OK, what really happened was that I got dumped by my boyfriend and started using the extra time, first, to go to services at the *chavurah*, and second, to begin having a Jewish social life.

I was still attending my parents' Seder and I was lucky to have open, curious, liberal parents who would welcome anything I brought, no matter how *meshuganeh*. Due to the Jewish awakening I was having, I wanted to mix it up. I wanted to make it more personal. I wanted to find a way to inject our participants' personalities into the seder. Learning about the orange on the seder plate[1] gave me the idea that anyone participating in a seder could bring any symbol that had personal meaning.My father led the Seder, as fathers in my Jewish world were wont to do (and often, still are). Even he wasn't entirely happy with the ritual as we were used to doing it. He cast about for more meaningful Haggadot from the various movements, but whatever Haggadah we used, we went around the table reading the passages aloud with the occasional interruption for a well-known song or maybe a question. And, as the Haggadah prescribes, at various points, he would ask participants to lift a symbol from the seder plate and read the corresponding passage.

I thought: If we could lift and explain a traditional object, then why not lift and explain an item that represented freedom to each of us in a more personal, contemporary way? So one year, I sent an email to all our

---

[1] See "Why an Orange?" by Susannah Heschel in this volume.

invitees a week before the Seder, and asked everyone at the seder to think of one personal item that represented freedom for them, and bring it for our new "Freedom Plate." To my surprise that year, everyone arrived at the Seder with their items! No eye-rolling ensued (as far as I know). Here's what my Ma says about that first time:

> I remember that I was in treatment and put my chemo-therapy pills on the plate. Annie put her contraceptive pills on the plate, and Dad put his bike lock keys. Dave played a tape of the MLK speech, "I Have a Dream." Someone put money on the plate. It made the Seder more personal and made the people feel closer.

One thing the Freedom Plate has demonstrated over the years is the dual nature of liberation and oppression. Life is so complicated, so full, so fraught. Every item on the Freedom Plate had, and continues to have, elements of freedom, but also of bondage. So too with the traditional Seder plate and the ritual items of Pesach. In Judaism, every coin has two sides! Just as we lift the matzah and say the *motze* in praise of God for providing bread, we also note that matzah is the bread of our affliction. As we lift the chemo medicine from the Freedom Plate, we thank God for the modern medical miracle, and we bemoan the fact of cancer, knowing that our health is tenuous. And participants with enough means are deeply grateful and relieved to have the freedom associated with money, which is also the hallmark of oppressive capitalism for so many. Modern slavery and freedom are discussed at the table as these profoundly ambiguous symbols are raised.

Through the years, when we invite our family and friends at the Seder to talk about what items they brought for the Freedom Plate, I've also seen the power of personal perspective. Whereas having to undergo the suffering of a lengthy chemo treatment could be seen by some as deeply oppressive and physically horrible, my mother's ability to put her pills on the Freedom Plate expressed gratitude and her love of life. In this way, we all learn more about each other during the evening.

I've also learned how powerful rituals—and ritual items—are to helping us tell stories about our lives and finding meaning in them. Passover is an (the) Exodus journey we are commanded to take in one night, for "In every generation every person should feel as if they, themselves had gone out from Egypt—*Mitzrayim*." Mitzrayim translates both to Egypt and to "narrow place." And so we do take that journey. We not only tell the story, we *eat* the Matzah, a dry cracker in place of bread, to internalize the suffering. We dip bitter herbs in salty tears and eat those, too. Many of us experience drudgery as we clean the house, rushing to get everything done, sniping at each other about the chores.

For many, Seder can be about how we experience being Jewish, especially because, for some people, attending a Seder may be the most meaningful and powerful Jewish celebration they attend all year. The Freedom Plate is also a great vehicle for non-Jewish participants and those who have never experienced a Seder to contribute in a genuine way. And the ritual of the Freedom Plate can allow participants a safe setting for sharing themselves and their intimate thoughts and feelings with others in a meaningful way. As my cousin said:

> The seder experience for me previously was more of a learning about Judaism. What changed by your Freedom Plate is my experience became more focused on connecting with my loved ones at a deeper level. I feel more connected to our extended community of family and friends with cherished stories about meaningful moments in their lives. For me, I shared my freedom at discovering marriage as a beautiful, cherished freedom by explaining my delight in being married to Peter and learning what a happy marriage feels like.

Indeed, one year Peter and his then-girlfriend Liz each put their brand new divorce papers on the Freedom Plate. The next year they held their marriage license aloft.

My sister-in-law:

> I came from a tradition where seders were about eating special food, singing Hebrew songs that I didn't understand and lots of laughing with extended family. It was a lot of fun, but there was no discussion about what it was all about. The Freedom Plate was an express way for me to discover what Passover really was about. It started before I even got to the Seder, thinking about what I was going to bring for the Freedom Plate. All of a sudden, on my own time, whether I was driving or in the shower, I contemplated what makes me feel free. One year, I remember choosing my new business plan and recognizing the freedom I was feeling to be able to

take that step. When I shared that story I burst into tears. I hadn't really appreciated what I was doing in that way before.

The Freedom Plate has allowed us each to truly express our gratitude for freedom in our lives. At the Seder, as the Haggadah says:

It is our duty to thank, praise, laud, glorify, raise up, beautify, bless, extol, and adore *YHWH / Yahhh*, [Interbreathing Spirit of all life] who made all these miracles for our [ancestors] and ourselves; *YHWH / Yahhh* brought us forth from slavery into freedom, from sorrow into joy, from mourning into festivity, from darkness into great light, and from servitude into redemption.

Each of us is still on that journey. For as in the Bible, journey, struggle, becoming who we are—collectively and individually—didn't end the day we left Egypt. Nor does it end with the conclusion of the Exodus narrative. Or the conclusion of any struggle.

While we experience personal struggles and the oppression of our own communities deeply, growth, struggle, oppression and the fight against it occur all around us. Our friend Adam, whose family now regularly attends our Seder, said:

> My most powerful contribution to a Freedom Plate was a piece of Haitian Casava bread. The casava root is poisonous prior to careful preparation by the desperately low-income households that rely on it. Casava bread, which looks much like *shmurah matzah*, is truly a bread of affliction. It was very meaningful at the time to represent the struggles of my Haitian friends at that year's Seder with a piece of their bread.

The Freedom Plate help us use the Seder to expand, to learn about each other, Judaism, the world. And sometimes it causes us to contract, because oppression is sitting at the table. My brother writes:

> Last year, I had decided that I would symbolically put my parents on the freedom plate—both to honor them as people who have taught me to experience and cherish freedom in a multitude of ways, and also because they represent the genetic lottery of freedom, and my plan was to acknowledge that no matter how much I have worked and created my own privilege, it is deeply rooted in the fact that I was born into the right family in the right time and place and all of

the doors of opportunities that opened for me. Nice idea, right? Both honor my parents and recognize the fundamental unfairness of privilege.

However, at this family Seder, with my white, educated, upper-middle-class family, we also had some family friends who were non-white, and quite economically challenged. This included kids who have experienced being separated from their parents into the foster care system, and their loving parents who have had to fight to "prove" that they are suitable to take care of their own children.

I knew just a bit of the many, many arbitrary cruelties of the social services system they had experienced, along with the daily extra obstacles faced by the poor who have so many fewer resources to meet them. I talked about the ways my parents had taught me to pursue and cherish freedom, but the second part of my Freedom Plate spiel stuck in my throat and I couldn't even say it.

Perhaps it was the right decision under the circumstances, but it really got me thinking about a whole new dimension to my comfortable life in a white-privilege culture—that I was prepared to acknowledge the arbitrariness of my privilege if it was only among my cohort, but I couldn't face up to it in front of people who experience the other side of the coin. A whole new experience of what freedom means in our society.

After a few years of experimenting with the Freedom Plate, it became ritually enshrined in our Seder every year, and friends started using it at their Seders. I summoned the courage to post about it. On April 7, 1996, it gained even more notoriety when Rabbi Arthur Waskow posted this note on the Shamash Listserv:

> My previous post recalled from last year someone's pro-posal of a "Freedom Plate" beside the Seder Plate, con-taining the specific freedom-evoking objects of the Seder folks—but I couldn't recall who proposed it. It was Martha Hausman. Great idea, powerful addition to the liturgy in our house. — AW

In my family, the Freedom Plate has given us the opportunity to cel-ebrate the personal ways we have each traveled "from darkness into great light" but also to feel ongoing striving for freedom. Because when we are each commanded to "feel as if [we, ourselves] had gone out from Egypt" it is actually the case that that this "going out" from Mitzrayim, a narrow place, is not in the past. We are still and will always be, in one way or another, on that journey personally and along with friends, family, community, humanity.

How to have your own Freedom Plate:

1. A week before your Seder, send an email to everyone invited, asking each person to bring one item that symbolizes freedom in their lives.
2. On the night of the Seder, set aside one large empty platter or dish for your Seder participants to put their items on the Freedom Plate.
3. Depending on the number of guests you have, choose a few moments during your Seder to invite each person to hold up their item and explain why they brought it for the Freedom Plate. We don't necessarily go in order around the table, and one, or a few, people might explain their submissions at any point in the Seder when moved to do so. Ideally, each person will speak, but some people may not feel like sharing and at our Seder, that's OK. Another way to do it is to have the leader, if there is one, hold up an item and ask if its owner would like to explain. So the leader might say, "Oh, here's a sneaker! Who can explain why it represents freedom?"

Four New Questions for the Passover Seder

Rabbi Arthur Waskow

1. Why do we break the matzah in two before we eat it?

Matzah, the pressed-down bread that embodies the "fierce urgency of Now," was both the bread of the oppressed and the bread of freedom.

If we keep the whole matzah for ourselves, it remains the bread of affliction. Only if we share the matzah can it become the bread of freedom. We must break the matzah in two in order to share it with each other.

If we hold all our abundance, our prosperity, for ourselves, the withholding brings forth anger and resentment, guilt and fear. The abundant bread becomes the bread of affliction. Only if we share our abundance with each other can it become the bread of freedom.

If we gobble all the abundance of our Mother Earth for human society alone, leaving no space for other life-forms, the Earth will choke and curdle. Whatever bread may barely grow will bear affliction. Only if we share our air, our water, with the myriad shapes of life will all this growing birth our freedom.

If we hold our own knowledge, our own wisdom, for ourselves alone, we end up in a Narrowness that enslaves us. Only if we share our wisdom with other traditions, other communities—only if we open ourselves to learn from them—can our wisdom lead to freedom. [*Mitzrayim*, the Hebrew word for Egypt, actually means "Tight and Narrow Place."]

If we try to hold the whole land for ourselves, even the Land of Israel, the land will remain a land of affliction. Only if we share it with another people can it become the land of freedom.

And so, at the beginning of the Seder we break the matzah, and at the end of the Seder we share its pieces with each other, to eat the bread of freedom.

2. Why is there *charoset* on the Seder plate, and why do we linger on its delicious taste?

Because *charoset* embodies the delicious Song of Songs, which itself celebrates the embodiment of love among human beings and love between the earth and human earthlings. All the many recipes for *charoset* draw on the ingredients named only in the cookbook of the Song of Songs—wine, nuts, fruit, spices.

We are taught to recite the Song of Songs during Passover in order to remind us that the joy of freedom cannot be celebrated in human societies alone; as in the time of Eden, all Earth must sing for joy.

In Eden, the Garden of Delight, we humans tried to gobble all the fruitfulness of Earth. So Eden ended with an Earth turned stingy and with half the human race subjugated to the other half. Passover calls us to Eden once again, where love and freedom join in fuller celebration.

3. What are the plagues that today new pharaohs are bringing upon all Earth and human earthlings?

[Wait for answers. Some possible answers:] Undrinkable water poisoned by fracking. • Asthma: Lungs suffering from coal dust and gasoline fumes. • Suffering and death still haunting fish, birds, vegetation, and human beings from the oil blowout in the Gulf of Mexico 2010. • Smashed mountains and dead coal-miners in the lovely hills of West Virginia. • Summer-long intense heat wave in Europe, killing thousands of elders. • Unheard-of floods in Pakistan, putting one-fifth of the country under water. • Superstorm Sandy, killing hundreds in Haiti and America. Typhoon Haiyan in the Philippines, killing more than 6,000 people. • Years of drought, parched fields, dead crops, and wildfires in Africa, Russia, Syria, Australia, and California—in some, setting off hunger, starvation, civil wars, genocide.

[Pause. Everyone breathes. Then the community says in unison:]

And we pledge ourselves to act so that the Tenth Plague does not happen.

4. When the community rises and goes to open a door to the outside, to welcome Elijah, they say together this Question:

Why do we welcome Elijah the Prophet to the Seder?

Someone gives the answer:

> Just a few days ago, this past Shabbat, we read the last passage of the last of the Prophets, Malachi, who proclaims on behalf of the Breath of Life: "Before the coming of the great and awesome day when the Breath of Life may become a Hurricane of Change, I will send the Prophet Elijah, to turn the hearts of the parents to the children and the hearts

of the children to the parents, lest the Earth be utterly destroyed.

As we open our door to the winds of the world, so we open our hearts to the future, to the hearts of our children and their children. And we open our hearts to our parents and their parents, to the wisdom of many generations.

[All come back to the table. Elijah's Cup, filled and set aside early in the Seder, is now passed around the table. Each person pours a little of Elijah's Cup into their own wine cup. Then all lift their cups and all say in unison:]

"We open ourselves, each one of us, to take on the joyful task of Elijah. We open our hearts to our parents and our children, to heal the Earth and ourselves from her suffering."

[Those present say aloud some action they will take.]

5. These are four questions. Are there any other questions?
That is the newest question. What are the other questions that arise for us? Wait for the answers of new questions.

The #FreedomSeder50

#FreedomSeder50: "Making our Days Radically New as They Were 50 Years Ago"

Rabbi Phyllis Berman and Vivienne Hawkins

It all started with Rabbi Arthur Waskow, just as it had fifty years ago when he was a progressive activist utterly newly venturing into Jewish life. For more than a year, he had been imagining a 50th anniversary of the Freedom Seder that wasn't a repetition of what had been radical in 1969 but would itself be radical in 2019.

"Commemoration through Emulation," he said.

He imagined that as the original Freedom Seder had been held in an African-American church in 1969, to break new ground in honoring a community under attack in 2019, this Interfaith Freedom Seder must be held in an African-American mosque. He knew that just as the original Freedom Seder was held on April 4, on the first anniversary of the murder of Reverend Dr. Martin Luther King, the new Seder must be held on the Sunday closest to that dreadful moment—April 7, 2019. It would have been too complicated to do a Seder, usually a home ritual for Jews, on a Friday night when observant Jews would not be traveling or turning on electronics (until possibly the *Year of the Pandemic*).

He knew that to make the new Seder as challenging and transformative to our times as the original had been in 1969, it needed to go even further in lifting up and reawakening the teachings of Dr. King—under far worse attack now than a year after King was murdered. So Arthur was clear about the keynote speaker: Reverend William Barber, an African-American prophet from North Carolina, architect of the Monday Moral Majority actions in a state whose government didn't represent a majority of the people, and co-chair of the new nationwide Poor People's Campaign modeled for today after King's Poor People's Campaign.

With that, we were off and running. We turned to Masjidullah, a masjid/mosque of African-American Muslims who, with many other Jewish and Christian congregations, are active members of POWER (Philadelphians Organized to Witness, Empower and Rebuild), a Philadelphia-area faith-based community organizing group that includes about 40 congregations representing 50,000 people across socio-economic, cultural, racial, religious, and neighborhood lines.

Masjidullah's building was itself an embodiment of multireligious commitment: It had begun in 1947 as Temple Sinai, a synagogue; it became a church, the West Oak Lane Church of God, in 1973; and in 2013 it became Masjidullah. So it has truly been, in the words of the psalmist, a "house of prayer for all people."

Masjidullah took its relationship with the world seriously enough to define the mission of one of its Imams as pursuing Social Justice. When Masjidullah's Imam Abdul-Halim Hassan responded with excitement to hearing Arthur explain that the murder of Dr. Martin Luther King in 1968 was his inspiration for the original Freedom Seder, we all knew we had found the right home for this 50th anniversary event.

From that beginning, we knew that this Seder needed to be organized around the traditional **Four Cups** of grape juice and not—in a mosque—of wine, since Islamic law forbids the use of alcohol. The four cups were to be symbols. Three of those symbols came from what Dr. King had called, in his "Beyond Vietnam" speech at Riverside Church in New York City in 1968, the "deadly triplets" of American desecration—Racism, Materialism, Militarism—as virulent now as in 1968. Now, however, in 2019, we added a fourth desecration—Sexism —more acknowledged in 2019 than it had been in 1969, despite its presence in all of our history.

Everything unfolded one step at a time from there. First, we agreed that there would be three other main speakers besides Rev. Barber: Dr. Debbie Almontaser, founder of the first Arabic-language public school in New York City; Rev. Liz Theoharis, co-chair with Rev. Barber of the Poor People's Campaign; and Ana Maria Archila, co-director of the Center for Participatory Democracy, who was one of the two women who famously confronted Republican Senator Jeffrey Flake of Arizona in a U.S. Capitol elevator, thereby delaying (but unfortunately, not stopping) the 2019 Senate's confirmation of Brett Kavanaugh for a seat on the U.S. Supreme Court.

Then the planning committee for the event met—including Rabbi Mordechai Liebling of The Shalom Center board, Reconstructionist Rabbinical College student Lizzie Horne, Arthur, and Phyllis. We brainstormed together ten Philadelphia-based organizations whose work was focused on eliminating an oppressive aspect of Racism, or Militarism, or Materialism, or Sexism—plagues upon Humankind or Earth that were contemporary versions of the **Ten Plagues** recounted in a traditional Passover Seder.

At that meeting, the Seder began to take its shape. Drawing on the teachings of the Buddhist teacher/activist Joanna Macy, we understood that change happens through a four-fold process: we must begin with joy and love for the world; only then can we move on to the reality of its pain and our sorrow for its wounds; from there we're able to open our eyes to "see anew" what's true; and from there to commit ourselves to actions that bring about change.

(After that planning meeting, I, Phyllis, began to think about who could emcee the event in the way we were imagining it. It had to be a person without a lot of ego, who didn't need to bring in his/her own agenda, but who could hold the structure of our plan. How could I explain what I knew was needed to another person? So I decided, despite my discomfort in front of a big audience—and still recovering from hip replacement surgery—that I was the one, because I understood the importance and value of that role. I wanted to be able to invite people into a reflective silence after they heard each speaker, before they spoke and listened to an unfamiliar partner, before they imbibed the grape juice, or the bitter herb, or the sweet charoset, or the hastily-baked matzah. No one was more surprised than I to see 400 activists respond silently each time I invoked a reflective silence!)

"Why is this night different from all other nights?" we asked together, as has been done for millennia at the start of a traditional Seder. Our answers to the **Four Questions** at this 50th Interfaith Freedom Seder, however, were not traditional.

We began to imagine which of the four speakers might address each of the central aspects of this Seder: Four Cups, Four Questions/Answers, Four "Deadly Quadruplets" eating away at American society—understanding (even before the Uprising after the murder of George Floyd a year later) that Racism was part of every aspect of what's poisonous in our country.

Logistically, we knew that this Seder, like all others, needed music; needed the involvement of all 400 people there, not just as listeners but also as speakers; and needed some basic Passover Seder symbolic foods. And then we got practical: unlike many home Seders, this one could not go on all night. In fact, we had negotiated the space at Masjidullah only until 9:30 pm.

One of our concerns was that The Shalom Center needed this event to function both as an agent of religio-political transformation and as a fundraiser to support other of its transformative projects. We had to explore how to set prices for participation that would both invite a wide swath of people from the Philadelphia community (and beyond, though before all of us were so comfortable with livestreaming) and bring in sufficient funds.

So we set the cost of the Seder ceremony itself at an amount that would just cover space and table/chair rentals. We also invited people who lived too far away to be physically present to tune in to the Seder by live internet feed, for a low per-person fee based on the number of spectators at that livestream site. And we invited activist groups to cosponsor the event and to place paid ads in a program booklet that brought their work to a wider audience and doubled as a Haggadah ("Telling-of-the-Freedom-Tale").

We decided to offer an optional dinner preceding the Seder that would cost participants an amount somewhat beyond the out-of-pocket food costs. We also asked some Shalom Center supporters for large contributions in honor of the event and its fifty-year history. We also published commemorative messages in the event program for a fee.

Our dual purpose was achieved: We brought about both deep spiritual uplift, moving people into fuller action for social change, and a financial success great enough to fund other transformative efforts by The Shalom Center.

Looking carefully at the time frame for the Seder, we decided to have dinner first at 5:00 pm for the 200 people who registered for both dinner and Seder. We decided the Seder itself would run from 7:00-9:30 pm for the additional 200 people who registered. Everyone had to pre-register in order for us to have the right number of tables, chairs, food, etc. and to be sure we had the space—not unlimited—at Masjidullah for those registered.

Throughout this process, the logistics would have been unworkable without the exceptional experience, organizational skills, and cooperative work ethic of Viv Hawkins, The Shalom Center's Program Coordinator. She put together online programs to register people, answered countless questions by phone and email, ordered supplies, set costs and paid bills, put together the Haggadah as a program booklet, made complex arrangements with Rev. Barber's staff in response to ever-changing plans for his arrival, created name tags, and in all ways created miracles. Terry Burgin, an organizer for POWER, and Lizzie Horne reached out to area congregations and organizations to publicize the event.

To stay within our 150-minute Seder time limit, we cut the number of ritually meaningful foods on the traditional Seder plate down to the most essential to make the crucial spiritual points: grape juice, *charoset* (the sweet paste usually made with wine, nuts, raisins, apples, and spices—now replacing wine with grape), bitter herb (in the form of horseradish) and matzah (flat unleavened bread baked in a spirit of fierce urgency). Finding *charoset* that was "kosher for Passover" and also, no doubt for the first time in history, "*halal*"—proper according to Muslim law—was its own adventure! We cut the Ten Plagues and their representatives down from ten to five because of the limits of time, fitting at least one plague into each of the four sections of the Seder. We gave every speaker and musician a firm time limit which was honored by almost everyone.

In the brief transition from dinner to Seder, we listened to music played by Masjidullah's band, The Children of Adam. After we all recited the traditional opening question, we recited together the first of four answers: **On this night we share our joy and love of one another and for the natural world**. Then people at the same table were invited to take one partner (someone they didn't know) and share briefly something that gave them joy. Then, the charoset (sweet and delicious) was passed around for everyone to ingest the joy and pleasure. (All the ceremonial foods eaten at a traditional Seder are intended to give each participant a direct experience of the story that recalls the movement from enslavement to freedom: awakening to newness, recalling bitterness, tasting sweetness, rushing to take in what's still only partially baked.)

From there, we moved to the second answer, reciting together: **On this night we share our pain and suffering of each other and the world**. We began by focusing on **Racism** in its many forms (including systemic oppression of African-American, Latinx, and Native communities in education, employment, the "justice" system from police to courts to prisons, and in voter suppression, religious bigotry, Islamophobia, Antisemitism, and anti-immigrant hatred, to mention just a few).

Dr. Debbie Almontaser, as a Muslim and an immigrant to the U.S., spoke about her experiences of Islamophobia, followed by two brief plague speakers: Jessica Way, a public school nurse, focusing on the unequal funding in Pennsylvania for big-city school systems with a majority of Black/Brown students, and Rabbi Shawn Zevit, focusing on Antisemitism not only as experienced in the killings at Tree of Life Synagogue in Pittsburgh, but throughout the speaker's childhood.

All of us together recited the following words in English—"Blessed are You, Breath of Life, our G!D by whatever Name we call You, Who brings forth the fruit of the vine"—over the first cup of grape juice as we committed ourselves to End Racism. Rabbi Zevit played music as people drank the juice.

Still sharing **pain and suffering**, we turned to **Militarism** (including gun violence, ICE, militarization of police, vast sums spent on extremely dangerous nuclear weapons), for which Rabbi Arthur Waskow was the main speaker. As plague speaker, Chantay Love, of EMIR Healing Center, shared her family's experience of the gun violence that ended her brother's life.

Everyone silently shared the bitter herb representing the bitter sharpness of life as Cantor Jack Kessler played music. Then all recited the words we had said in English above before drinking the first cup of grape juice, this time in Hebrew (transliterated into English) for the second cup of grape juice, as we committed ourselves to End Militarism.

Continuing to share pain and suffering, we turned to **Materialism** (including asthma caused by environmental racism, the opioid epidemic, homelessness, the gulf between the hyperwealthy and the majority of people, planetary danger of climate chaos imposed by greedy companies), for which Rev. Liz Theoharis was the main speaker. The plague speaker, Rev. Greg Holston, talked about environmental racism that caused deaths from cancer of several of his mentors and the suffering of his daughter from severe asthma until his family moved to a different neighborhood.

People silently reflected on the pain and suffering caused by both Militarism and Materialism and then shared their responses with someone else they didn't know at their table. Then, reciting the words in Arabic (transliterated into English), we drank the third cup of grape juice, as we committed ourselves to End Materialism.

Continuing once more to share pain and suffering, we turned to **Sexism** (including sexual harassment, molestation, rape, violence against LGBTQ folks, and gender inequality in pay and roles) represented by Ana Maria Archila. The plague speaker, Chris Bolden-Newson, focused on the pressure forced on Black boys growing up to be aggressive rather than gentle and loving.

Together, people recited the words in Spanish over the fourth cup of grape juice, as we committed ourselves to End Sexism, while Rev. Rhetta Morgan sang.

Together we recited the third and fourth answers to the original question:

On this night, we open our eyes to new ways of seeing what's true.

On this night we define our commitment to act for justice, peace, and healing.

The combination of music, of sharing, of listening to powerfully painful speakers, of embodying foods that represented the ecstasy and the agony, might have been enough, but it was all prelude to the final speaker, Rev. Barber, who gave a prophetic charge to action as the climax of seeing the truth of the world around us and the need for a "fusion politics."

All of us were transfixed; time stood still; the ancient prophet Jeremiah came alive through Rev. Barber as he called us all "to go to the palace, to tell the king" that what he's doing is immoral. (Hundreds of people did, indeed, gather across the street from the White House six weeks later, on June 12, 2019, to do just that!)

Later Rev. Barber said he felt that, as in Pentecostal tradition, the Holy Ghost enveloped him as he spoke—for him it was the first time that had happened outside a Christian prayer context. And many of the 400 present said that they themselves felt that as everyone present rose to affirm their highest selves in speaking and in silence, the *Ruach HaKodesh*, the Holy Interbreathing Spirit of the World, was present in them all.

We recited the blessing in English over wheat, which is the main ingredient in most bread and matzah. We ate the matzah, baked in no more than 18 minutes—the bread of the poor that when we share it becomes the bread of urgency, the bread of freedom. We sang a joyful "Go Down Moses" together with two additional verses:

> *When Israel was in Egypt's land, Let My people go.*
> *Oppressed so hard they could not stand, Let My people go.*
> *Go down, Moses, way down in Egypt's land.*
> *Tell old Pharaoh: Let My people go!*
>
> *The pillar of cloud shall clear the way, Let My people go.*
> *A fire by night, a shade by day, Let My people go.*
> *Go down, Moses, way down in Egypt's land.*
> *Tell old Pharaoh: Let My people go!*
>
> *As Israel stood by the water-side, Let My people go.*
> *At God's command it did divide, Let My people go.*
> *Go down, Moses, way down in Egypt's land.*
> *Tell old Pharaoh: Let My people go!*
>
> *When they had reached the other shore, Let My people go.*
> *They sang the song of freedom o'er, Let My people go.*
> *Go down, Moses, way down in Egypt's land.*
> *Tell old Pharaoh: Let My people go!*
>
> *Act now so Earth be bondage free, Let ALL My peoples go.*
> *And let all life be free to Be, Let air and water flow.*
> *Rise UP, People—Rise up in every land.*
> *Tell ALL Pharaohs: Let My creation grow!*
> **As we live here in America, Set our people free!**
> **In all our colors we Resist, from Sea to Shining Sea!**
> **Rise up, O People, Rise up all across our Land—**
> **Tell new Pharaohs, your oppressions will not stand!**

And we went forth, ready to act on the inspiration of #FreedomSeder50.

One more delight that arose from the process: When Arthur and I, Phyllis, began our negotiations with the administrative staff of Masjidullah, we didn't know anyone there, and they didn't know us. On the surface, one could say, we were divided by race and by religion. However, as we worked together, we saw that we were connected by spirit and even by style. To my great delight, I found that Sister Ayesha Muhammad, the woman who coordinates rental arrangements at the mosque, was my kind of planner—detailed and thorough. We loved working together and recognized one another as soul sisters. She and her husband came to our family Seder at home, and Imam Abdul-Halim and his wife came to an intimate Shabbat dinner at our home. When an interfaith/interracial event yields an interfaith/interracial friendship, the Messiah must be right around the corner with a wide grin on her face!

The Mosque and the Seder

Imam Abdul-Halim Hassan

The significance of holding the Freedom Seder at an African-American Muslim Masjid was not only historic but profound. For it reflects the Prophetic message found in all the scriptures of the ONE G-D called by many names, where The One says this:

The Torah's Exhortation, "Do not stand still when your neighbor's life is in Danger" (Leviticus 19:16) is a commemoration of the actions of our brothers and sisters of all faiths who were called to Action. This Call came forth not only from Reverend Barber during the Freedom Seder, urging us to gather at "the palace" of a corrupt and murderous king in Washington, D.C. That call goes forth from all who continue to stand arm in arm with good people of different faiths challenging the forces of evil which try to separate us so that they may try to divide and conquer.

The same scheme of division and arrogance is what Satan used to trick our Father ADAM to get him out of the Garden. It is the Band of the Faithful whose spiritual awakening caused a renewed commitment to not only the faiths but to the different tribes to get to know each other as G-D commanded in Quran in Surah 49 ayat 13 where G-D says:

> O Mankind We created you from a single [pair] of a male and female and made you into nations and tribes that you may know each other [not that you may despise each other]. Truly the most honored of you in the sight of G-D is whoever is most righteous of you, and G-D has full knowledge and is well acquainted with all things.

The things that connect us as One Human Family can NEVER be broken by Time, Distance, Economic Status, Race, Religion or any other distinctions placed upon us by Man or Jinn. The recent Pandemic that we The World are experiencing is further proof that what affects One in the Family affects ALL in the Family. Only through mutual cooperation, compassion, and concern will we be able to overcome the trials and traps that Satan—the Adversary—sets for the people of Faith!

I am truly grateful and humbled to have been a Part (however small it was) of that righteous and sacred event and to have made lifelong connections with like-minded people of G-D who I continue to pray for and I hope will pray for me.

Remember the Poor

By Rev. Dr. Liz Theoharis

It was an honor to participate in the Freedom Seder 50 held at Masjidul-lah in Philadelphia and hosted by The Shalom Center under the leadership of Rabbi Art Waskow on April 7, 2019. It was an honor because of the evening itself, the one it was remembering from 50 years earlier, and the history of Seders celebrated through the ages that inspire contemporary prophets to engage in the work of justice and liberation.

I spoke at the Seder about the plague of poverty, along with Rev. Dr. William J. Barber II, as Co-Chair of the Poor People's Campaign: A National Call for Moral Revival, a campaign that is taking up the last campaign that Rev. Dr. Martin Luther King Jr. waged before he was killed for trying to unite the poor. I celebrated the Seder as a Christian preacher who has participated in a multi-religious movement for most of my life, including in an abandoned church in North Philadelphia in the 1990s where homeless Christians, Muslims, Jews, agnostics and atheists organized, lived, built a beloved community together, and debated the religious response to poverty, oppression and homelessness. I came to the evening and reflect on it now as a biblical scholar whose scholarship has largely focused on a particular Passover Seder—the last meal that Jesus celebrates with a group of his disciples in the house of Simon the Leper in the poor town of Bethany.

As a scholar of New Testament and Christian Origins, I understand the Bible as an inspired book that tells stories of poor and oppressed people banding together, with God on their side, to build movements for libera-tion and freedom. The Exodus is a foundational story of God opting for the poor and oppressed, the Deuteronomic Code—with frequent references to the deliverance from Egypt—instructs that how you care for your neighbor is how you honor God. The Christian gospels—drawing on the tradition of Isaiah and the Deuteronomic jubilee—proclaim bringing good news to the poor, and the Jewish Apostle Paul's epistles teach followers to offer mutual solidarity through the collection for the poor.

Yet, in our world today, the Bible is often interpreted in ways that justify inaction in the face of poverty, argue that poverty is eternal, and claim that if God wanted to end poverty and oppression, God would. Politicians and faith leaders put forward ahistorical, non-contextual, and unethical (mis) interpretations and (mis)appropriations of biblical texts, such as Matthew 26:11 and John 12:11 ("the poor will be with you always"); 2 Thessalonians 3:10 ("If you do not work, you shall not eat"); Matthew 25:29 ("For to all those who have, more will be given, and they will have an abundance; but from those who have nothing, even what they have will be taken away"). And some of the only Christian preachers talking about poverty are those who condemn the poor as sinners; very few talk about how poverty itself is a sin against God that could and should be ended.

I have spent much of my life exploring the story from Chapter 26 of the Gospel of Matthew about an unnamed woman who anoints Jesus during his last Passover Seder. It is in that story that we encounter the peculiar little line, "the poor will be with you always" (Matthew 26:11), which evangelical leader Jim Wallis calls the most famous Bible verse on poverty.

The passage, "the poor will be with you always," takes place in the context of the Last Supper, a Passover Seder itself, during which a woman comes and pours an alabaster jar of rare ointment on Jesus' head. With this action, the woman anoints Jesus. He becomes Christ (literally meaning "anointed") in this scene. But the disciples don't understand the significance of the anointing, of Jesus' impending execution at the hands of the state, or of the larger social and economic critique of charity being made in this moment. They criticize the woman for wasting the ointment (using *apoleia*—the Greek word for "destroying") by pouring it on Jesus' head, anointing him prophet, and preparing him for his death and burial at the hands of the Roman Empire.

The story takes place in the house of Simon the Leper in the Town of Bethany (*Bet 'ani*—meaning "House of the Poor" in Hebrew), directly after Jesus turns over the tables of moneylenders in the Temple and challenges the religious and political authorities for impoverishing the people, especially during a Passover celebration of liberation. During the Last Supper, when Jesus says, "the poor will be with you always," he is responding to his disciples, who are criticizing the unnamed woman for wasting the ointment. They say that if she hadn't broken the jar, they could have sold it for a year's salary and given the money to the poor.

Significantly, this misunderstood verse actually echoes the jubilee codes which call for radical economic redistribution as a central requirement for community prosperity. Millennia later, I hear those echoes once again when I read Dr. King's statement on true compassion from his sermon at Riverside Church on April 4, 1967. This may, in fact, be Rev. Dr. King's interpretation of this story of the unnamed woman:

A true revolution of values will soon cause us to question the fairness and justice of many of our past and present policies. On the one hand, we are called to play the Good Samaritan on life's roadside, but that will be only an initial act. One day we must come to see that the whole Jericho Road must be transformed so that men and women will not be constantly beaten and robbed as they make their journey on life's highway. True compassion is more than flinging a coin to a beggar. It comes to see that an edifice which produces beggars needs restructuring.

This idea of earning money and giving away the proceeds to the poor remains the dominant way that we try to address poverty today— by doing charity work, buying and selling and then donating, and never questioning how poverty is created in the first place. When Jesus says, "the poor will be with you always," he is quoting Deuteronomy 15, which says that there will be no poor person among you if you follow God's commandments—to forgive debts, release slaves, pay people fairly, and lend money even knowing that you won't get paid back. Deuteronomy 15 continues, saying that because people will not follow those commandments, the poor will never cease to be in the land. Then, directly after this breathtaking analysis, Judas betrays Jesus by turning him over to be crucified, an act of execution that only the empire has the power to enact—a punishment that is reserved for those individuals who the empire deems insurrectionists, revolutionaries, and freedom fighters.

Thus, throughout the Bible, and in this story, we are reminded that God hates poverty and has commanded us to end it by forgiving debts, raising wages, outlawing slavery, and restructuring society around the needs of the poor. We are reminded that charity will not end poverty and that inaction will keep poverty with us always. We are reminded that God's identification with liberation is a threat to empires and is located among those who have been cast to the underside of history.

Indeed, we are instructed to remember. Memory in the Bible is closely connected to the question of liberation and of freedom movements taking collective action against poverty, slavery, and oppression.

During the Freedom Seder 50, we read Exodus 13: "Remember this day on which you came out of Egypt, out of the house of slavery, because the Lord brought you out from there by strength of hand." In the passage that directly follows the one already quoted from Deuteronomy 15, the Deuteronomic Code reads, in reference to freeing slaves, "Provide liberally out of your flock, your threshing floor, and your wine press, thus giving to him some of the bounty with which the Lord your God has blessed you. Remember that you were a slave in the land of Egypt, and the Lord your God redeemed you." And the very next chapter, Deuteronomy 16, begins with the commandments concerning Passover as a remembrance of liberation from bondage. Psalm 112 connects justice and memory when it explains, "for the righteous will never be moved; they will be remembered forever." In the Christian Testament, we have the central Pauline teaching being about remembering the poor: "They only asked one thing, that we remember the poor..." (Galatians 2:10).

And at the end of the story of the unnamed woman, we hear about memory once again: "Truly I tell you, wherever this good news is proclaimed in the whole world, what she has done will be told in remembrance of her" (Matthew 26:15).

In Matthew 26:13, when Jesus states that what the unnamed woman has done will be told in memory of her, he uses the Greek word *mnēmosynon*, meaning "memory" or "memorial offering."[1] This same word is used in Acts 10:4, when an angel of God tells Cornelius that his alms and generosity to the poor have ascended as a memorial offering to God. The use of *mnēmosynon* also echoes Exodus 12 and the manna scene of the Exodus event in the Septuagint (the Greek translation of the Hebrew Bible that was the version of the Bible in which Jesus and his followers most likely had used *mnēmosynon* and memorial offering). Indeed, in the world view and religious knowledge of Jesus and his disciples, the echoing of the language of memory used for the Exodus would have been a direct evocation and reminder of God's dissatisfaction with the practices of Egypt/Rome and the divine desire for liberation. The Exodus tradition and its celebration through Passover provides the foundational narratives and instructions on how to respond to poverty and oppression, from Deuteronomy to the Prophets to the Christian Testament. In criticizing his disciples for their belief that charity, rather than a transformational social movement, could end poverty, Jesus reminds them of a core teaching of the Passover celebration. Rev. Dr. King, explaining why a Poor People's Campaign was necessary in 1967, described that same lesson in this way: "The way to end poverty is to end the exploitation of the poor."

All of this reveals a bedrock liberatory biblical tradition that is almost entirely obscured or denied today. In my scholarship and in my twenty-five years of organizing among the poor, I have come to recognize the power of this hidden history and what it tells us about the leading role of the poor

---

[1] Also Mark 14:9.

and directly affected in society today.

When I think on this long history, I am also reminded of the movement for liberation that the first Freedom Seder was a part of near the end of the 1960s. This was an explosive time when many were demanding a move from an era of reform to one of revolution. A year-and-a-half before the Freedom Seder, Dr. King began calling for a Poor People's Campaign that would bring together the poor and dispossessed of the nation across lines of division. In December 1967, less than four months before his execution, he wrote:

> The emergency we now face is economic, and it is a desperate and worsening situation. The dispossessed of this nation—the poor, both white and Negro—must organize against the structures through which the society is refusing to take means which have been called for, and which are at hand, to lift the load of poverty. There are millions of poor people who have little or even nothing to lose. If they can be helped to take action together, they will do so with a freedom and power that will be a new and unsettling force in our complacent national life.

Today, the memory of that revolutionary moment still reverberates, and King's societal diagnosis still rings true. Indeed, the injustices and plagues of biblical times and of contemporary history are still alive and well in our day. Consider these facts:

- 43.5% of Americans, or 140 million people, are poor or low income

- 51% of children live in poverty and/or food insecure households

- The United States spends $630 billion each year for the military

- $183 billion for education, jobs, housing and other basic human needs

- Pollution caused 9 million deaths last year and 4 million American families were exposed to unsafe drinking water

In such a time as this, people of all faiths are called to come together and remember the word of God and the prophetic commandment to build a liberation movement in our lifetime.

One such movement is the Poor People's Campaign: A National Call for Moral Revival, that has developed out of years of organizing with poor communities across the United States. We have joined together with those whose water has been shut off in Detroit; families who have lost loved ones because of the lack of health care and Medicaid expansion in Vermont, Pennsylvania, North Carolina, and Alabama; immigrants at the US/Mexico Border; whole communities in Lowndes County, Alabama and rural areas across the country who are living in raw sewage and with tropical diseases that had once been eradicated; hundreds of thousands of people whose votes have been suppressed because of racist gerrymandering, the ending of early voting and same-day registration, and closed polling places; homeless encampments under attack in Washington state, Oregon, Colorado, California, New Jersey and New York; and many others.

The Poor People's Campaign believes that we are living in the midst of a "kairos moment"—a time of great change and transformation, when the old ways of society are dying, and new ones are being born. In this time, we must change the moral narrative of the nation and break through the collective trauma and historical amnesia of a nation that is soul-sick with itself. For too long, we've been told that "poverty is the fault of the poor." The dominant narrative in this nation remains that if millions of people just acted better, worked harder, complained less, and prayed more, they would be lifted up and out of their miserable conditions. Those who would prefer to hold onto their riches tell us that we live in a world of scarcity and that it's not possible for everyone to survive and thrive.

And yet, America is the richest nation in the world. This country exists in historic abundance and has the resources to protect the environment and ensure dignified lives for everyone. It's not a question of economic possibility, but of moral and political will, as more and more of our wealth flows into the pockets of a powerful few and into our bloated Pentagon budget.

These are moral issues and we must call them out. But simply articulating an agenda and a vision for a better world is not enough. We also need moral action. We are required sometimes not just to dissent, but to disrupt that which is already disrupting and destroying many millions of lives.

In the summer of 2018, from Mother's Day to the summer solstice, thousands of people in 40 states committed themselves to a season of direct action to launch the Poor People's Campaign. For six consecutive weeks, tens of thousands of people gathered in state capitals across the country and in Washington, D.C., for nonviolent moral fusion, direct action, weekly mass meetings, teach-ins, and cultural events. The result was the largest and most expansive wave of nonviolent civil disobedience in 21st-century America.

More than just a series of rallies and actions, a new model of organizing in this country has been catalyzed. From Alaska to Alabama, California to the Carolinas, Flint, Michigan, to the Oak Flat lands of the San Carlos Apache, people are coming together to organize moral outrage about poverty, racism, ecological devastation, and militarism into a "new and unsettling force"—to turn the poor into agents of change rather than objects of history.

Now, we are continuing to build and organize. In over 40 states, we are developing the groundwork for a mass movement through community canvasses, public hearings, actions, demand deliveries, national emergency truth and poverty bus tours, and by registering people for a movement that votes. In June 2019, we convened over a thousand community leaders in Washington, D.C. for a Poor People's Moral Action Congress. And we're now readying ourselves for a nine-month national tour that will build toward a massive Poor People's Assembly and Moral March on Washington on June 20, 2020.

Indeed, there is a moral movement afoot in this country with poor people in the lead.

This is a movement where Indigenous, Latino, Black, Asian, and poor white leaders are finding common cause. It is a movement that stands on the shoulders of the freedom fighters who have come before us—including those who have gathered in freedom Seders throughout the ages, from Bethany to Philadelphia. Those leaders, and the leaders who are emerging today, remind us of that most basic and holy of moral imperatives: that everyone has a right to live and that those who believe in freedom cannot rest until it comes to everyone.

"Only Prophets Can Stand Up Now..."

Reverend William Barber II

Excerpt from speech at the
50th anniversary of the Freedom Seder, April 12, 2019

Note: Text in bold denotes shouting. Text in all caps denotes emphasis.
Politicians can't deliver this message. The Prophetic Community must do it.

Only prophets can stand up now and take on the false prophets and say No and tend to matters of justice. Set things right between the people.

Rescue victims from their exploiters. Don't take advantage of the homeless, the strangers, orphans and widows. AND STOP MURDERING!

And so, for freedom's sake, for justice's sake, for truth's sake. For the sake of the present, for the sake of the future. For the sake of all those whose blood we stand in, that they shed before we ever got here. We must deliver Jeremiah's message in the 21st century and demand change. Because this truth has in it hope. The rest of the verse is, IF the leaders listen, this nation will be well. But the Bible also says, if they don't, this nation will be abolished.

But the prophets always believed, if I tell the message, there's going to be a remnant that'll hear it. Ah. And so, it's time. Not to sit back and just let things happen. It's time for us to still believe up above my head, there's music in the air. There must be a God somewhere.

I know, I know, we are in this acute time. And I got my brothers and sisters, my Atheist family. We walk with them. I love them. I'm not talking about anybody else. I'm just talking about me right now. When I see some of the demonic stuff that's happening in the name of policy and the way in which people are being controlled by something that cannot be human and there's wickedness in high places, and they're willing to control and destroy the lives of people, I must believe there's a counter force in the universe. I hear that force calling.

Tell them, living wage is a guaranteed protection for the poor, **My orders.**

Tell them not destroying this society and environment is **My orders.**

Tell them, Labor rights and affordable housing is **My orders;**

Tell them, fair policy for immigrants is **My orders;**

Tell them, equality in education is **My orders;**

Tell them loosening the prisons that have locked too many of our people up is **My orders.**

Tell them, **healthcare for everybody is not Bernie's orders, it's My orders. TELL THEM!**

Fighting the proliferation of guns is **My orders. TELL THEM!**

To stop lying about Muslims, being anti-Semitic toward Jewish people, and stop punishing Palestinians and applauding Netanyahu, those are My orders!

Expanding voting rights, they're God's orders; protecting women, God's orders; Loving the LGBTQ community; **If I made them, you better love them. God! My orders!**

Equal protection under the law is non-negotiable. THOSE ARE MY ORDERS!

We got to deliver it to the courts, deliver it at the ballot box, deliver it at the pulpit, and deliver it to the State House, to the White House, to the Capitol House, which is our house anyway.

So, Arthur, you invited me and I went to fasting and praying. The Lord spoke to me and I confirmed it with someone else. I ain't told this to nobody else. He said, you can't do this tonight and leave it there. So, since we've got Muslims here, Christians here, Jews here. Ramadan is over.

Arthur, I'm asking you in the 50th year. You and your partners and others who are here. Liz. On June 5th, let's put 1,000 Rabbis and Imams and Christian pastors in full vestment and walk down the center street of Washington, D.C. and **deliver God's orders.**

One thousand of us, unified in the name of the God that is; and is above everything. I want to work on it. I don't know what it will do but I know what's going to happen if we don't do it. The leaders will say they didn't know. It's time for us to make sure that ain't no excuse that anybody can ever claim that they didn't know what God wanted.

Jeremiah is calling but we are his sons and daughters and the same God of Jeremiah is calling us today. Go down to the King's palace and tell him what My orders are and then watch Me go to work on the heart of this nation.

And the message in the Bible, it reads like this:

These are God's orders. Go down to the Royal Palace; and deliver this message; and say to the rulers: Listen to what God says. Oh, King of Judah, you who sits on David's throne, you and your officials and all the people who go in and out of these palace gates. This is God's message.

Attend to matters of justice. Set things right between people. Rescue victims from their exploiters. Don't take advantage of the homeless. And the stranger, and the immigrant, the orphans, the widows. And stop murdering. And if you obey these commands, then kings who follow in the line of David will continue to go in and out of these palace gates mounted on horses, and riding in chariots; they and their officials and the citizens of Judah. But if you don't obey these commands, then I swear, God says, THIS place will end up a heap of rubble.

This my friends, I believe, is where we are. And the pathway to real freedom given to ancient Israel needs to be given to America today. Notice, God gives orders to the prophets, go publicly, and tell the kings. GO PUBLICLY.

The first pathway to freedom is not just voting. I know you all get mad, but hear me. I believe in voting. I fight for voting. I know it. I've been in the trenches. My life has been threatened for fighting for the right to vote. I've been told I'd be dead in three months for challenging; but I know that voting alone is not what's going to help it, because as Rabbi Heschel says, **Until you have prophetic imagination, you will not have a prophetic implementation.**

We must not only vote, we must register people for a movement that can change the entire narrative of why we're voting both sides of the aisle, Democrat and Republican. Otherwise, the poison of the system itself will contaminate everybody and we can do both at the same time.

The first pathway to freedom is to take an unyielding freedom and justice message directly to the seats of power. Look at this text. Apply it to the 21st century. Don't send a letter. Don't send another damn tweet. Don't send an email. Don't send a nice prayer. Don't have a service away from the White House. **NO.**

God's orders to us, the prophetic remnant, is to go down to the king's palace and interrupt what's going on with a message of freedom and justice. And if we don't want to do that, we don't really want freedom.

The Eleventh Plague: Virtual Seders

A Seder for Healthcare Workers During a Plague

Denise L. Davis, MD

I knew at age 12 that I wanted to become a medical doctor, fantasizing how secure I would be in that role. These were my dreams during my parents' divorce, as their conflicts tore the fabric of our family, and I began to believe that becoming a physician would make me whole. Indeed, practicing medicine has forged much of my development as a person, helping me to listen with less judgment and respond with more courage and compassion. I am a general internist and my subspecialty is communication in healthcare, a discipline that benefits me enormously, as I continue to wrestle with the most effective and equitable ways to communicate with patients/families and with my colleagues and students.

In a sudden, wrenching upheaval in 2020, healthcare workers in the U.S. have been tested by the Covid-19 pandemic. Many healthcare workers have sickened, and some have died. Most of us have felt vulnerable, and sometimes I have felt very alone with my fears.

During this public health crisis, Passover 2020 arrived, and I was determined to enjoy some connection with my chavurah. I hosted an outdoor, carefully socially distanced Seder to keep me and my guests safe, separate, and together. I was struck by how my experiences, as the only healthcare worker at the Seder, informed my emotional and spiritual experience. As we said the kiddush and read the Shehechianu (we didn't sing the prayer because the act of singing would generate the transmission of viruses in a more powerfully contagious way) my heart began to break, and my feelings began to break open. To experience in my bones the gift of reaching a moment of celebration again, which is what the Shehechianu prayer is about, did not allow me to pray in a perfunctory way, after having been exposed to 3 colleagues ill with Covid-19 the previous week. I was deeply emotional reflecting on my health and on the fact that I still existed in the land of the living.

I left the first-night Seder needing an experience that could speak to my terror and grief, and I wanted to share those experiences with my colleagues in medicine and nursing who were navigating suffocating, overwhelming difficulty every day. I called on my prior Jewish experiences that were innovative, subversive, and fresh, and channeled my distress into composing a 20-minute Seder for healthcare workers, inspired by Rabbi

Zalman Schachter-Shalomi's z"l (of blessed memory) inspiring and approachable teaching of "20-minute davvenen/intense praying." One third of an hour seemed just the right amount of time to allow a few moments of reflection and storytelling, employing the metaphors of Pesach, as we gathered virtually.

As an African American Jewish woman, active in a Jewish organization dedicated to illuminating the racial and ethnic diversity of Jews, I intentionally gathered a multi-racial, multi-religious group. Distilling some of the symbols of the holiday into accessible metaphors for all participants was challenging and incomplete, and I know that on some levels I failed to flesh out some important and meaningful conversations present in a traditional 3-4-hour Seder. So be it. It was a pilot, and it fed my soul.

As affirmation and sweetness (Kiddush), gave way to gratitude for being alive during a time of widespread, life threatening illness (Shehechianu), we washed our hands in a mindful way for a full minute, noticing the sensations, which was an experience wholly different than our usual sanitizing for the sake of infection control. Karpas was the metaphor of spring, and the possibility that humankind would someday recover and heal from an unknown period of illness.

Matzah is the most basic food—bread made hastily from flour and water. We spoke of the basics we needed and deserved as healthcare workers—physical protection from infection, and the respect and appreciation of our leaders, not the coverups that corporate healthcare Pharaohs demanded and enforced with gag orders and the firing of whistleblowers. Instead of the 4 questions, we engaged each other with a big question: "How are the experiences of Covid-19 in urban hospitals, where members of Black and Latinx communities are dying at much higher rates than other racial groups, the same and/or different than previous plagues?"

The Magid, the story of Exodus, became our own stories of how we had begun to overcome some challenges during this crisis. I spoke about how, as a 60-ish year-old single mother, I had been so fearful of contracting the virus that I shook with fear the first week of the outbreak. I was seeing my patients behind a mask while thinking anxiously about other staff members in my clinic having already been diagnosed with the coronavirus. As a senior faculty member, telling the story was challenging for me because it challenged the rigid hierarchy of academic medicine, as I revealed my anxieties with trainees and colleagues as my witnesses.

In a 20-minute ritual, time is of the essence, and the Seder plate symbols were crystallized into single words that summarized the themes. Participants shared a "word necklace" that expressed what they were taking from the Seder experience that was *personal*. It is said that on Passover every person should feel as if they had personally come through a *Mitzrayim*—a tight, oppressive place.

The words "In Times Like These" begins the song by Mavis Staples played at the end of this ritual. In these times of healthcare workers sacrificing and struggling, dedicating themselves, speaking with outrage, and living with vulnerability, the lyrics reminded me that we all need someone to lean on. Even the healers.

20-minute Seder for Health Care Workers

Welcome

Introductions: Your names and one experience this year with early springtime.

Affirmation: (Said to yourself or another person) You are a blessing.

Sweetness: I am inviting you to this possibility of a sweet moment, even as we are navigating great difficulty.

Being present and grateful to be alive: Grateful in this present moment, we celebrate this meaningful and vulnerable life, with each other, our fellow healers.

Handwashing: silently and mindfully for 1 minute, then lifting our hands without words.

Spring: There is a promise that winter will eventually recede, and spring will come.

Nourishment: In the midst of a crisis, we hope to be nourished by our most basic needs being met: feeling physically protected *enough* in our work; aiding and witnessing the recovery of some of our patients; comforting the sick who are near the end of their lives; the appreciation and respect of our leaders.

The Big Questions: Though we often feel we are responsible for answers, for these minutes let's focus on a question: "How is this experience of the current pandemic different from other experiences in healthcare?"

Our stories: This is a time of great challenges. "Think in quiet for a moment about a challenge you have overcome recently related to the Covid-19 pandemic." All participants have about one minute each to speak without interruption. Listeners are invited to respond to the speaker with "Thank you."

Symbolizing our experiences: Bitterness, Urgency, Oppression, Courage, and Resilience describe some of the myriad experiences we've had and will continue to have in healthcare during this crisis— and in future crises.

Harvesting our experiences: "What is one word that describes something you will take with you from this 20-minute ritual?"

Closing Quotations:

"Celebration is a confrontation, giving attention to the transcendent meaning of one's actions."
—Rabbi Abraham Joshua Heschel

"We must accept finite disappointment, but never lose infinite hope."
—Rev. Dr. Martin Luther King, Jr.

Crossing the Red Sea to Create the Post-COVID World

Seventh night Seder Online April 14, 2020/5780

Rabbi Shawn Israel Zevit

In looking at Torah and Midrash through the lens of mythic understanding, it is possible to discover in the ancient stories a model, a paradigm, for seeing the deeper patterns of spiritual evolution unfold in our own lives. The idea of mythic reenactment of an ancient tale is fully consonant with what we learn at the Passover seder: *hayav adam lirot et atzmo k'ilu hu yatzah mi-Mitzraim*—"It is incumbent upon each person to see oneself as if they themselves had left Egypt." This notion suggests that each time we retell the story of the Exodus, and (hence) the subsequent Crossing of the Red Sea, we are invited to find personal, contemporary spiritual connection and meaning for our own lives.

As a kavannah, a framing for the 2020 Shalom Center offering in the dislocating pandemic times we were navigating, Rabbi Arthur offered the following:

> What is special about the Seventh Day? According to tradition, that was the day the Children of Israel, fleeing slavery, reached the Red Sea. Behind them was Pharaoh's Army, racing to force them to return to their accustomed slavery, with its perks of onions and garlic. Before them was the unknown. The Sea that might be New Birth, if the birthing waters broke. Or the Sea of Drowning if they didn't. The Sea of Freedom—maybe. The Sea of Active Hope. The Sea of Sharing Life with all life-forms, not imposing slavery and forcing plagues on Earth as well as Humankind.
>
> The entire human race stands now, today, at that moment. The Coronavirus Plague has been a lightning flash, illuminating the darkest hidden places of our world. Domination. Subjugation. Fear. AND joyful neighbors, ready to help each

other if we need the help and simply ask. That joy is also hidden from us in the race for domination.

We can go forward into wilderness, the unknown—that is what freedom is. We can go forward seeking to create the Loving and Beloved Community. Or we can go back to the world of Pharaoh: Subjugation, and the Plagues both social and biological that Subjugation brings us. That will do us in.

The reality is we are all slaves to something—to work, or a relationship, to fear, or food, to a lack of discipline, or too much discipline, to love, or a lack of love. The word *Mitzrayim* (Hebrew for "Egypt") means limitations and boundaries and represents all forms of constraints that inhibit our true free expression. Our people's redemption from Egypt teaches us how to achieve inner freedom in our lives. Enslavement is a habit that needs to be broken and transformed over an extended period.

Building on the groundwork Reb Phyllis and Reb Arthur had already laid, we worked to construct a flow for the program that invited us to reflect on and be in relationship with the way our world now and move into prayers, poems, dialogue, and invocation to the world we hope will emerge once we actually cross the sea out of the place we are wedged in now, and into what revelation awaits us with our active participation.

And so what follows is not my analysis of the evening. It is the flow of the two hours we spent together with hundreds online and now hundreds more who have watched the Seder since that time, using the link provided in this article. I found the whole evening moving, inspiring, multifaceted in content and approach, affirming and prophetically agitating towards action.

Some of the material is in full in this essay, while other elements are best watched, or linked elsewhere, to avoid a literal transcription of the evening that would keep us somewhat removed from the experience which is animated by tone, nonverbal communication, and energy dynamics between the participants. In a couple of places, such as the quoted material from Rabbi Waskow and Rabbi Prager—it is the words they used as a template for what they shared. In the case of Rabbi Gold—afterthoughts she sent to me.

We tried not only to chronicle the Shalom Center Seder itself using available technology that allowed us to gather in cyberspace during a pandemic—but we also greeted the future in the now. This *Olam Habah*, or as Reb Zalman Schachter-Shalomi z"l interpreted it, the future's call or the world coming towards us—as opposed to an afterlife or post-messianic world—was hastened by a global health challenge, not simply invented as a response to it. Many of us acknowledge and are already well into rethinking and planning for a new age of in person and online spiritual community in both tandem and tension with each other.

Our journey together was itself a process of discovery in the interchange of ideas, creative expression and sacred conversation. As in the Seder (meaning order) tradition handed down to us, of fifteen stages along the way of the reliving of Exodus and grappling with the poverty and afflictions of our time, I sectioned this Seder into fifteen parallel stages. My hope is that you will use the first part of this article as a preface and preparation, cueing up the video to then watch using the outline in the next part as your guide as you move through the experience we were blessed to have had live that evening.

As you begin whatever journey will unfold for you, I offer you Reb Arthur's invitation:

I invite you—encourage you, implore you!—to watch it.

https://youtu.be/YVZcYEDApVs

Feel free to share the link with all your friends. *Feel free to pause the video to discuss it with your housemates, to call your community and watch it together in your separate places (and, I pray, together—when safer and healthier times allow). With blessings to move forward in the steps of Nachshon ben Amminadav. —Shalom, Arthur*

THE SHALOM CENTER'S SEVENTH NIGHT SEDER

Rabbi Shawn Zevit: welcome and intro to the Seventh Night Seder

Cantor Linda Hirschhorn: invocation with "Circle Chant"[1]

Circle round for freedom,
circle round for peace.
For all of us imprisoned,
circle for release.
Circle for the planet,
circle for each soul.
For the children of our children,
keep the circle whole.

Part 1: THE REALITY WE FACE NOW

[1] Music and lyrics, Linda Hirschhorn, 1989.
https://www.youtube.com/watch?v=6I-UiDzeexU
http://www.lindahirschhorn.com/cds/linda_hirschhorn_songbook/circle_chant.html

Rabbi R. Lee Moore:
Poem "And They Assembled" by Rabbi Tamara Cohen[2]

And Moses said *dayam*, enough.
Enough: enough.
Stop, withdraw,
bring/do/perform/gather no more.
Let the silver glare of a silent sanctuary,
the gold blue of a plane-less sky
the garnet sheen of an empty concert hall
be our sacred offering,
meager gifts of absence from wise and less wise-hearted people.

Please God let our ceasing be enough.
Let our hospital beds be enough.
Let our slow awakening to the interconnectedness of every living being
be enough
Let a pillar of stillness rest at the entrance to every home and prison.
Let this plague pass over us, enough of us.
Enough.

Report from Larry Bush, retired editor of *Jewish Currents*:
Susan Gross and I have been waiting for about two years for a man who has been in prison for more than 25 years to be paroled and come stay with us until he can navigate the world on his own. This is an excerpt from a letter Susan received from him today (he's in a medium-security New York State prison, and he's nearly 70 years old):

> I am sorry to further inform you that Coronavirus has al-
> ready gotten root in this facility and is spreading like mushrooms.
> About 55 to 60% of prisoners have been, to some degree, exposed
> to the virus and are suffering from it. Every morning a dozen
> inmates rush to the Facility's clinic for some kind of help. But there
> is NONE. Those few prisoners with high fever or other severe
> symptoms are held back in the isolation unit, and others are sent
> back to the population with a handful of Ibuprofens. There are
> rumors that five or six inmates have already passed. There is no

[2] https://www.truah.org/resources/and-they-assembled-prayer-covid-19-2020-rabbi-tamara-cohen/

testing being done and no one knows who is positive. Everybody is cranky, and the moods are grim. I don't believe people on the outside really know what is going on in here!

Although I have been feeling sick and miserable with headaches and body pain for the past few weeks, I haven't bothered going to the clinic or complaining to anyone. There is no point to it! I just stay in bed a lot, hope to eat a little (absolutely no appetite) or sleep. I pray that whatever has gotten me sick leaves me by itself.

Rabbi Arthur Waskow: Prelude to crossing the Sea

Mah nishtana? How can we make the days that are coming different from the nights that went before—nights like the Ninth Plague—so thick with the darkness of domination and death that we could not see or know each other, even though we and all life-forms are shaped in the Image of God? (Thanks to the film "Revolution of the Heart" for shaping these questions.)

1. **After the pandemic passes, what are the changes in your life and in the world that you want to continue, instead of "going back to normal"?**

2. **How would you describe the world that you want to live in after Covid-19?**

3. **How can we be active participants in co-creating that world?**

4. **Where do we go next and how can we best use this time during shelter-in-place to help make that new world possible?**

On that night 3,000 years ago, as the hoofbeats of Pharaoh's Army beat doom as they clattered to catch up with the band of frightened fleeing Israelites, the question was what choice to make:

Should they surrender to Pharaoh's chariots and return to slavery and to the rampant death that had swept across the Land of Narrowness? Or should they plunge into an unknowable future marked by the Sea of Reeds? Could they cross the Sea, or would they perish in it?

One activist took the chance: He walked into the waters. Not till he was up to his nose, on the verge of drowning, did the Great Breath of Life, the Inter-breathing Spirit of the world, the Wind of Change, blow a path between the waves. The people went forward.

We face three great interlocking crises:

1. Worsening inequality and declining democracy in the U.S. and many other countries—a trend that has hushed and hesitated responses to the other two crises.

2. Coronavirus Plague and many others brought on or worsened by our own pharaohs.

3. Climate Crisis.

The Plagues we suffer, like the Plagues of old, are not only dangers; they beckon us to transformation.

The agonizing outcry of a young Black American suffocated by physical racism, "I can't breathe!" is repeated in thousands of human beings invaded by the Coronavirus that has been worsened by governmental greed for power—"We can't breathe!" say those dying—and by Earth's outcry as the life-giving cycle of Oxygen and CO_2 between plants and animals gets stuck on CO_2 emission. Earth's whole being cries out, "I cannot breathe!" as the planet heats and the climate crisis becomes a crisis in God's Self, in the *Ruach HaKodesh,* the *Ruach HaOlam,* the Holy Breath.

In the spirit of the Haggadah's invitation—"Let all who are hungry, all who are in need, come to celebrate Pesach"—we are not charging a fee for this Seder. We do invite all of any spiritual or ethical community who in this moment are intellectually, emotionally, or spiritually hungry for community and hope and Spirit—or who want to learn how to deal with physical hunger in your community that has been greatly worsened by the pandemic.

Let me add a personal note. In 1969, I wrote the original Freedom Seder and a band of Jews and Christians, Black and white, joined to mark the first anniversary of the murder of Rev. Dr. Martin Luther King. Hundreds of us met in a Black church in Washington, D.C. We had no idea that this Freedom Seder would become the spark and seed for many new *Haggadahs* seeking freedom from wars, from racism, from oppression of immigrants and asylum-seekers, from subjugation of women and the LGBTQIA community, from wounding Earth itself. Freedom not only *from* but *for*—yearning for and actively reaching toward what Dr. King called the Beloved Community. Now it is even clearer that the Beloved Community must bring together respect and compassion around the great wide world. The world of pharaohs and their plagues endangers us all. The world of Inter-breathing enlivens us all.

Time to choose. Shalom, salaam, paz, peace, namaste! —Arthur

See the Seder video for these contributors' content:

R. Simcha Zevit: Muriel Rukeyser (Miriam poem) https://jwa.org/

R. Mordechai Liebling: Social plagues today and **Faryn Borella** (RRC rabbinic student)—contemporary plagues—the ten equivalents today (see video).

R. Shawn (facilitating): Conversation among us. Where are we now in light of our current reality (roundtable inc. Lynne Iser, Rabbi Simcha Zevit, Rabbi Joanna Katz and others) (see video)

Rabbi Rayzel Raphael: Song—"By the Shores"[3]

By the shores, by the shores,
Of the Red, Red Sea,
By the shores of the Red, Red Sea
The light of day lit up the night
The children, they were free.

CHORUS: And Miriam took her timbrel out and all the women danced. (2X)
Va- te-kach Miriam ha-nivea et ha tof b'ya-da, va'taytzeh-na col ha-nashim ah-cha- re-ha.

They danced, they danced
Oh, how they danced
They danced the night away
Clapped their hands and stamped their feet
With voices loud they praised.
They danced with joy
They danced with grace

They danced on nimble feet
Kicked up their heels, threw back their heads
Hypnotic with the beat.
CHORUS
They danced so hard, they danced so fast
They danced with movement strong

---

[3] © by G. Rayzel Raphael 1984 https://www.shechinah.com/
(https://www.youtube.com/watch?v=BRCrx7PSiJY

Laughed and cried, brought out alive
They danced until the dawn.
Some carrying child, some baking bread
Weeping as they prayed
But when they heard the music start
They put their pain away.
CHORUS
Enticed to sing, drawn to move
Mesmerized by such emotion
The men saw us reach out our hands
Stretching across the ocean.
As they watched, and they clapped, they began to sway
Drawn to ride the wave
and all our brothers began to dance
They dance with us today!
They danced, we dance
Shechinah dance
They danced the night away
And all the people began to sing
We're singing 'til this day!!
FINAL CHORUS: And Miriam took her timbrel out and all the people
danced. (2X)
*Va-te-kach Miriam ha-nivea et ha tof b'ya-da, v'a'taytzeh-na col anashim
ah-cha-re-ha.*

Part 2: HOPE, FAITH AND ACTION MOVING FORWARD

R. Marcia Prager:
Prayer as Spiritual Activist Resource for Our Time

Just a week ago, Wednesday night, the full moon of the month of Nisan
rose round and brilliant in the azure blue-black of the night sky. This full
moon calls us to the "Great Telling"… to gather in our Seders and relive
the great tale of slavery and liberation.

The holiday is Pesach—translated as Passover. But in Hebrew there
is a fabulous play on words, for in Hebrew the verb *sach* means "to tell;"
peh is "mouth." Thus, Pesach summons each of our mouths to be a "mouth
that tells!"

The story of *Yitzi'at Mitzrayim i*s one of the great power-tales of human
history, yet that story owes its pervasive power to the *present*—because of
its power to evoke our own stories.

And this Pesach, of course, was different than any other. Every Seder felt to me like a wave of hope cresting from the sea of the pandemic. Remarkably, in the midst of adversity more frightening than anything many of us have ever known, we found ways to forge communities of love, fellowship, and inspiration that surpassed our expectations.

Personally, because of surgeries in the past two years, I guess I am pretty high risk. I am quite thoroughly volitionally quarantined. It is easy for me to slide into terror and pull inwards.

Yet the story I really want to tell is a story of *resilience, love, and courage*—a story of communities of caring that rise to meet even unanticipated needs, and acts of group and individual heroism—especially on the part of the medical folk who, like Shifra and Puah, risk their lives to save lives. At our P'nai Or Zoom Seder, 50 people, many of whom would have been alone, were welcomed into a very big room... with room enough for all...

We have each other and we are not powerless or alone.
When the full moon of Nisan rises, our birth as a people begins;
we start to move.

Tomorrow morning, the morning of the seventh day, midrash teaches us, we arrive at the shore of the Sea of Reeds—the deep water-filled marshy swamp-grass sea that is the archetypal impenetrable obstacle. We often sing our *Mi Chamocha* celebration song without lingering very long in terror. The dust storm and din of the Egyptian chariots bearing down on us ... we and our children facing death at the water's edge ... the panic, danger, and terror—gripping and real... like now.

Only one way forward... only one way towards freedom.
Literally or virtually holding each other's hands
—yes, with our terror—
yet also with courageous song—
we go forward.

The Reed Sea opens like a birth canal.
We pass through into a new reality, a new world that awaits us.

What forces now imprison us? Yes, we are hunkered down in our homes, for those of us who are privileged enough to have safe homes... We work from home and meet on Zoom, for those of us who are privileged enough for these options. Conditions of class and race make stark the benefits of privilege and the risks of being less than privileged. The dangers are all too real.

And we learn from another wordplay that the word Pharaoh is like the Hebrew word oreph, which means the back of the neck—that part of the brain that controls imagination. Bondage to the "Pharaoh Within" is a bondage to illusions of powerlessness. We become enslaved to false and limiting ideas.

They say that this pandemic will change our society forever. Nothing will go back to being the same. If we live—as I hope I and you will —we can and will reshape the national conversation. This calamity reveals the urgent need for universal health care... for social programs that flatten the curve—not only of infection, but of class, gender, race, and privilege... Enhanced need for environmental protections...

We are neither alone nor powerless. Reb Zalman would always remind us of how powerfully our prayers and celebrations "charge the electromagnetic field of the possible future." That possible future is pulling us strongly! Wow, is that magnet getting charged!

See the Seder video for these contributors' content:

- Daniella Forstater and Hazzan Jack Kessler: Contemporary Greta/ Prophetic haftarah (see video)
- Rabbi Arthur Waskow: The Lightning-Flash—Lessons from Coronavirus Plague (see video)

~*~*~*~*~

Rabbi Shefa Gold and Rachmiel O'Regan chant "*Ki aza kamavet ahava*"[4] from Shir HaShirim—the strength and power of love to move us forward.

Rabbi Shefa Gold reflects on the Seder

Looking back at our past selves, I am struck by how much we all knew and yet didn't know. We didn't know what was coming, and yet we all knew enough to dig into the resources within us and within our inheritance that would help us to meet the challenges ahead. The verses that I chose to chant, "For love is as strong as death," from the Song of Songs, was prophetic in that the next few months would bring so much death from

---

[4] (https://www.rabbishefagold.com/shs-commandment-6/)

Covid-19, beyond what we could have imagined.

Even though I didn't know what was coming, I knew that LOVE was what we would need to walk through this time, with courage, compassion, and open-hearted perspective. Since that night of crossing the sea and stepping into the wilderness, The Song of Songs, our core text of love, has risen up to a prominent place in my awareness, to save me, sustain me, and remind me of where to put my attention. It is love that moves me, sends me, and connects me to the wholeness of life, even through times of plague, division, injustice and sorrow.

See the Seder video for these contributors' content:

- **R. Phyllis Berman:** the Overstory: A Novel- the Love of Trees/ Real Community (excerpt) (https://www.goodreads.com/work/ quotes/57662223-the-overstory) (see video)
- **Conclusion: R. Shawn Zevit (**Yah Eloheichem Emet; (see video) https://www.youtube.com/watch?v=oYhLnOe0U-A) **and group-**clergy responding to our circumstances- what would help us go forward to a new society and how congregations can be a source for change moving forward? (roundtable) and **Circle Round for Freedom—concluding song**

Hassal siddur Pesach—and now our Seder has come to its completion. This year we were enslaved to systemic oppressions that have plagued us for decades, if not centuries. This year we were quarantined and challenged to balance collective safety and well-being with individual freedoms and perspectives. May the lessons we have learned from the narrow places of this past year and the experience of this Seventh Night Seder bring us all to a place of greater liberation, justice, love and compassion in the year and years ahead.

To this end, I offer my own prayer for all of us continually breathed into being through the Cosmic Constant, the Breath of All Life:

> *Gathering the mixed multitudes in my soul*
> *I rummage through my belongings*
> *In preparation for leave-taking.*

What aspects of myself
Do I need to make the journey?
What can I leave behind
To memory in the narrow places?
Maybe this year, we will go out together
In broad daylight
Not in the still of the night,
In no haste
Soul to Soul
Holding each other in loving compassion
Knowing we—the mixed multitude—
Will cross together
Finding home at last
In the depth of divine waters
That part willingly
On the shores of a wilderness.
What if no one need drown this year
And you need not weep
For any of your lost children
Or parts of your precious planet?
So, let us not leave in haste
And move in a mindful pace this year
Seeing the blessings and lessons that even
The narrow places have offered us.
For no place is without you
You who go by many names
Freedom, Liberation, Salvation
The Place—
Wherever we may be
On the journey.

Resources

https://youtu.be/YVZcYEDApVs

https://mishkan.org/

https://www.inquirer.com/news/freedom-seder-passover-rabbi-was-kow-masjidullah-philadelphia-20190408.html

http://www.thearconline.org/uploads/5/8/9/2/5892888/shevii_pesach_ritual_crossing_of_the_red_sea.pdf

Mystical Seders

Notes Toward Freeing the Seder

Rabbi Zalman Schachter-Shalomi, Ph.D.[1]

I have come today to Free you from the Maxwell House Haggadah. You are free to celebrate Pesach!

What is wrong with the Haggadahs we are used to? For one thing, the English is ancient: "vouchsafe" and "bestow." Even the plagues of the Egyptians cannot be understood: what is "murrain?" And the instructions are wooden. Why? Because when it was put together people wanted a definite, "Amy Vanderbilt" description of exactly how you do it. They did not want to be free to play, to elaborate.

But not only can you be free from those old and wooden Haggadahs, but you can be free to use freely the much newer, better Haggadahs, the ones with good translations and more openness. For like an ordinary siddur, the Haggadah is a cookbook. Try to eat what's on the page of even the best cookbook: the paper and the ink, they are neither nourishing nor tasty. You must take the words and make them three-dimensional, four-dimensional. Just so with a Haggadah. And at every Seder there may be a different way to bring the words off the page. Different spices, different timing.

For example, write down for yourself a word for a scenario of how you would like to do a handwashing around the table at the beginning of the Seder…OK. Have you got your word down? Here is mine: that we wash each other's hands. That instead of doing a perfunctory gesture, we do it as an act of love for someone. And your words, your ways, the ones that come out of your own feelings, are also fine.

Take your pencil and paper again. Ask yourself: What are your four questions? Your four questions about Judaism? If I want to know something this night, what is it I really want to know? Why is it different?—Life, I mean; why is it different from what I expected? Mark down four "differents," four "it isn't thus."

Maybe we could start, "What are the Four Questions for America today? Should hand-guns be permitted? Is electricity from a nuke kosher?" And you can't just do a Seder and talk about slavery and Pharaoh without going at some point to Auschwitz. At some point we must talk about

---

[1] Menorah: A Center for Jewish Renewal Nisan 5742, April 1982, Volume III, Number 4

how bad slavery is. What is the difference between slavery and righteous work—for there is work that we feel, if we do it and then eat, that we are not freeloaders on the universe. At which point does work break your body, at which point does it give you zest? When do you feel, *this is not the work I want to do, this is not the work I am meant to work, these conditions are not working conditions?*

We must address a question we hate to ask ourselves: What did I contribute to my enslavement? It's not just Pharaoh; there can't be an oppressor without there being someone who plays the other side: being oppressed. The world tries to keep us between two options: being the oppressor or the victim. Going out of Mitzrayim is leaving *Either/Or. Meytzar* is the narrow place, and *-ayim* is the "dual" ending for two-ness. *Eynaim,* two eyes; *oznaim,* two ears; *mitzrayim,* double narrows— Either/Or. Out of this tension only, this *Either/Or,* did I call out to G-d—and learn a third option. Not to be an oppressor or a victim, but my *self:* how to be this, that is my question at the Seder.

With whom do you have a Seder? With your *mishpocha*—family, but *mishpocha* sounds and is denser than "family," more like oatmeal that's been standing around for a day. You can't swim around so easily, you can't make changes so easily in a *mishpocha.* So it is with these people with whom it is so hard to make changes that you meet, to make changes, to make a new covenant for the next year, by which the sources of slavery could be eliminated from your life.

You have two Seders. So one you could do the way the family did, like *bubbe* and *zeyde.* Old tricks that you want the kids to learn, the same old melodies. That's the form you got, the form you have to transmit. But it's also very important to get together one Seder that is new, that is your own, that is a leaving of your own Mitzrayim.

How much to sing, how much to talk at any one point in the Seder? Keep a sense of leanness. If you overeat on karpas, you will have no room for the real goodies that come later. Build up to an experience and when you are in it just enough to give your buoyancy to the next one, you stop rather than let it run down.

The plagues. Are there any plagues we are experiencing here in America? Plagues, *takke,* not just incidents or accidents. I am sure that in Egypt there were people who tried valiantly to say, what should we do to restore the economy after this terrible mess of frogs? People who did not see it as a plague, as a smiting by the Ruler of all Space-Time. It takes a certain kind of belief to recognize that the signs of the times are a true feedback from the Universe.

Imagine: I have a headache. Why? Because my body wants to tell me something. Never mind. I take the extra-strength pain reliever, and I cut off the communication. "Head, I don't want you to tell me that you hurt." So then does the body have to scream tumor before the message gets through?

So, what are the plagues we turn off, we escape, we ignore? And as we discuss this, we can pour out some more wine from the cup for each of our own plagues. I hope at the end there's some wine left!

Let us turn to the foods upon the table.

We have karpas, a green vegetable like parsley that we dip in salt water—in our family a little vinegar too, for both the tears and the sweat. Let's say the kids are hungry and they start saying, "Is *that* all we have for supper!" And you say, "Could you imagine—that's all we had for supper!" Because you can't have the feast without having some element of the fast. We can't afford to ignore the dark side. And this fast beneath the feast—it runs all through the Seder.

We pour off the wine when we come to the plagues in order to say, "Yes, yes, I'm happy over what G-d did for me—but I do not want to drink in my cup of joy the sufferings of the Egyptians." So we should take just a minute to absorb what it would mean to have only a piece of parsley or potato for dinner—maybe that will bring up a discussion of Anne Frank or her family, or our own fears—a lost job, old people who are denied food stamps...

Rabbi Gamaliel says you've got to talk about these things on Pesach: the lamb, the matzah, the bitter herb. Why? The pass-over lamb, the one that was sacrificed so G-d would skip over our houses. The hardest question we have is, why us? Why *me?* If we get to believe in G-d at all, we do it "cosmic." G-d cares about the ecology in general, not my little toe. The Paschal lamb was about really believing that G-d really cares about *this* house. So we haven't done our Pesach homework unless we talk about this question.

Matzah. No salt, no yeast, no sugar. Water and plain grain meal. What's so nice? Nothing, except that the more you chew the sweeter it gets. First bite: nothing. Hemstitched cardboard. If you stay with it, chew and chew.

We bake it ourselves. When people were most worried about the purity of kashrut, they said don't bake your own, it might not be quite absolutely kosher. But once a year we must recall how food gets from the plant to our belly, no? Otherwise, we will begin to think food comes from the supermarket. So we get the grain, we look it over ourselves to make sure none has sprouted, we hand grind it, we kasher our ovens, we smell the marvelous smell, we bump into each other while some of us roll the dough and some of us make the holes and some of us put on a record, *Hallelujah, hallelujah*... because that's the right sound to do it with. [Karpov to Arthur Kurzweil: there were actual *matzah*-baking-songs, more elaborate than this, in Turkey, and the elderly ladies who sang them are on their way out or mostly so how can I get a grant to send me to record the matzah-baking-chants and be ethnomusicologist with tape recorder before these are (G-d forbid) lost forever?] All of this, I'd like to urge you to bake your own, and to use it for the celebration itself. It works.

For the first bite of matzah, keep in mind what the Zohar says: the first night it is the bread of faith. The Talmud says a baby doesn't know to say *Abba*, "Daddy," until it has first tasted the taste of grain. And the soul doesn't know how to say "G-d" until it has first tasted the taste of matzah. So when you eat that first bite of matzah, focus on it—silently—so it will feed your faith.

Three matzahs. Why? At one time, there were three sets of Jews: Kohen, the priest; Levi, the religious bureaucrat; Yisrael, the ordinary congregant. And which was on top? The priest made the rules, so the priest was on top and the Yisrael on the bottom. And in our day? Think for yourself... what kinds of people are we? And should some be on top? Let us not be sentimental—perhaps they should, perhaps not. It is a good question, one of the Four.

It goes deeper than this: The middle matzah we break, and the large piece we hide away. Why... I'm not going to tell you. Because it is important that at every Seder there should be a totally new reason for these things we do. Because somebody gave a reason in the thirteenth century, why should that be the reason forever? There was a very good reason for that person's understanding of the universe, but the Seder is bigger than that moment. The Seder is that continuity, that covenant, that household of Israel that keeps going on in freedom—so you have your own reason. Think: what is your own sense of "middle matzah?" What is broken? And why do you have to leave that for last?

Let us look at the three matzahs through Kabbalistic eyes. They are the three S'phirot just below the highest one. *Keter*, "Crown," the highest one—*Keter* is the circular crown made by the circle of everyone at the table—the whole *chevra*. The top matzah is *Chochmah*, intuitive wisdom. The middle one is *Binah*, the ability to distinguish or differentiate or analyze. *Chochmah* is right brain, *Binah* is left brain. The bottom matzah is *Da-at*, experiential knowledge. Conceptualization takes place in *Chochmah*, analysis in *Binah*, reality testing in *Da-at*.

From the third, experiential matzah we take two pieces. On one we put some bitter herb and some charoset and cover it all with the other piece of matzah, and we say, "In the Temple time this is the way Hillel, the gentle teacher, did it; he softened the bitter herb with the matzah of faith and the lamb of loving-kindness, *Chesed*." Eating that, we have it whole.

Bitter herb. Maybe dandelion greens from your back yard; it is good to teach yourself that you can survive on weeds, even bitter ones.

Horseradish. The rocket fuel invented in Eastern Europe. I don't know of anyone who ever actually died of it, but it feels that way. There is that moment when it chokes you in the throat and you don't dare to take a breath for fear you will poison your lungs. Aaaak! That's what the body does to teach you the real agony of the bitterness of the work that breaks the spirit and the body.

A story. We were in France, at a concentration camp, in the Vichy zone, mostly for Jews who had fled Austria or Germany. They gave us picks and shovels and told us to go out to the fields to remove the rocks. We were eager, because our diet was very poor—mostly peas and rice with holes from worms—and we thought we would get to grow some carrots, onions. What is a good Jew without an onion from time to time? So we went to work: chipper, eager. And we cleared away the rocks. Something to do. Otherwise we were cooped up, a family of seven in a stable for a horse.

We cleared the fields. And then the commander comes by and says, "I don't like this pile of rocks. Bury it deep underneath." We were not so chipper now, but still we did it in good cheer. And he told us to cover these rocks with cement, then cover it all with earth again. And we did it—happy.

Three days later he comes again, saying, "Where are these beautiful rocks from the field? Dig up these rocks, replace them in the field!" And otherwise we would be punished.

Can you imagine how the work tasted? I remember standing there, we had dug up already to the place those rocks had fused into concrete. He wanted us to break them up. I picked up my pick and hit down on the ground…so much frustration and anger. The last thing I saw was a spark where my pick hit the rock, and I fell in a faint.

My father wasn't permitted to bring me water and there I was till the evening, when a dog licked my face and I came to. For years I had migraine headaches that would begin when tension hit that point where the spark came out.

That is the kind of work, those are the kinds of conditions that many people must spend their lives under. Over and over again doing stuff you don't feel like doing under conditions you can't possibly work under.

Knowing you couldn't survive—it doesn't feel like you want to survive, but you know you couldn't survive unless you give in.

So: work that breaks the boy with frustration. We stimulate this story with the bitter herb. We tell this story *to our bodies* with the bitter herb.

Reb Nachman of Bratslav says, "Why don't most people make their way spiritually? Because when they have a spiritual experience they never tell their body about it." If they would tell the body about the spiritual experience, the body would become ever more willing to participate in a spiritual path and wouldn't rob you of the energy to follow it. And how do you tell your body? In body language.

Bitterness is the ingredient necessary to make change. Bitter is not bad. Some good is sweet, some good is bitter. *Bitter is not bad.* Children learn from the beginning to repress pain. We say, "I don't want my child to feel pain." But for me, whatever pain has to teach my child, I want it to teach quickly, so it doesn't pile up. This whole conspiracy of unconsciousness... *That* is not good.

Passover & Kabbalah: Freedom from Alien Authority, Liberty Toward Higher Purpose

Joel Hecker with Jeffrey Dekro

In the theopoetics of the *Zohar*, the world is divided into two realms: holy and demonic. The application of this binary to the essential narrative and practices of Passover imbues the pairs of Egypt/Israel and leaven/*matzah* with an appealing and compelling dynamism that can be readily applied to the practices of theology, psychology, and politics.

For the medieval mystics the domains of holiness and the demonic were states of metaphysical reality, but also states of consciousness— one could aspire to this one or slide into the other, with redemptive or cataclysmic consequences resulting from one's choice. This essay will consider the mystical tools surrounding Passover eating practices that enable one to shift from one spiritual space to the other, yielding different meanings of freedom. Specifically, I will consider the commandments of disposing of all leaven and refraining from eating leavened products for the duration of the festival; the consumption of *matzah*; and the eating of *manna*, a higher form of "bread," that nourished the Israelites in the desert after the Exodus.

Before reading the kabbalistic passages below, some preliminary remarks about Kabbalah are in order. Kabbalists read the Torah as if it were written as a code, divulging the concealed dynamics of Divinity and the opposing forces that operate in the world. Each word in the Torah is conceptualized as a reference to a divine property or as a pathway to connection to God. In this literature, symbolic terms from the material world are not mere conceptual signposts, but more like mystical portals that facilitate spiritual travel to different cosmic and psychic dimensions. As a result, even items as mundane as leavened bread or its counterpart *matzah* serve as vehicles for mystical union. Generally, the kabbalists speak of ten *sefirot*, divine qualities that are manifested in the world through different terms in the Torah and the commandments and, as we will see, different kinds of holy foodstuffs correspond to these different gradations within the divine being. There is a countervailing system of demonic *sefirot* which signify the workings of the Other Side, and there are foodstuffs—leaven in our case—that are associated with the spiritual degradation that those demonic *sefirot* represent.

Moving from One Domain to Another: Freedom from the Sitra Ahra

One of the pervasive motifs in the Zoharic kabbalah's treatment of the Exodus from the demonic realm and emergence into holiness is the use of the metaphors of leaven and unleavened bread (*matzah*) to symbolize these two dimensions. The following text is characteristic:

> Rabbi Hiyya opened, saying, "…it is written: *Seven days you shall eat it* [the Passover sacrifice] *with unleavened bread, bread of affliction (lehem oni)* (Deuteronomy 16:3)—spelled *lehem ani, impoverished bread*…Come and see: When Israel was in Egypt, they were under alien authority. When the blessed Holy One desired to bring them close to Him, He gave them the realm of *lehem ani, impoverished bread*…This *impoverished bread* is called, 'unleavened bread' (*matzah*)…"[1]
> This passage tracks the movement from domain to domain: beginning in Egypt, called here "the alien authority," referring to the demonic *Sitra Ahra* (Other Side), and then proceeding to the realm of *matzah* and *Shekhinah*. The entry into relationship with God is through the consumption of *matzah*—hardly an exciting food—which symbolizes *Shekhinah*, the feminine and most accessible aspect of Divinity. Both esoteric and populist, the *Zohar* provides dramatic impetus for avoiding leaven and eating *matzah*—one can attain union with *Shekhinah*.

In one Zoharic text the escape from Egypt is described as the emergence from three "knots."[2] One of the boldest features of kabbalah is the prominent role played by the demonic realm, called the *Sitra Ahra*, literally the "Other Side."[3] The frightening proximity to dualism of this theological approach depicts the ten *sefirot* of Divinity mirrored by a parallel set of *se-*

---

[1] *Zohar* 1:157a. All translations from the *Zohar* are from *The Zohar: Pritzker Edition*, trans. Daniel Matt, Nathan Wolski, Joel Hecker, Stanford University Press, 2004–2017.

[2] *Zohar* 2:38a.

[3] See Nathaniel Berman, *Divine and Demonic in the Poetic Mythology of the Zohar: The "Other Side" of Kabbalah* (Leiden: Brill, 2018).

firot on the demonic side. These three knots from the dark side are alluded to in Exodus 11:5: *the firstborn of Pharaoh…the firstborn of the slave girl… and every firstborn of the beasts.* In another text discussing these demonic knots, they are symbolized by three different terms for leaven: … a secret spoken by Rabbi Shim'on: "Why is it written: *Surely on the first day you shall remove leaven (se'or), from your houses, for whoever eats what is leavened (mahmetset) (Exodus 12:15)?*" Well, so I have established: This *se'or, leaven,* and this *mahmetset, what is leavened,* are a single rung; all of them a single other dominion—those rulers appointed over other nations. We call them Evil Impulse, Other Dominion, Alien God, Other Gods. Here too, *se'or, leaven; mahmetset, what is leavened; leavened stuff* (*chametz*—all is one. The blessed Holy One said, "All these years you have been under alien dominion, slaves to another people. From now on, you are free! *Surely on the first day you shall remove se'or, leaven, from your houses* (ibid.); *nothing mahmetset, that is leavened, shall you eat* (ibid., 20); *no chametz, leavened stuff, shall be seen in your possession* (ibid. 13:7)."[4] The *Zohar* interprets these three terms for "leaven"—*se'or, mahmetset,* and *chametz*—as symbols for demonic powers. Evil may originate in a metaphysical source, but it plays itself out through oppression by political powers or even psychically, through the *yetser ha-ra,* evil impulse. Through the elimination of these different forms of "leaven," the people Israel enact their own liberation from foreign influence.

The appearance of leaven as a symbol of the evil impulse first finds expression in a prayer attributed to Rabbi Tanhum in a midrashic text: "May it be Your will, *YHVH,* my God and God of my fathers, that You break and destroy the yoke of the evil impulse from our heart. For You created us to do Your will, and we must do Your will; You desire it and we desire it. So, who prevents it? The leaven in the dough."[5] This linkage of leaven and the evil impulse is expanded upon in kabbalistic writings. In a description of *matzah* and *chametz,* Joseph of Hamadan—an early 14th century Castilian kabbalist writing in a Zoharic circle— characterizes the tension between leavened and unleavened bread as a battle between holy and demonic angels, and also between the *yetser tov* and *yetser hara:*… *Matzah* is the side of purity, while leaven alludes to the camps of Samael

---

[4] *Zohar* 2:40a. Exodus 12:15 reads in full: *Seven days shall you eat unleavened bread; surely on the first day you shall remove leaven, from your houses, for whoever eats* חמץ (*chametz*), *leavened stuff, that person will be cut off from Israel—from the first day to the seventh day.* Here, the *Zohar* substitutes מחמצת (*mahmetset*), *what is leavened*—which actually appears several verses later (12:19)—for *chametz, leavened stuff.*

[5] JT *Berakhot* 4:2, 7d.

and to the evil inclination. *Matzah* alludes to the camp of Michael, the heavenly High Priest, and it annuls the evil impulse... accustom oneself to the camps of Michael, the High Priest; distance oneself from the camps of Samael, blessed God forbade us to eat leavened bread on Passover on account of its similarity to the evil impulse... As an egg's volume of leaven slowly transforms the dough,[6] so did the Evil Impulse, bit by bit, draw Adam and Eve according to its own will, causing them to err, bringing death to the world. So, in order to weaken its strength and to alleviate the burden of its yoke from us, our Creator, blessed God, commanded us to eat *matzah* on the eve of Passover, at the beginning of the year, in order to recognize, know, and to destroy the evil inclination, to despise evil and choose virtue... [We eat *matzah*] in order to uproot harmful spirits and the evil impulse from the world, and in order to inculcate the good impulse in the body. The *matzah* symbolizes the *Shekhinah* so that the blessed Holy One will cause His *Shekhinah* to dwell there...[7] In the symbolic world that Zoharic kabbalah inhabits and constructs, personal transformation occurs through interaction with various levels of spiritual reality—divine, angelic, and psycho-ethical. Through the elimination of leaven and the eating of *matzah* one's own body is transmuted through the elimination of the evil impulse and the absorption of the good impulse. Kabbalistic symbolism is not merely figurative. Rather it assumes a dynamic, isomorphic relationship between the symbol and the entity it represents. In the passage above, *matzah* simultaneously changes the individual and the world (healed through eradication of evil spirits), both serving as receptors of the unleavened bread's transformative effects.

A feature of the kabbalistic method is to construct a web of associations between different symbols so that an action that triggers a positive entity will similarly trigger a range of corresponding symbols. We have seen how the kabbalah adapted Rabbi Tanhum's metaphorical teaching regarding the yeast in the dough in a more mythical and literal vein. The *Zohar* offers the following adaptation of the teaching in a theological direction:

> It is written: *No molten gods shall you make for yourself* (Exodus 34:17), and it is written: *The Festival of Matsot you shall keep* (ibid., 18). What does this have to do with that? Well, they have established as follows: Whoever eats *chametz*,

---

[6] An egg's volume (*ke-zayit*) is a standard rabbinic measure for prohibited foods.

[7] Menachem Meier, ed., *A Critical Edition of the Sefer Ta'amey Ha-Mizwoth (Book of Reasons of the Commandments) Attributed to Isaac ibn Farhi*, Ph.D. Diss. Brandeis University, 1974, 221–223.

leavened stuff, on Passover, it is as if he fashions an idol to worship. For so is the mystery: *chametz* on Passover is tantamount to idolatry—it is idolatry![8] When Israel went out of Egypt, they left their domain—alien domain, the domain called *chametz*, evil bread. That is why idolatry is called so, and this is mystery of the evil impulse, alien worship, also called leaven. This is the evil impulse, for so it functions in a person, like leaven in dough: entering one's innards little by little and then increasing, until the whole body is permeated by it. This is idolatry, of which is written *There shall be no alien god in you* (Psalms 81:10)—literally![9]

This teaching builds upon the identification of the evil impulse with the Other Side, a connection originally ascribed to Resh Lakish in the Talmud: "Satan, the evil impulse, and the Angel of Death are one and the same."[10] In the *Zohar's* rich web of connections, leaven, idolatry, evil impulse, and Egypt are banded together. In this way, foodstuffs, theology, spiritual behavior, and geography are all allied in the depiction of a demonized world. If one transgresses the laws of Passover by eating leavened products, one has strengthened the evil impulse, and ingested idolatry. Idolatry is thus not a matter of dogma or creed, but rather a feature of behavior, manifest through performance and bodily conduct, and internalized into one's own physicality and personhood. The *Zohar* arrives at this understanding through a hyperliteral reading of the verse in Psalms. Though its simple meaning is usually understood to mean *There shall be no alien god vekha, among you,* read hyperliterally it yields *There shall no alien god vekha, within you.* Since leaven symbolizes the demonic Other Side, eating it provides a dwelling place for idolatry within one's gut. Further, the individual transforms incrementally as the evil impulse worms its way into one's physical being. Leaving Egypt had signified a departure from that domain; eating the wrong food at the wrong time constitutes a symbolic return to that headspace. In this sense, knowing something in one's gut is taken very literally. In the *Zohar's* topography, when leaven enters the body, providing physiological residence for the demonic idol,

---

[8] On the link between the two consecutive verses in Exodus, see BT *Pesahim* 118a. Cf. *Zohar* 2:124a. The second verse reads in full: The Festival of matzot shall you keep. Seven days you shall eat matzot as I commanded you, at the fixed time of the month of the New Grain, for in the month of the New Grain you came out of Egypt.

[9] *Zohar* 2:182a.

[10] BT *Bava Batra* 16a.

one simultaneously enters into the domain of Egypt.

Purposeful Freedom

One of the effects of the receiving of Torah is political freedom, in the *Zohar*'s words, "freedom from subjugation of foreign kingdoms." In the material we examined above, we saw how the culinary progress from *chametz* to *matzah* corresponds to a rooting out of malevolent impulses and the infusion of the good. "Leaven" had deleterious effects, signifying destructive internal desires and oppressive nations. One can mark several stages in the Israelites' march toward freedom and connection: the first is the departure from the slavery and the realm of impurity; second, coming under the wings of *Shekhinah*; and, third, is the trajectory from *matzah* to *mitzvah*, a movement in which the Israelites transcended their slave-consciousness, and more clearly identified with their roles as covenantal partners with God with the receiving of the Torah and the assumption of *mitzvot*. It is a transition from pure receptivity and passivity to one of responsibility and participation.

The association of freedom with the giving of Torah derives from rabbinic literature, playing on the phrase *engraved upon the tablets* from Exodus 32:16:

> Do not read *harut, engraved*, but rather *heirut, freedom*. Rabbi Yehudah, Rabbi Nehemiah, and the Rabbis [disputed the matter]. Rabbi Yehudah said, "Freedom from the Angel of Death." Rabbi Nehemiah said, "Freedom from kingdoms." The Rabbis said, "Freedom from suffering."[11] In this midrashic riff, Torah is associated with freedom, but freedom is still defined negatively, in terms of "freedom from…" In the kabbalistic material to come, we witness a more optimistic and responsibility-oriented notion of freedom.

One instance of the second stage can be found in a Zoharic section called *Piqqudin*, Commandments:

> The twenty-seventh commandment: to eat *Matzah* on *Pesach*, for it is a remembrance throughout the generations about the mystery of faith. We have already established that at that time, Israel departed from the mystery of alien gods

---

[11]   *Vayiqra Rabbah* 18:3.

and entered the mystery of faith.[12] In Zoharic kabbalah, entering "the mystery of faith" designates the beginning of a relationship with Divinity in its most immanent aspect. In this passage, *matzah* marks not only a departure, but also an entry under the wings of *Shekhinah*, the starting point of the *sefirot*. Similarly, we read:

"*On the fourteenth* (Leviticus 23:5... for then one eliminates leaven and leavened stuff; and Israel escaped from an alien domain, uprooting themselves from it and uniting with *matzah*, the holy bond."

This is the beginning of the Israelites' relationship with God, once they have extricated themselves from the physical and cultural oppression of the Egyptians.

The third stage of freedom calls for a fleshing out of the dream. For the medieval kabbalists, that meant the fulfillment of the entirety of Torah, the bourgeoning opportunities for connection to God through Torah and commandments. The continuation of one of the texts cited above expresses this progression most effectively. In Rabbi Hiyya's homily about the *impoverished bread* the passage continues:

This *impoverished bread* is called *matzah*, "unleavened bread"... First, they approached *matzah*... first *matzah*, then *mitzvah*...

Similarly, when Israel left Egypt, they knew nothing until the blessed Holy One gave them a taste of the bread of this *earth*, as is written: *Earth, from which bread emerges* (Job 28:5). Then Israel entered into knowing and perceiving the blessed Holy One...Israel did not know or perceive supernal matters until they ate supernal bread, whereupon they knew and perceived that realm.

The blessed Holy One wanted Israel to know more of the realm befitting this *earth*, but they were unable until they tasted bread from that realm. Who is that? Heaven, as is written: *I am going to rain bread from heaven for you* (Exodus 16:4). Then they knew and contemplated that realm. Before eating bread from these sites, they knew and perceived nothing.[13]

---

[12] *Zohar* 2:41a (*Piqqudin*).

[13] *Zohar* 1:157a–b.

Two binaries provide the structure for this excerpted homily: *matzah/mitzvah*, Earth/Heaven, with a pair of divine *sefirot*, the feminine and masculine *Shekhinah* and *Tif'eret* concealed behind these symbols. In the kabbalah's decidedly patriarchal and heteronormative orientation, Israel begins their spiritual ascent through encounter with the *Shekhinah*, eating *matzah* that comes from the earth, and then progresses to the bread that rains down from heaven. They begin with *matzah*—symbolizing *Shekhinah*, the entry to the divine realm; then they proceed to prepare themselves for *mitzvah*. The text presents the move as if it were a mere linguistic increment, the addition of the letter *vav* completing their journey. Grammatically, the letter *vav* signifies the conjunction "and," but in kabbalah it does extra work, serving to join mythically the transcendent and immanent, the masculine and feminine valences of Divinity. The addition of the *vav* to the Israelites' mission brings them in concert with the mystical ideal of divine harmony.

The move to *mitzvah* corresponds to their eating of manna, food from heaven, which in turn symbolizes *Tif'eret*, the masculine potency of Divinity. Only through eating this heavenly food did the Israelites come to know the "realm befitting this *earth*," signifying *Tif'eret*. Tracking their development through foodstuffs, the *Zohar* perceives that what the Torah is really teaching is an evolving understanding of God. While they were slaves—oppressed physically, culturally, and spiritually—the Israelites knew nothing. Reinforced here is the notion that a change in political status is significant, but it is only the beginning of the way toward true enlightenment.

This transition of foodstuffs and consciousness is also represented through the graduation from *matzah* to leavened bread, offered at the holiday of Shavu'ot, fifty days after Passover. After providing various rationales for the spiritual superiority of *matzah*, the *Zohar* is forced to wrestle with the fact that leavened loaves are brought to the Temple as part of the sacrificial rite on Shavu'ot:

> On *Pesach*, Israel left the bread called *chametz*, leavened stuff, as is written: *No chametz, leavened stuff, shall be seen with you* (Exodus 13:7), and similarly: *Whoever eats chametz* (ibid. 12:15). Why? In honor of that bread called *matzah*. Now that Israel had attained higher bread, shouldn't *chametz* have been abolished and not be seen at all? Further, this offering was *chametz*, as is written: *Semolina they shall be, leavened they shall be baked* (Leviticus 23:17). And further,

now on this day the evil impulse was nullified, and Torah, called "freedom," appeared.

This may be compared to a king who had an only son who became ill. One day he craved food. [The royal advisors] said, "Let the king's son eat this healing food, and until he eats it, no other food or nourishment should be found in the house." So it was done. Once he had eaten that remedy, they said, "From now on, he may eat whatever he desires and it cannot harm him."

Similarly, when Israel went out of Egypt, they did not know the essence and mystery of faith. The blessed Holy One said, "Let Israel taste a remedy, and until they eat this remedy, no other food should be visible to them." Once they had eaten *matzah*, which is a remedy for entering and knowing the mystery of faith, the blessed Holy One said, "From now on, *chametz* is suitable for them and they may eat it, because it cannot harm them"—especially since on the day of *Shavu'ot* supernal bread is available, a cure for all![14]

The passage is explained by Daniel Matt. "All leaven (which symbolizes the demonic power) is forbidden on *Pesach*, in honor of *matzah*, symbolizing *Shekhinah*. Why then, on *Shavu'ot*—which is linked with the higher nourishment of manna and Torah—is *chametz* permitted? Moreover, why is *chametz* actually brought as an offering? Furthermore, at Sinai Israel was liberated from the evil impulse, which is symbolized by *chametz*, so the presence of leaven is troubling."[15] While at first deprived of true spiritual knowledge, the Israelites were first given the "remedy" of *matzah*, to bring them into knowledge of God gradually. Once they had tasted the elevated food of Torah, they could even withstand leavened bread, now purified of its temptation. The ostensibly startling reversal is an astute insight into a certain understanding of freedom. Even the most nettlesome ingredient—leaven —can be integrated into one's "diet" at the opportune time, with proper regimens and disciplines in place.

---

[14] *Zohar* 2:183a–b. Still suffering from a slave mentality, the Israelites were ignorant of true faith; so God prescribed for them the remedy of *matzah* and forbade the presence of any *chametz*. Once they were cured and purified, they were permitted to eat *chametz*—especially since at Sinai, on the first *Shavu'ot*, they could taste the supernal nourishment of Torah, the ultimate cure.

[15] Daniel Matt, *The Zohar: Pritzker Edition*, vol. 6, p. 29, n. 74.

Conclusion

The discussion above considers the two primary forms of freedom that the *Zohar* considers with regard to the holiday of Passover: freedom from external, political oppression, or from internal impulses that run counter to our best interests, and freedom to engage with God in a mature and responsible covenantal relationship. The arc from one to the other can be traced through the different kinds of food that the Israelites consume on their journey from slavery to freedom—*matzah*, manna, and unleavened bread. The kabbalists aimed to cultivate a different kind of consciousness in relationship to these commandments, resulting in freedoms of political, psychological, and social-ethical styles. Rabbi Yaakov Leiner, the Radzyner Rebbe, taught that the Exodus is referred to fifty times in the Torah to indicate the never-ending task of seeking freedom: each time we experience a dimension of freedom, there is a feeling of astonishment, but as the revelation becomes clearer, the surprise diminishes. May we continue to seek freedom, always seeking the astonishment that new freedoms can provide.

The Future: Spirit, Ritual, Politics

Liberating the Future: Passover and Beyond

Rabbi Arthur Ocean Waskow

Fifty years after the original Freedom Seder, thousands of Jews all across the United States observed Tisha B'Av in a new way. Traditionally, it was the midsummer fast day of mourning the destruction of two ancient Holy Temples in Jerusalem. In 2019, they observed the day by demonstrating against a major high-priority policy action of the then government of the United States—its oppressive and deadly treatment of refugees and immigrants. In some of these demonstrations, dozens of Jews were arrested as part of the protests.

There were two remarkable aspects of these events: that for the first time in history, large numbers of Jews and many of their major institutions publicly, clearly, vigorously, and concertedly opposed a major policy priority of the U.S. government; and that in doing so, they drew on the religious teachings and spiritual practices of a Jewish holy day in an effort to change public policy.

In many of these gatherings, the participants spoke of the Jews who had been driven from shattered Jerusalem into death marches toward exile in Babylon and toward enslavement in the Roman Empire, mentioned dozens of passages of Torah demanding love and decency toward refugees and immigrants, cited thousands of years when Jews were expelled from various countries and became refugees, remembered how the United States had rejected refugees from Nazi Germany and sent them back to concentration camps and then death camps, and recalled how their own grandparents and great-grandparents had immigrated in terror and poverty to America.

All these memories were about the specific life experience of Jews and the Jewish people. Yet the protests were focused far more universally—toward an oppressive U.S. government and the oppression of a non-Jewish ethnic group. "Never Again Means Anyone" and "Never Again Means Now" were watchwords of the protests.

Why would I bring this up at the end of a book about liberating the Passover Seder?

Because the Freedom Seder also liberated a new way of thinking about all the Jewish festivals and fast days. The wall between "ritual" and "politics," between "spirituality" and "social justice," first began to crumble, then came crashing down.

In 1969, nowhere that I have been able to find did any Jewish community think or act as if Tisha B'Av had to do with anything other than those ancient Temples. By 1972, the same group of people in Washington, D.C.—about forty altogether—who had organized and led the Freedom Seder were gathering on the steps of the U.S. Capitol to fast in sorrow for and opposition to the U.S. War Against Vietnam. They drew an analogy between the Roman Empire's salting the soil of what Rome called "Palestine" so that the Jewish farmers could not grow food, and the U.S. Government's pouring Agent Orange onto the forests of Vietnam, thinking that to kill the forests would kill the Vietnamese revolution.

Already, earlier in 1972, the same small band of Jews had sparked a somewhat broader celebration of Tu B'Shvat, the midwinter Jewish festival of the RebirthDay of Trees and of the Divine Tree of Life, by condemning the destruction of those trees in Vietnam. They pointed out that the Torah (Deut. 20:19-20) explicitly forbids the killing of "enemy" trees even or especially in time of war. So they organized "Trees and Life for Vietnam," convinced the renowned Rabbi Abraham Joshua Heschel to become Honorary Chair of the Campaign, raised money to support reforestation in Vietnam, and sent delegates to Paris to give the money in equal shares to representatives of the Democratic Republic of Vietnam, the National Liberation Front, and a group of Vietnamese Buddhist monks led by Thich Nhat Hanh. On Tu B'Shvat itself and its adjacent days, they brought the feminist and politically strongly progressive Congresswoman Bella Abzug and neo-Hassidic Rebbe Shlomo Carlebach to speak at different times on Judaism and the war. This time it was a reinterpretation of both a medieval mystical celebration of God as the Tree of Life and the modern Zionist redefinition of the day as a time to plant trees in the Land of Israel that moved in a universal direction.

By the summer of 2010, the universalization of Tisha B'Av had taken a small step forward, beyond 1972. Earlier in the summer, the BP Big Oil blowout of an oil well in the Gulf of Mexico had engulfed and killed eleven BP workers on the oil rig and tens of thousands of fish and birds in the Gulf region, leaving many businesses along the Gulf shores in financial downfall. The U.S. government was doing little to help—especially little to protect the future of Earth's oceans and marine workers and businesses from similar disasters.

So about 300 people, led by Jews using the symbols and practices of Tisha B'Av but including many adherents of other religious and spiritual traditions and many secular environmentalists, gathered on the steps of the Capitol. They spoke of the destruction being imposed on Temple Earth. They heard and joined in the wailing chant of a new "Lament for Earth" written by (now Rabbi) Tamara Cohen in the style and wailing melody of the ancient Book of Lamentations. The use of Rabbi Cohen's text for a more universal Tisha B'Av slowly made its way into the more experimental arenas of Jewish life.

In 1969, the original Freedom Seder was like a crystal dropped into a super-saturated solution. Many parts of the American Jewish community—especially but not only many of its young people—had soaked themselves deeply in the need to turn away from America's "original sin"—racism—and the need to end an illegitimate and obscene war. Although many Jewish institutions had to some extent supported the Black-led freedom movement in the South, very few were willing to condemn the U.S. War Against Vietnam. Yet many outside the official leadership burned with passion to redress those wrongs, and were convinced that the values they espoused were rooted in Torah and in Jewish history.

So the Freedom Seder crystallized those urgent feelings, and the result was a sudden transformation in the ways in which many Jews thought and felt about "ritual" as a frame for social activism. The first result was a profusion of activist Haggadahs that were utterly clear about their Jewish roots and strongly committed to their universalist flowering. The new understanding of "activist ritual" kept cooking in the community. And for many young Jews half a century after the original wave of Seders, the encounter at Standing Rock with Native/Indigenous spirituality fused with resistance to corporate plans for earth-wounding oil pipelines once more soaked the community in the passion for activist ritual.

As a handbook of "how" to liberate Passover, this book has drawn on many experiments in the past half century. I want to end by turning our gaze into the future:

Some world-spanning banks invest hundreds of billions of dollars in corporations that burn Earth, destroy communities, and kill people. On Sukkot, the earthy harvest festival, Jews celebrate by building *sukkot*—temporary, vulnerable, open-to-Earth huts with leafy, leaky roofs; by waving in the seven directions of the universe the Four Species branches of palm, willow, and myrtle, and a lemony etrog (citron); and by chanting prayers called "*Hosha Na*—Please save" Earth from locusts, droughts, invasive worms, and other plagues.

What would happen if groups of Jews walked into offices and branches of those banks waving the branches, singing songs of sacred Earth, chanting prayers to save us from burning fossil fuels, demanding that the banks stop lending money to the Carbon Pharaohs and instead lend money to neighborhood solar co-ops, to companies building wind farms, to projects of reforestation?

In American society, every other year Sukkot comes a few weeks before a major national election. What if we were to commit ourselves to "Share Sukkot/Green and Grow the Vote" as part of the Jewish observance of the holy day? What if the building of sukkot in all our communities were connected with the values inherent in the festival and with outreach to make sure that undervoting communities—our own youth, the poor, and those racially marginalized—were especially encouraged and aided to vote?

What are those values? Torah teaches that the band of runaway slaves that made up the refugees from the Tight and Narrow Place—*Mitzrayim*, Egypt—lived in *sukkot*. What does that mean Sukkot teaches about responding to refugees? Sukkot is about the harvest. What does that teach about feeding the hungry? The Hoshanot "Save us, Save Earth" prayers—what do they teach us about saving Earth from CO2 and methane, from "forever plastics" and carcinogenic chemicals?

Traditionally, the offering of 70 bulls during Sukkot was connected to prayer for the prosperity of all the "70 nations of the world." And we pray, "*Ufros alenu sukkat shlomekha*—Spread over all of us the sukkah of shalom." What if we were to hear the truth that it is the very vulnerability of the sukkah, not the seeming impregnability of a fortress, that —when shared with others—makes for peace? Together, these two teachings make the foundation of a loving and respectful "foreign" policy.

On Yom Kippur, Jews read aloud a passage from the Prophet Isaiah (57: 14-58: 14): that cries out:

> *Do you think that when God called you to fast on Yom Kippur, that meant drooping your head like a bulrush, wearing sackcloth and ashes? No! It meant feeding the hungry, clothing the naked, housing the homeless, breaking the handcuffs clamped on those imprisoned by the powerful.*

What would happen if in many synagogues, at that point in the regular service, groups of people went out from their synagogues into the streets, chanting these passages from Isaiah, picketing a business that is stealing its workers' wages, standing in tears at a prison notorious for its physical and psychological abuse of prisoners?

At the synagogue celebration of B'nai Mitzvah, what would happen if the young persons growing into more responsibility, together with their families, integrated into their celebration an outcry from the last of the ancient Hebrew Prophets (Malachi 3: 23-24):

> I will send you the Prophet Elijah to turn the hearts of the parents to the children and the hearts of the children to the parents, lest the Breath of Life come as a Hurricane of Destruction and smite Earth with utter desolation.

What if the adults and youngsters present on that day said aloud they would take on the mission of Elijah, and named one act to save Earth that they would commit to doing?

Let us in fear, hope, and the trembling that infuses both of them reexamine our celebrations of Pesach. What does it mean for the American Jewish community to celebrate the Festival of Freedom in a society that is still caught in the history of slavery and racism? We began with memories of a Freedom Seder that took some partial account of this reality by weaving other struggles for freedom—especially the Black American struggle—with the ancient celebration of liberation from slavery to Pharaoh. In America, the triumphant observance of that freedom is for Jews the crowning achievement of that ancient struggle. For Jews!—but for Blacks? For the Indigenous Peoples? For brown-skinned Spanish-speakers? For Muslims? For the rural "old Americans," forgotten and left with dwindling life spans to die of alcohol and drugs and despair?

What would Pesach become if "*Lo dayenu*—NOT enough for us"— were as important as "Dayenu"? What would it mean for every Seder community to spend one day of Passover in action on the streets—not only remembering, but *embodying* the freedom journey? For as the traditional Haggadah says: In every generation, every human being must act as if we, not our forebears only, move from slavery to freedom!

In short, what would it mean if large parts of the Jewish community, working with other communities to heal sufferings that afflict all peoples, were to reenergize the powerful rituals that were themselves originally crystals of life, and point them toward seeking justice, compassion, healing, and peace?

I have asked "what would it mean?" up till now from the "outside" of spiritual experience—adopting spiritual practice to meet a "political" need. Suppose we ask what would its *meaning* be, from the inside out? That is, what is the spiritual truth of a reconfiguring of these rituals into activist change?

Often I hear people contrasting spirituality and politics: spirituality as an individual's experience of awe toward something fuller than the self—beyond self and society—contrasted with politics as filled with fearful defenses against being overwhelmed by something in society bigger than oneself.

I think this is a misperception. I suggest we think of spirituality as both an individual and a social/political possibility. As a single person, I can feel awe at the astonishing complexity and grandeur of my community and of the universe, of each of which I am a sacred and a necessary part. (The "sacred and necessary" does not permit me to oppress or be oppressed.) If I can experience and affirm this role, the expression of it is my individual "spirituality."

As a society, the same: With our unique culture, if we affirm the unique cultures of other communities within the One and affirm for each its own reach toward the One—its own pursuit of its own spirituality—we can together strive toward a "communal spirituality." That striving is the society's "politics."

The goal of that striving is not a God Who is Adonai or Melekh, Lord or King. It is a theology of Ecology as world view, social and cultural as well as biological—not a world view grounded in Hierarchy and Subjugation. We each in our own culture need to look inward as well as beyond ourselves to encourage the language and symbols and behaviors that call forth that response.

At our best, this is how "ritual" and "politics" fit together. Each is an expression of its own and of the other's spiritual life.

About the Authors

Rabbinic Pastor Matia Rania Angelou, Eshet Hazon, is a published poet, ritual artist, and healer certified in Applied Resonance Therapy and SpiritSong Authentic Voice. Matia serves as a Mikveh Guide at Mayyim Hayyim Community Mikveh where she writes ceremonies for ritual immersion. She works as a Mashpiah Ruchanit: Spiritual Director, is a Hospice Chaplain and Bereavement Counselor, and teaches chant and meditation at Makom Hazon.

Emily August is the Director of Communications and Public Engagement at the National Museum of American Jewish History in Philadelphia, her institutional home for more than a decade. She serves on senior management team, leads the Museum's communications and public programming efforts, and directs special projects such as its annual Freedom Seder Revisited and Jewish American Heritage Month. Her prior work focused on regional economic development programs and non-partisan voting rights initiatives. Emily graduated from the S.I. Newhouse School of Public Communications at Syracuse University.

Rev. William J. Barber II is a Protestant minister and political activist. From 2006-2017, Barber served as president of the NAACP's North Carolina state chapter, the largest in the South, and from that base organized the Moral Mondays nonviolent challenge to institutional racism and poverty and their enforcers in the North Carolina legislature. He is the President and Senior Lecturer at Repairers of the Breach and co-chair of the Poor People's Campaign: A National Call for Moral Revival. He also serves as a member of the national board of the NAACP and the chair of its Legislative Political Action Committee. He has pastored Greenleaf Christian Church (Disciples of Christ) in Goldsboro, NC since 1993.

Rabbi Phyllis Ocean Berman was ordained a rabbi in 2005 by ALEPH; she serves as a *mashpia ruchanit*—spiritual director—for those in the ALEPH Ordination Program and others. She was a founder and for 37 years co-director of the Riverside Language Program in New York City, and directed the summer program at Elat Chayyim spiritual retreat center for many years. Rabbi Berman co-authored *A Time for Every Purpose Under Heaven, Tales of Tikkun*, and *Freedom Journeys*. She is a meditator, chanter, swimmer, baker, prayer leader, mentor, and Savta (to 5 grandchildren). "Big talk" with friends, family, and strangers feeds her soul.

Reena Bernards is an intergroup facilitator, writer and family therapist. She is adjunct faculty at the University of Maryland. She has provided trainings on Race and Inclusion for organizations including the National Institute of Mental Health. She created the Common Ground workshop for Braver Angels. She was the former Executive Director of New Jewish Agenda and co-coordinator of the project that led to The Shalom Seders, published by Adama Books.

Rabbi Ellen Bernstein founded Shomrei Adamah, Keepers of the Earth, the first national Jewish environmental organization (1988) and has been writing, teaching, and organizing around the intersection of Judaism, Bible and Ecology ever since. Her books include *The Promise of the Land: A Passover Haggadah* and *The Splendor of Creation*. She is an advisory committee member to the Yale Forum on Religion and Ecology.

Rabbi Tamara R. Cohen is a rabbi, educator, writer, and activist, working towards more just, inclusive, and liberatory practices, rituals, and community. She is VP and Chief of Program Strategy for Moving Traditions and serves on the board of Women's March, Inc. A graduate of the Reconstructionist Rabbinical College, Sarah Lawrence and Barnard, she lives in Philadelphia with her partner Gwynn Kessler and their children Tobias and Kliel.

Denise Davis, M. D. is Clinical Professor of Medicine at University of California San Francisco and teaches workshops nationally on compassionate communication skills in healthcare. She is a member of Temple Beth Abraham in Oakland, California and is an alumna of Elat Chayyim Center for Jewish Spirituality.

Jeffrey Dekro studies and teaches Zohar, Kabbalah, and midrash. He had a 40-year career as an activist and nonprofit entrepreneur. Dekro founded and led The Shefa Fund for eighteen years. In that role, he established TzEDeC, a Jewish-sourced low-income community+economic development fund, and the Isaiah Fund, the first national faith-based loan fund for major disaster response. He closed his career by serving for three years as the initial Director of Faith-Based Initiatives for Calvert Impact Capital.

Cat Essoyan was raised in Egypt and Lebanon. Catherine Essoyan has concentrated professionally on Middle East conflict resolution. With a Yale BA and a Harvard ME Studies MA, she spent 10 years at American Friends Service Committee, three running an East Jerusalem legal aid office. Since 1992, at Oxfam Novib, she has focused on Middle East and North Africa, on governance and conflict.

Al Hajj Imam Abdul-Halim Hassan was the Acting Resident Imam of Masjidullah from 2003-2005 and the elected Resident Imam from March 2005-March 2009. He was the first Imam elected by the people in the city of Philadelphia. Imam Hassan is deeply involved in Interfaith relations in and around Philadelphia. He has been on the planning committee of the Philadelphia Interfaith Peace Walk for more than 15 years. He was instrumental in Masjidullah's being one of the founding members of POWER (Philadelphians Organized to Witness, Empower & Rebuild) and now serves on the Mass Incarceration committee. He acted as liaison from Masjidullah to arrange the 50th anniversary Freedom Seder, which was held at that mosque.

Martha Hausman represents clergy in contract negotiations and coaches, consults, and conducts negotiation training. Martha practiced as a lawyer, in both Washington and New York and has also held various Jewish communal positions. In addition to her law degree, she has a Masters in Jewish Studies. Martha enjoys bringing a combination of legal background, Jewish knowledge, and rabbinic family experience to help facilitate important life transitions for her clients.

Viv Hawkins works and prays to inspire, encourage, and empower people, individually and corporately, to live into our most sacred selves in harmony with creation. Having served The Shalom Center for nine years, she now provides integral coaching for spiritual changemakers. Details are available at LifeCallsCoach.com and ReleasingMinistry.org.

Joel Hecker, Ph.D., is Professor of Jewish Mysticism at the Reconstructionist Rabbinical College. Among his publications are *The Zohar: Pritzker Edition*, Vols. XI & XII; and *Mystical Bodies, Mystical Meals: Eating and Embodiment in Medieval Kabbalah*. Dr. Hecker has been a research fellow at the Center for Advanced Judaic Studies at the University of Pennsylvania and the Shalom Hartman Institute; Visiting Instructor at the University of Pennsylvania, the Jewish Theological Seminary, and Yeshiva University.

Susannah Heschel, Ph.D. is the Eli M. Black Distinguished Professor of Jewish Studies at Dartmouth College. The author or editor of numerous books and articles, she is a Guggenheim Fellow. Her scholarship focuses on

Jewish and Christian interactions in Germany during the nineteenth and twentieth centuries. She is the daughter of Rabbi Abraham Joshua Heschel, one of the leading theologians and Jewish philosophers of the twentieth century, and has edited several volumes of his essays. She also edited one of the earliest collections of essays on Jewish feminism.

Avi Katz, who created the graphic on the front cover, is an Israeli illustrator who originally created the illustration for The Shalom Center's Interfaith Freedom Seder for the Earth, celebrated in Washington, D.C. in 2009 on the fortieth anniversary of the original Freedom Seder. The graphic is Copyright (c) 2009 by The Shalom Center. Katz has been a major illustrator for *Davar*, the *Jerusalem Report* and the *Jerusalem Post*, and has won numerous national and international awards for his illustrated books .

Susala Kay is one of the founders of JeWitch Collective and JeWitch Camp. She is also a Priestess in the Reclaiming tradition and a retired clinical psychologist. She can be reached at jewitchyritualist@gmail.com. To find out more about JeWitch Collective visit www.jewitch.org. Info about JeWitch Camp is at www.jewitchcamp.org.

Rabbi Sharon Kleinbaum was one of the first openly lesbian American rabbis. She serves as spiritual leader of Congregation Beit Simchat Torah in Manhattan. She became CBST's first rabbi in 1992, arriving at the height of the AIDS crisis when the synagogue was in desperate need of pastoral care and spiritual leadership. Rabbi Kleinbaum has been an active campaigner in both the Jewish community and the public sphere for human rights and civil marriage for gay couples.

Rabbi Mordechai Liebling is the Director of Reflection and Renewal at POWER Interfaith. He was the founder and director of the Social Justice Organizing Program at the Reconstructionist Rabbinical College for 10 years. Prior to that he was the Executive Vice-President of Jewish Funds for Justice (now Bend the Arc). Earlier he was the Executive Director of the Jewish Reconstructionist Federation. He serves on the boards of The Shalom Center and of the Faith and Politics Institute. He was the founding chairperson of Shomrei Adamah: Guardians of the Earth and a co-founder of T'ruah: The Rabbinic Call for Human Rights. He is married to Lynne Iser and together they have five children.

Born but not raised Jewish, **Stephanie Loo** got her Jewish education as an adult through her ex-husband Philip Ritari (z"l), Havurat Shalom, ulpan (Brookline and Jerusalem), teaching Hebrew school under Matia, and a Yiddish song circle. At the Hav she met Debra Cash and Ronnie Levin, members of her current Rosh Hodesh group, who host dynamic

Passover seders. In recent years, Stephanie's spiritual focus has shifted to her work at the Asperger/Autism Network (aane.org), a non-profit founded by a Jewish social worker and a Jewish psychiatrist.

Rabbi Rachel Grant Meyer is a social justice activist, community organizer, rabbi, and educator. She hopes to help Jews of all ages live their most authentic life using Judaism as a guide. A graduate of Columbia University, she was ordained by Hebrew Union College-Jewish Institute of Religion in New York City. Currently, Rabbi Meyer serves as rabbi-in-residence at HIAS, the Jewish refugee agency. Her writing and commentary has been featured in such publications as *The New York Times, Mashable, The Forward,* and *The New York Daily News,* and she is the author of several essays that appear in printed volumes through the CCAR Press and Ben Yehuda Press.

Letty Cottin Pogrebin is an author, journalist, lecturer, and social activist. From 1970-1980, she wrote a column for Ladies' Home Journal called "The Working Woman." She became a founding editor of Ms. magazine in 1971, and a cofounder of Ms. Foundation for Women and the National Women's Political Caucus. She has written eleven books,[3] and was an editorial consultant for the TV special Free to Be... You and Me (as well as for the album and book associated with it) for which she earned an Emmy.

In 1976, the first women-only Passover seder was held in Esther Broner's New York City apartment and led by Broner, with 13 women attending, including Pogrebin. Her essay in this collection is drawn from her memoir, *Deborah, Golda, and Me: Being Female and Jewish in America.*

A. Daniel Roth has been working to establish participatory communities rooted in education and action for more than two decades in Canada, the United States, and Israel-Palestine with the aim of building a powerful movement for equality and self-determination for all peoples in the place they call home. Daniel is the co-founder of Solidarity of Nations - Achvat Amim, a movement building framework based in Jerusalem, a founding member of This is Not an Ulpan critical language learning cooperative, and a founding member of All That's Left: Anti- Occupation Collective. His writing and photography is at adanielroth.com

Rabbi David Saperstein as rabbi, lawyer, and Jewish community leader served for almost forty years as the director and chief legal counsel at the Religious Action Center (RAC) of Reform Judaism.

There, he advocated on a broad range of social justice issues. He directed a staff who provided extensive legislative and programmatic materials to synagogues, federations and Jewish Community Relations

Councils nationwide, coordinating social action education programs that train nearly 3,000 Jewish adults, youth, rabbinic and lay leaders each year.

When in 2014 he retired from the RAC, President Obama named and the Senate confirmed Saperstein to be the first non-Christian to hold the post of United States Ambassador-at-Large for International Religious Freedom.

Rabbi Saperstein has served as president of the World Union for Progressive Judaism and on the boards of the NAACP, Common Cause, and People for the American Way.

Rabbi Shalom Schachter received his ordination from ALEPH in 2005 after commencing rabbinic studies in Chabad. He is a union labour lawyer representing primarily female health care workers. He is the Toronto Board of Rabbis representative to numerous interfaith social policy advocacy groups. Shalom sued the Canadian Government to secure paid parental leave for all parents. His motivation was to model a role for fathers as women cannot truly take an equal role in society outside the home until men play an equal role in maintaining the household and in child-rearing.

Rabbi Zalman Schachter-Shalomi, z'tz'l, was born in Poland in 1924 and grew up in Vienna. As a teen-ager, he fled Vienna with his family after the Nazi Anschluss, was interned in Vichy France, and fled again to the United States in 1941. He was ordained to the rabbinate in 1947 by the Lubavitch Hassidic community under the tutelage of the sixth Lubavitcher rebbe. His life and thought were transformed by encountering Rev. Howard Thurman, Dean of the Chapel at Boston University (also MLK's primary teacher), and he began to share spiritual learning with Christian, Muslim, Buddhist, Hindu, and psychedelic mystics, and with Jews of many persuasions. He wrote *Fragments of a Future Scroll* in 1975, *Paradigm Shift* in 1993, and many essays during those decades as well as other books and essays thereafter to prophesy and help create a major transformation of Jewish life. As a traveling organizer, Reb Zalman inspired local havurot and congregations that became the B'nai Or and then the P'nai Or Religious Fellowship, and the movement known as Jewish Renewal. In 1993 P'nai Or merged with The Shalom Center (led by Rabbi Arthur Waskow) to create ALEPH: Alliance for Jewish Renewal. Reb Zalman taught for many years at the University of Manitoba, then Temple University in Philadelphia, and then Naropa University in Boulder, Colorado. His essay in this volume was written for Menorah magazine in the early 1980s. He died in 2014 shortly before his 90th birthday.

Jess Schwalb (she/her) is a writer and researcher from Washington, DC. A former *New Voices Magazine* fellow with *Jewish Currents*, she has written about the history of Black-Jewish relations, campus Jewish organizing, and megadonor Israel politics. She currently works on fair housing and lives in Chicago.

Rabbi Jeff Sultar, ordained by the Reconstructionist Rabbinical College, serves as the spiritual leader of Congregation B'nai Jacob in Phoenixville, Pennsylvania. He has worked for the Green Menorah Program of The Shalom Center and for Shomrei Adamah, and has served as campus rabbi at Choate Rosemary Hall and Cornell University.

Rabbi Robert dos Santos Teixeira, MPIA, MA, MSW, LCSW, is a psychotherapist and a rabbi. He is the author of *The PSALM™ Cards and Messages from the Psalms,* a tool for prayer and meditation, and he is the founder and spiritual director of Seek My Face, a community of Christians and Jews who come together each day to pray the Book of Psalms in its entirety.

The Reverend Dr. Liz Theoharis is Co-Chair of the Poor People's Campaign: A National Call for Moral Revival with the Rev. Dr. William J. Barber II. She is the Director of the Kairos Center for Religions, Rights, and Social Justice at Union Theological Seminary. Liz is the author of *Always with Us?: What Jesus Really Said about the Poor* (Eerdmans, 2017) and co-author of *Revive Us Again: Vision and Action in Moral Organizing* (Beacon, 2018). She is an ordained minister in the Presbyterian Church (USA).

Rabbi Brian Walt is rabbi emeritus of Mishkan Shalom, an activist congregation in Philadelphia and the founding executive director of Rabbis for Human Rights/ North America (currently T'ruah). He was an activist for justice in South Africa, where he grew up, in Palestine/ Israel, and in the United States since 1974.

Rabbi Arthur Waskow, Ph.D., wrote the original Freedom Seder in 1969 and a number of adaptations of it in the years since. He founded (1983) and directs The Shalom Center. In 2014 he received the Lifetime Achievement Award as Human Rights Hero from T'ruah: The Rabbinic Call for Human Rights. Among his 26 books are *Seasons of Our Joy, Down-to-Earth Judaism, The Tent of Abraham, Godwrestling — Round 2,* (editor) *Torah of the Earth,* and *Dancing in God's Earthquake: The Coming Transformation of Religion.* He taught from 1982 to 1989 at the Reconstructionist Rabbinical College and in 2017 was awarded its premier honorary degree, Doctor of Humane Letters. He cofounded the National

Havurah Committee, Rabbis for Human Rights/North America (now T'ruah), and ALEPH: Alliance for Jewish Renewal.

Rabbi Shawn Israel Zevit was ordained by the Reconstructionist Rabbinical College and by Rabbi Zalman Schachter-Shalomi. He rabbis at Mishkan Shalom, Philadelphia, integrating meaningful spiritual living, life-long learning, community organizing, and acts of caring, and social justice. He is co-director with Rabbi Marcia Prager of the Davvenen Leaders Training Institute; a member of ALEPH Hashpa'ah (Spiritual Direction) Training Program; and co-chair of the Faith Leader's Caucus of POWER, a multireligious, multiracial coalition of activist congregations in Philadelphia. He is also a Menschwork co-founder and leader in the annual Jewish Men's retreat; author of essays in the books *Brother Keepers* and *Offerings of the Heart*, and song-composer and liturgist of numerous musical recordings at www.rabbizevit.com

Also by Rabbi Arthur Ocean Waskow from Ben Yehuda Press

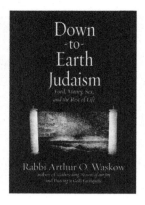

Down-to-Earth Judaism:
Food, Money, Sex, and the Rest of Life

A classic exploration of the pillars of a spiritual life in the real world and the guide-posts that mark the communal path for the modern Jewish practitioner.

"A full-bodied vision of Jewish life today."
—Rodger Kamenetz, author of *The Jewish in the Lotus*

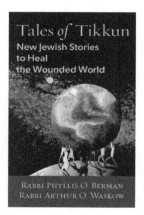

Tales of Tikkun:
New Jewish Stories to Heal the Wounded World
by Rabbis Phyllis O. Berman and Arthur O. Waskow

This book of new Jewish tales fashioned from ancient stories aims to repair our past, renew our future, and captivate our imaginations. The eleven stories in this volume draw from and expand the midrashic tradition of Jewish creativity. They include a a mythical quest to save the world from modern-day rising oceans, retelling the Torah's most difficult stories in a way that makes them whole and healing, and even an imaginative yet shockingly plausible vision of the Messianic age.

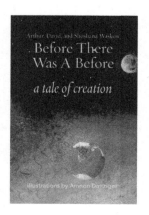

Before There Was A Before:
A Tale of Creation
by Arthur, David, and Shoshana Waskow

Arthur Waskow and his children reveal creation as a soul-stirring act of love and need, showing anew the interrelatedness of all life in this book for parents and their children to read together.

"I enjoyed reading it very much indeed."
—Madeleine L'Engle, author of *A Wrinkle in Time*

Passover books for your family from Ben Yehuda Press

**More Than Four Questions:
Inviting Children's Voices to the Seder -
A Conversational Haggadah Companion**
by Sharon Black

"Although it's meant to be a supplement and not a replacement, if I had to choose between it and a rote, by-the-book option, I'd pick *More Than Four Questions in a heartbeat.*"
—Jay Michaelson, *The Forward*

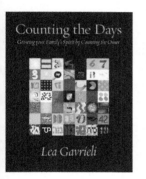

**Counting the Days:
Growing Your Family's Spirit by Counting the Omer**
by Rabbis Lea Gavrieli

"Counting the Days offers a powerful way to bring the spiritual practice of counting the omer to the whole family with depth and meaning. It's a must-have in the Jewish home."
—Rabbi Danya Ruttenberg, author, *Nurture the Wow*

Passover in a Pandemic
by Avram Mlotek and Ally Pockras

Because of the Covid pandemic, Reva can't celebrate Passover with her Bubby, her beloved grandmother.

"Has Bubby ever been alone for a Passover before?" she asks her parents. The answer is yes, and as Bubby tells the story of a Passover in her childhood, Reva learns an important lesson about resilience.

Also available in a Yiddish edition.